A Portrait of Aristotle

Bust of Aristotle, Kunsthistorisches Museum, Vienna
(*Reproduced by courtesy of the Museum*)

A PORTRAIT
OF
ARISTOTLE

Marjorie Grene

THE UNIVERSITY OF CHICAGO PRESS

THE UNIVERSITY OF CHICAGO PRESS, CHICAGO 60637

© 1963 by Marjorie Grene
All rights reserved. Published 1963

Midway Reprint 1979
Printed in the United States of America

ISBN: 0-226-30822-7
LCN: 63-5556

To
my children
RUTH and NICHOLAS

Acknowledgments

I am indebted to Professor Charles Kahn of Columbia University and Mr. Gershon Weiler of the National University of Australia for their careful criticism of my manuscript. Whatever the deficiencies of the book, it has certainly benefited very greatly from their assistance. Professor Kahn has been especially generous in supplementing my scanty Greek. Mr. Eustace D. Phillips of Queen's University and Mrs. Otto von Simson have also read the manuscript in part and have advised me on some points of translation and terminology.

I am grateful to my students from the Departments of Philosophy and of Scholastic Philosophy for the stimulation they have given me in developing the ideas set down here. I also wish to thank the American Philosophical Society for a grant in aid of research in the philosophy of biology, and Bryn Mawr College, especially the President, Miss Katharine McBride, and the Chairman of the Philosophy Department, Professor Milton C. Nahm, for their generosity in awarding me the Lucy Martin Donnelly Fellowship for the year 1960–61 'in order to do some writing which I might not otherwise have done'. This is not the writing I meant to do when I visited Bryn Mawr in October 1960, but it was done during the tenure of the Fellowship, and their hospitality and encouragement certainly helped me to do it.

The title was suggested by the late Robert Redfield's distinction, in *The Little Community*, between 'portraiture' and 'analysis' in anthropology. A similar distinction seems to me apposite in philosophical studies.

ACKNOWLEDGMENTS

References to Aristotle and Plato are given in the traditional numeration. Other quotations are acknowledged by reference to the number of the title in the bibliography at the close of the book: thus, for example, '76 110–11' refers to title 76 in the bibliography, pages 110–11. I am indebted both to the Loeb Library and to the Oxford University Press for permission to quote from their translations; this debt is further specified, and gratefully acknowledged, in the Bibliographical Note, p. 253.

Queen's University
Belfast

Contents

CONTENTS

I

On Interpreting Aristotle

---

1. 'Aristoteles ex Aristotele'

How does one person come to understand another? We can have no direct access to another person's character, to what he 'really' is, yet we do sometimes come to know people. How do we do it? By taking their expressions, their gestures, their words, their actions as clues to what they are. We read our experience of them as meaning the persons they are, much as we read words on a page as meaning what they say. The very fact that we may be deceived in our interpretation shows that our effort to understand is a meaningful one. Were it meaningless, we could not recognize that our reading might be correct or incorrect, true or false. As in the interpretation of an ambiguous picture, or the weighing of evidence for a theory, so here too, there is a venture to be made.

Trying to understand a philosopher is the same sort of task. The central problems that absorb his interest, the teachers who have taught him, the books he has read, the structure of his arguments, all these provide relevant clues for answering the central question: what sort of thinker is he? It may be objected that a philosophical system is an impersonal entity. What Hegel liked for breakfast, or how he treated his wife, has nothing to do with the nature of his system of thought. And of course, in trying to understand a philosopher we are not trying to understand a person in as complete a way as when we try to understand a friend. It may be that his character as a husband and father, for example, has no bearing whatsoever on his character as a thinker. Even here, however, it depends

13

on the philosopher. In the case of Søren Kierkegaard, to understand his relation to his father, his broken engagement to Regine Olsen, his inability to take up the ministry: all this contributes to our understanding of his thought. Existential dialectic, being existential, is like that. And I should guess, also, that almost anything in Plato's life—certainly his political experiences, both at home in his youth and later in Sicily—has an important bearing on the philosophical problems that concerned him. The philosopher of the Forms was always concerned for the cave; it was the very darkness of the cave that drove him to brave the ascent to the sun and the Good. Even the most detached philosopher, moreover, philosophizes out of his own being, and voices that being in his philosophy. Descartes's mathematical discoveries have their eternal validity, but Descartes's philosophy, his pursuit of a universal mathematics, expresses the confidence of the mathematical discoverer in the validity of mathematics as a model for all knowledge, a belief not then, or now, or ever, to be shared by all men alike. To understand Descartes is to know, as one might know a friend, or better perhaps an academic colleague, a certain Frenchman of the seventeenth century, and in so doing to understand also a certain sort of reflective mathematician's mind.

If this is true, then there is not a philosophy, or the philosophy, but there are philosophies, i.e. there are, and have been, philosophers, and the critical assessment of the history of philosophy becomes very germane to, if not identical with, philosophy itself. Western philosophy becomes, on this view, a conversation of western man with himself, a conversation about pervasive and difficult if not insoluble problems, which has been going on for the past twenty-five hundred years, and in which, as twentieth-century people reflecting on the same or similar problems, we take our place. To understand a past philosopher is difficult, because he lived long ago, and his problems, his interests, his language, his solutions, are different from ours. Yet it is possible to understand a past philosopher, because the conversation of philosophy has been continuous, and we ourselves are taking part in it. As we might read a friend's personality in his letters, we can still read such a philosopher's thought in his words. We can still question him, and he can answer.

What we want to do in the case of our interpretation of Aristotle, therefore, is to read the thinker in his works. We could not do this so easily for the earliest Greek philosophers, for Anaximander, for example, of whom we have two sentences, with difficulty even for Parmenides, of whose great poem we do possess extensive fragments. But for Aristotle, once philologians have established the extent of the genuine material at our disposal, the task ought, on the face of it, to be easier. The texts may be crabbed, but if they are Aristotle's, we should be able to follow the maxim of an eminent nineteenth-century critic, and interpret 'Aristotelem ex Aristotele'.

2. The problem of Aristotle's development

Our task is not to be approached, however, as directly as we might wish. Parallel with the continuous conversation of philosophy, there is the formidable accretion of scholarly literature about philosophy, and especially in the interpretation of Aristotle: the last forty years have seen changes here with which every new interpreter must reckon.

Until recently the traditional Aristotelian Corpus was taken to represent, by and large, a systematic unity. Some of its contents, admittedly, seemed spurious, and some, notably the *Politics* and *Metaphysics*, oddly organized, to say the least. Yet the philosophy of the high middle ages, and an important strand of western thought ever since, was founded on the impression of system in the works of Aristotle, as restored in Latin translation to the West. True, Aristotle could not have been Christianized without the heritage of Augustine and Plotinus, that is, without neo-Platonism, but it was the Aristotelian universe revised in a Christian sense that thinkers of the seventeenth century in part accepted, in part attempted to destroy. And the unity of this world, in its marvellously careful

15

and manifold articulation, has long seemed evident to students of the Corpus, whatever the contradictions or oddities of a few apparently spurious bits. After all, the simple fact that Aristotle fills his works with cross-references suggests overwhelmingly that, in the sum total of them, he knew what he was at. Take as one example the outline of the works on natural science at the beginning of the *Meteorology*:

> We have already discussed the first causes of nature, and all natural motion, also the stars ordered in the motion of the heavens, and the physical elements—enumerating and specifying them and showing how they change into one another—and becoming and perishing in general. There remains for consideration a part of this inquiry which all our predecessors called meteorology. It is concerned with events that are natural, though their order is less perfect than that of the first of the elements of bodies. (338 a 20 ff.; Oxf.)[1]

There follows an outline of the *Meteorology* itself, and then Aristotle continues:

> When the inquiry into these matters is concluded let us consider what account we can give, in accordance with the method we have followed, of animals and plants, both generally and in detail. When that has been done we may say that the whole of our original undertaking will have been carried out. (338 b 5 ff.; Oxf.)

The topics mentioned in the first sentence of the *Meteorology* do in fact correspond to the subjects of a series of treatises: the *Physics*, *On the Heavens* I and II, *On the Heavens* III and IV, and *On Generation and Corruption*. Thus we have here a neatly organized programme for treating one by one each of the branches of 'physics' or 'second philosophy', and the works referred to carry out the programme rigorously and on the whole consistently. The biological works also, when Aristotle comes to them, are again organized not only tidily, but with typical Aristotelian tidiness, the subjects being treated with reference to the relation of form and matter, and with reference to such concepts as final and efficient cause.

Or consider the organization of Aristotle's logical writings,

---

[1] Translations not specified as being either Oxford or my own are from the Loeb Library. See Bibliographical Note, p. 253.

traditionally referred to under the title of the *Organon*. We have first a book dealing with single uncompounded terms, then one dealing with the combination of two terms to form a proposition, and with the immediate inferences possible between pairs of such propositions, then a pair of books dealing with the arrangement of three terms to form arguments, the doctrine of the syllogism, then another pair of books telling us how to string sets of these triads of terms together in the best possible way, that is, in such a way as to produce demonstrative science; then a treatment of dialectical syllogism, the second-best method of argument, which is still valid, but not built on the right sort of first principles and therefore not scientific; and finally a treatment of logical fallacies. Such a scheme suggests the grasp of a varied material by a single systematizing mind.

The publication in 1923 of Professor Werner Jaeger's *Aristoteles* has changed all this, and has produced a deluge of exegetical literature with a new and more 'historical' slant. It is the growth of Aristotle, not the system of Aristotle, which the scholars influenced by Jaeger's work attempt to understand. For Professor Jaeger introduced to students of Greek philosophy an Aristotle deeply influenced in his youth by the teachings of Plato's Academy and growing toward a more 'scientific' or 'empirical' temper in his later years—a direction carried further by his friend and successor Theophrastus. Aristotle's so-called esoteric or popular writings, in particular, Jaeger argues, i.e. the dialogues which we possess only in fragments, and also certain parts of other works, notably the *Metaphysics*, are Platonic in doctrine. The dialogues, for example, convey a belief in the separateness of soul from body typical of the Academics. Similarly, in the case of *Metaphysics* Lambda we have a proof of God typical of the theological interest of the Platonic school. The latter interest, together with occasional references to the Platonists as 'we', serves to mark, in Jaeger's view, the early portions of the *Metaphysics* from the later, more 'scientific' parts. This theory of Jaeger's, basing the relative dates of parts of the *Metaphysics* on the internal evidence of differences in style or doctrine, opened the door to similar treatments by other scholars of other Aristotelian works. In a number of exact and exacting studies, the ethical, psychological and biological works have been similarly analysed and dated on internal grounds, and an entire new literature of Aristotelian exegesis has arisen, founded on this method. Any interpreter of Aristotle must take account of the existence of this body of literature.

Before taking up my central theme, therefore, let me notice some of the pros and cons, as they seem to me, of this sort of historical interpretation, both of philosophers in general, and of Aristotle in particular.

3. *Pro Jaeger*

On the credit side, it must be said, firstly: any method of exegesis which brings the thinker to life is preferable to one that leaves his words stiff and dead on the page. My analogy between knowing a friend and knowing a philosopher has already emphasized this point. If instead of taking the Aristotelian Corpus as a paper-and-ink computer, we try to understand the thinking of the man behind it, we have taken the first and essential step toward knowing what all the paper and ink is about. Much of Aristotle's logical writings, for example, can be translated into a modern formal language; but this is logic, or at least a small branch of it, not Aristotle. To understand any man's thinking, moreover, is, or may be, to understand his growth, for, as Aristotle himself well knew, thinking is a form of life, and all life consists in development, or rather in a cycle of development followed by decay.

Over and above this general historical thesis, moreover, there are difficulties in interpreting the Aristotelian writings which especially suggest some such developmental approach. The *Metaphysics* in particular is indeed a strangely patchy work. On an initial book introducing the nature of the subject as 'wisdom' and, as in most Aristotelian introductions, investigating the opinions of the philosopher's predecessors, there follows a small interpolated book, then a book of 'problems' or 'knots' to be untied, only a few of which are explicitly referred to later in the treatise. Next comes a book dealing principally with the problem of first principles, then the so-called philosophical dictionary, then a book which in part harks back to the first, third and fourth books, but in part seems to form a bridge to the next series. The next three, Zeta, Eta, Theta, form a relatively continuous argument, but instead of referring directly to the 'knots' of Book Beta, their argument is based explicitly on the meanings of 'Being' listed in the 'dictionary' of Delta (as is Epsilon also). The next book, Iota, can with some stretching be fitted into this series. Next, Kappa is itself a patchwork of summaries in part parallel to Beta, in part taken from another work altogether, the *Physics*. Next, Lambda treats the nature of God and the intelligences that move the celestial spheres, but seems to stand as an independent argument, though in part presupposing the arguments of Nu, which, however, follows it in our text. Mu attacks the Platonic theory of ideas, in part repeating Alpha. What is one to make of this conglomeration?

One plausible answer is to say that doctrines of various dates have been put together, whether by Aristotle himself for lecturing purposes, by Theophrastus, or even by the editors of our texts in Rome of the first century A.D. These pieces fit, as it were, into a jigsaw puzzle in the fourth dimension: they show us Aristotle's thought, not in extension at any one date, but in development from one phase to another.

How do Jaeger and his disciples know how to date the particular pieces? The evidence they use is mainly doctrinal. In fact, not even the cross-references weigh against doctrine, which comes first. Thus if Aristotle, in a given passage, states an 'early' view, and in the same passage refers to a work that states a 'later' view, then the cross-reference is said to be an 'interpolation' by an editor, since it is the recognizable shift in doctrine that forms the basic 'evidence'. So in the light of an hypothesis about the direction of Aristotle's intellectual development, an overall test for dating is established, and then various passages are fitted into the corresponding periods: in general, the Platonic and other-worldly earlier, the 'scientific' and empirical later.

Take, for example, the conflicting statements of Aristotle about the subject-matter of metaphysics, that is, in his language, first philosophy. This is sometimes described by Aristotle as theology, sometimes as the science of being *qua* being. But which is it? Let me expand the question a little before sketching the historical critic's answer.

Every special science, for Aristotle, has a special subject-matter, which can be carved out from the rest of reality and studied in the light of its own appropriate premises. Thus the subject-matter of 'physics', *natural* science, is *natures*: the internal starting-points of change in things which contain such a principle. The subject-matter of mathematics (or at least of a part of it) is the quantitative aspect of natural objects considered in abstraction from everything except their quantity. But there are three theoretical philosophies, physics or second philosophy, mathematics, and first philosophy or wisdom. What is the special subject, the subject-genus, of the last of these, which in Aristotle's view is the first and highest of the three? Aristotle describes it at least once as the science dealing with the highest genus: and that seems to be pure form, the unmoved mover of all moving things, God. First philosophy, then, is theology. Elsewhere, however, Aristotle insists that first philosophy has no subject-genus. It deals, as we shall see later, not with any single species of being, unambiguously carved out of a wider genus, as we carve the species man out of the genus animal, but with the much more difficult and only indirectly accessible subject 'being *qua* being'. It deals with the being of all things, not with any one being, even with God, who is still one being among others, even though the most perfect and best. How can we resolve this contradiction?

Jaeger's answer is to say that Aristotle has changed his mind. In his early days as a brilliant young Platonist, the Academician described by Plato as 'the mind of the school', he shared with his fellow Platonists their interest in the Divine. The highest, the first philosophy, was the study of

God: that study on which Plato in his old age founded his state, so that unpersuadable atheists must be imprisoned or even put to death. Later in Aristotle's life, when his early medical background came to have its due influence and he developed further than any man had ever done (or had ever expressed) a passionate interest in the detailed structure and functioning of living things, his interest in the supersensible source of reality waned and the vision of a science of things, of all things, seen as well as unseen, took possession of him. First philosophy then descended from its Platonic heaven and became the science of being *qua* being, with the stress, in *Metaphysics* Zeta, on sensible substances, the individual living things with which the beaches and pools of his Aegean haunts had been so richly stocked.

No wonder, then, if this is the true story, that the text we call the *Metaphysics* is such a jumble, for it consists of fragmentary documents representing different stages in the development of Aristotle's thought. And if this is so, the text can be sorted out in the light of the nearness to or distance from the Platonic period of each book, or chapter, or even paragraph. Discrepancies in style or doctrine can thus be used to explain the patchwork character of the traditional text. Lambda could not be integrated with the argument of Zeta, for example, because it is an early piece, theological in its emphasis. Nor could Zeta refer back to Beta, since meantime Aristotle had developed his views so much further in an empirical and 'scientific' direction.

Thus difficulties of organization are explained by drawing out apparently doctrinal differences and referring them to different periods for their composition. Where it is in the first instance doctrinal differences that need explaining, the historical hypothesis seems even more plausible. For if a philosopher asserts both A and non-A, one would like to think, not that he does not know a contradiction when he meets one, but that he once believed A and later non-A. That seems the simplest explanation for the multiple definition of first philosophy of which we have just been speaking. Or again, the discrepancy between the two accounts in the *Metaphysics* of the unmoved mover can be similarly explained. All movers, according to Aristotle, must have something to move them; but an infinite regress for him is inconceivable. So there must be a first mover which causes all other things' motion but is himself unmoved. (This is a very crude rendering of Aristotle's argument, which I shall try to make more intelligible in another context.) It is God, or the unmoved mover, whom Aristotle discusses in book Lambda of the *Metaphysics*. But in some passages he speaks of a single such divine source of movement, while in another place he specifies a number of such entities, one for each celestial sphere. How can the same thing, that is, the origin of movement in the universe, be both one and many? Clearly, to see one of these opinions as later than the other at once resolves the difficulty.[1]

There are many such seeming discrepancies in Aristotle's views of this or that. Consider, for example, his view of the soul: remembering always that behind him there is a long tradition in which ψυχή (soul) means something much broader than 'soul' in the Christian sense. ψυχή is first 'breath', something like the breath of life, we might say very generally, the principle of life. That is in fact (except for rational mind) how Aristotle takes it. Yet his theoretical account of it seems to differ in different texts. In the *Parts of Animals*, for example, when he inquires where the seat of the soul is in the body, his account of the relation of soul and body is to some extent unlike the account of the treatise *On the Soul* (*De Anima*). For in the latter work he defines soul as the activity of the body and (except for reason, which constitutes a problem in itself), so intimately linked to body that the question of their separation cannot even arise. In one of his rare metaphors the austere philosopher rails at those who would make the soul an entity with a separate existence in its own right:

> That is why we can wholly dismiss as unnecessary the question whether the soul and the body are one: it is as meaningless as to ask whether the wax and the shape given to it by the stamp are one, or

---

[1] But cf. H. A. Wolfson (116) and p. 226 below.

generally the matter of a thing and that of which it is the matter. (412 b 6–8; Oxf.)

For soul is simply how a living body works: that is what it comes down to in the end. Moreover, soul in this sense could not be in one part of the body rather than another; the organizing principle of a whole cannot be located in one part of it, it *is* just that whole *as* functioning. In the *Parts of Animals*, however, and in some parts of the *Shorter Treatises on Nature* (*Parva Naturalia*), Aristotle speaks of soul as if it were some sort of semi-detached something that had got into the body and had its seat in some particular part of it. A striking example is the opening chapter of the treatise *On Youth and Age*, etc.:

> We have elsewhere given a precise account of the soul, and while it is clear that its essential reality cannot be corporeal, yet manifestly it must exist in some bodily part which must be one of those possessing control over the members. (467 b 13ff.; Oxf.)

This organ, it turns out here as elsewhere, is the heart. Now the tone and tenor of this doctrine sounds to us less 'modern' and sophisticated than the rigorously functional psychology of the treatise *On the Soul*; so it seems plausible to ask: could not the doctrine of the localization of the soul represent a middle period in Aristotle's development, when he had outgrown the primitive dualism of Plato, but had not yet developed the full functionalism of his mature psychology? The reference here to the 'precise account of the soul', moreover, clearly cannot be a straightforward one, for the texts do plainly oppose one another; there must have been an earlier draft of the psychology, to which Aristotle is referring here; or else this is an interpolation by an editor.

This and others like it are peripheral puzzles, however, compared to the central and, on the face of it, glaring contradiction at the root of Aristotle's thought. We may present this apparent contradiction here briefly in two steps, and consider how an historical approach of the Jaegerian type might help us to alleviate if not to resolve it.

Knowledge, for Aristotle as for Plato, must be both

infallible and real, that is, it must be a grasp of real things. Guesswork and opinion are not knowledge, nor would a purely formal system, like a modern logical calculus, qualify for this honorific name. What real things can we know for certain? The flowing world of sense, Plato believed, lacks the stability of the purely knowable; it flits by, dreamlike, taking shape with every man's illusion. Only general conceptions, not this man but humanity, not this pleasure but good itself, are knowable. Such generals, of course, for Plato were Forms, the really real objects of knowledge, separate from the perceived and perceptible world, but lending it somehow such approximation to reality as it could achieve. Aristotle, while rejecting the separation of the Forms, yet agreed with his teacher that the objects of knowledge must be permanent and stable. But particulars, except in the heavens, change size and shape and quality as well as place, are born and die. As particulars, therefore, they would be only perceived, not known. Only universals are objects of knowledge. Yet Aristotle did deny the reality of the Platonic Forms; only individuals, he insists again and again in the *Metaphysics*, are fully real. Beings in the primary, the genuine sense are individual things such as this man, this horse, this ox. 'Man, this man, existent man' are one and the same. The Platonic conception of a Man, self-existent, really real, in which all men 'participate' is for Aristotle redundant and absurd. Substances: particular, separately existing things, capable of assuming and losing contrary qualities: Callias ruddy, turning pale; Socrates young, growing old—of such as these the catalogue of realities is made. So once more, Aristotle, most meticulous of dialecticians, seems to be asserting, within the compass of a given work: knowledge is of the real and universal; but whatever is real is not universal; therefore if knowledge is of the real it is not of the universal, if of the universal, not of the real. Yet knowledge by definition must be both. Here is a contradiction indeed! Aristotle has proved laboriously in Book Gamma that the Law of Non-Contradiction is fundamental to all meaningful discourse. No meaningful proposition can assert of the same subject in the same respect an attribute and its opposite. Yet when we put his statement, about universality and knowledge and reality alongside one another, he himself seems to be doing just that.

The contradiction becomes even more open and obvious, moreover, when we put the *Metaphysics* alongside the first treatise of the logical writings, the *Categories*. The basic distinction among all the things there are, for Aristotle, is that between substance and the accidents of substance, between the things which in some sense exist independently and the 'things', quantities, qualities, positions, relations, etc., which can exist only as belonging to those independent entities. First philosophy, as the study of being *par excellence*, is the study of substance, and in the *Metaphysics* Aristotle asserts over and over, in contradiction to the Platonists, that only individual things are substances. Universals are not so. This is quite clear and unambiguous. In the *Categories*, on the other hand, he designates individuals—this man, this horse—by the term 'first substance' and universals, i.e. species and genus—man, horse, animal—he describes as 'second substances'. If the *Categories* belong to the genuine Corpus (and the first nine chapters are generally accepted as Aristotelian even if not Aristotle's), this puts a glaring contradiction at the head of the Logic itself.

But what if Aristotle grew slowly away from a Platonic faith in universals as the really real? What if he came only gradually and late to a livelier appreciation of concrete, sensible realities: this octopus, that dogfish, or this man? If this is the way it happened, and the traditional Corpus represents all stages of the Philosopher's career, then of course the passages stressing the reality of universals must be early and the denial of substantial status to general concepts comes correspondingly late. The conflict which has beset interpreters for centuries falls away. Instead of working within a rigid frame somehow constraining, against reason, forces that press in opposite directions, we find ourselves climbing a gentle slope of growth and maturation, the deep seas of Platonism behind us and the indefinite horizon of science itself ahead. The prospect is alluring.

4. Contra Jaeger •

The genetic method, then, appears to solve many puzzles. On the other side, however, we must weigh the drawbacks of this kind of criticism against its successes in smoothing out the critic's task.

There are at least four objections that count heavily against Jaeger's view. First, the alleged pattern of development is by no means unambiguously plain. Scholars disagree emphatically among themselves as to the relative dates of the various parts of the Corpus. It is an important part of Jaeger's view, for example, that the theology of Lambda is early; yet Professor Guthrie argued in an article published in 1933 that it is in fact later, a mature doctrine, developed not out of a Platonic interest in the other-worldly, but out of a down-to-earth materialism. Even earlier, in 1927, an Austrian philologian, Hans von Arnim, had demonstrated, in a paper which does not appear to have been refuted by Jaeger or his adherents, that Jaeger's chronology for the composition of the *Metaphysics* is circular! That is, the sequence deducible from Jaeger's argument would be: ΝΛΑΚΒΓΕΙΝΛ. The details of this allegation are hard to confirm from Jaeger's text; but what does emerge quite clearly from von Arnim's analysis is the following circularity. In the first book of the *Metaphysics* Aristotle bases his account of his predecessors on his doctrine of the four causes as expounded in Book II of the *Physics*. Now in Book Alpha Aristotle refers to the Platonic school as 'we', and this, according to Jaeger, marks it as early. The dialogue *On Philosophy*, which criticizes the Academy more unsympathetically, must be later than Alpha. But in the second book of the *Physics*, Aristotle refers to the dialogue *On Philosophy*; so he must have written *Physics* II after that dialogue. Thus we have the series of relative dates of composition:

1. On Philosophy
2. Physics II
3. Metaphysics Alpha
4. On Philosophy

Admittedly, von Arnim himself was convinced that the genetic type of interpretation was the correct one; only he based his theory of Aristotle's development on the various ethical writings, rather than on the *Metaphysics*. The disagreement of the geneticists, therefore, does not necessarily demonstrate the incorrectness of all genetic hypotheses. It does point, however, to a second and more fundamental difficulty, a difficulty inherent in the use of internal evidence alone for dating texts. Internal evidence is uncontrolled (in fashionable language, 'unfalsifiable'). Once one is started on this kind of reasoning, there is no knowing where to stop. In another famous instance of such historical interpretation, Professor Kemp Smith's analysis of Kant's *Critique of Pure Reason*, there are at least a few small pieces of external evidence to pin the thesis to, such as a letter dated 20 May 1778, or an official document signed by the Rector of the University of Königsberg and dated 20 January 1780. Kant made notes on these scraps of paper, and these at least, therefore, can be dated with certainty. But in the case of Aristotle there is not even this slender bit of extraneous evidence upon which the historically minded scholar may construct his intellectual biography. It is the text itself and the text alone from which the various periods must be elicited. Even in the case of Plato, where the external evidence is ampler and the stylistic changes more definite, there is relativity enough in the dating of the dialogues. In the case of Aristotle, the field seems open altogether, especially when not only different works, but parts of the same work are set against one another and 'dated' by standards which they themselves provide. Even the cross-references are not left intact as quasi-external pointers; as I have already mentioned, they are explicitly subordinated to differences in doctrine: if there is a reference to a 'late' work—a work which on the particular scholar's theory should be later—it is diagnosed away as a 'later interpolation'.[1] The whole procedure finally issues in a

---

[1] This may seem advisable sometimes, as in the passage from *Youth and Old Age* already quoted; but on other occasions, where the difference in doctrine is

sort of Heraclitean flux: from one page to the next one is never reading the same Aristotle, and finally there is no Aristotle left to read at all.

This is literally so, for at least one student of these matters, Joseph Zürcher, has concluded after ten years' extremely detailed study of Aristotle's style and teaching that it was not Aristotle at all but his pupil Theophrastus who wrote most of the Corpus as we have it. And this is indeed the logical outcome of the Jaegerian approach. On the one hand, there is no external control to prevent such an absurd conclusion. And on the other hand, the philosophical principles back of Jaeger's theory lend themselves to just such a view. Aristotle developed from a Platonist, an other-worldly visionary, into a scientist, a down-to-earth observer of the concrete natural scene. But the element of systematic metaphysics is even less, the naturalist's curiosity about particular phenomena even more marked in the works of Theophrastus than of the traditional 'Aristotle'. So if we separate all metaphysical, i.e. Platonic passages from the 'scientific', i.e. Theophrastean passages, we have no Aristotle left. Or rather, we have Aristotle a disciple of Plato, whose friend Theophrastus was a scientist. And, of course, Theophrastus did succeed Aristotle as head of the Lyceum, and it was, tradition tells us, Theophrastus's copy of Aristotle's manuscripts which was taken away by Theophrastus's nephew to the Troad and recovered for the West in the first century B.C. What more likely than that the scientist Theophrastus should in fact have inserted many of his own opinions into the lectures of his predecessor? Why should he confine his lectures to metaphysical nonsense which he knew to be false? And yet out of respect for the founder of the school he might retain some of the more speculative and Platonizing expositions of the original lecture course. Theophrastus was not in any case a man to over-systematize. Philosophical inconsistencies would not worry him if there was plenty of factual detail there to interest the practical

less striking, the balance ought on the face of it to be the other way. Cf. e.g. *On Breath* 474 b10.

student of nature. So the inconsistencies of our Corpus are explained not by the development of an early into a maturer Aristotle, but by the fusion of some early Aristotelian, i.e. Platonic texts with later, scientific, i.e. Theophrastean teachings.

I am by no means competent to criticize this classical Bacon-wrote-Shakespeare theory on its own philological grounds, but whatever its merits or demerits in detailed analysis of texts, it does furnish, it seems to me, a most instructive object-lesson for the inherent arbitrariness of this form of historical critique. It suggests, even short of the author's extreme conclusion, the most general and basic objection to the interpretation of the Jaeger school. That is: that instead of leading the student to do his best to understand the philosopher in question, it makes him try his utmost to dissolve the thinker he is studying into many opposing thinkers and finally to legislate him out of existence altogether. True, even the greatest philosopher may contradict himself; and where he does so, we may well suppose, as a working hypothesis, that he has changed his mind. But there must be some coherence, some unity rich enough to be meaningful and illuminating, in some one stage of his thought, if he is to come through to us as a great philosopher at all. There must be some such richness and coherence in any one work which *is* one; and there must even be, it seems to me, one theme running through the philosopher's development, one predominating line of thought, one sovereign intellectual passion, of sufficient bearing on the persistent problems of philosophy to make him the philosopher he is. The genetic approach, however, turns its back on such a unity. It dissolves its subject into a bewildering plurality of subjects, before ever having made the effort to understand who in truth he is and what in truth he has to say, what he had to say, in his time, to those who heard and read him then, and what he has to say, at a greater remove and with a greater imaginative effort on our part, to us who read him today. Much labour and skill have been expended in the historical interpretation of the Aristotelian texts; but useful though the results may be in subordination to the task of understanding Aristotle, they are not a substitute for such understanding. Critical analysis is essential to history; but it should be criticism subordinate to an aim that is essentially anti-critical: i.e. the imaginative projection of the historian into the situation of his subject, his sympathetic identification with him. While remaining ourselves, with our twentieth-century standards and beliefs, we must, if we would understand a dead philosopher, yet put ourselves intellectually in some sense in his place; and this we cannot do if our principal attention is directed to denying rather than asserting his identity. It is logically possible, though, I should think, highly improbable, that there is no unified Aristotle, but we should not let ourselves be led into the byways of geneticism until we have made a serious effort to discover him if he does exist.

The theory of the 'multiple authorship of Homer' offers an instructive parallel. Consider one aspect of this story. The occurrence of stock lines and phrases where they were inappropriate seemed to suggest a use of one man's phrases by another, and it was therefore 'evidence' for the denial that there was one Homer who composed the *Iliad*. One of the decisive steps in overthrowing this theory was Milman Parry's careful study of Serbian folk poetry, where the poet uses similar traditional phrases or epithets in singing *his* poem. Such a minstrel, using traditional phrases as matter for his own creation, was Homer. In other words, to assimilate the seeming inconsistencies of the fixed lines there is no need to deny the existence of the poet, but only to understand the techniques of his kind of traditional poetry. Something similar might be true of Aristotle. As we shall see shortly, the solution suggested by Owens for interpreting the organization of the *Metaphysics* is essentially of this kind. Following his lead, we can imagine one Aristotle who used the several texts comprising our *Metaphysics* in a rational and orderly way.

Before suggesting such a solution, however, I must mention two further objections to the picture of Aristotle as Jaeger has drawn it. Apart from the objections already mentioned (the uncertainties of internal-evidence dating, and its tendency to dissolve its subject), Jaeger's model seems to me improbable on two counts, one philosophical and one historical.

The picture of a development from Platonic 'metaphysics' to observation and 'science' is based on a shallow view of both. All science rests on some metaphysics, some vision of reality. Moreover, the vision of modern science in its most authoritative branches, that is, first and foremost in mathematical physics, is in several important ways more Platonic than Aristotelian: in its reliance on mathematical forms as the instrument of all science, for example, or in its scepticism about the power of language (even formal language) to enunciate once for all the definitive answer to its problems. Further, the naïve positivist model of science which seems to underlie Jaeger's theory presents a gross over-simplification of scientific procedures. Science, Jaeger seems to believe, consists in observing the 'facts'. This was the conception that led the chemist Ostwald, as late as 1910, to deny the existence of atoms because no one had ever seen them. Science is by no means as simple as that. Even if scientists were mere fact-finders, moreover, this conception would have little to do with *Aristotelian* science, which, as we shall see, differs deeply both from modern scientific disciplines as they have come to be practised in the past three hundred years, and from the simple positivist ideal which has seldom been practised anywhere.

Finally, and this is the objection bearing most closely on my thesis in this book, if Aristotle did develop, did it really happen in this fashion of a slow drift from a 'Platonic' to a 'scientific' attitude?

Perhaps it is reasonable to believe that while Aristotle was still a member of the Academy he was sympathetic with the beliefs of that school. The dialogue *Eudemus* does include a proof of immortality, for example, closely parallel to Plato's in the *Phaedo*. Even here, however, as Jaeger himself points out, it is a Platonic argument strikingly Aristotelian in the economy and dryness of its logic. In fact, there have now emerged a handful of scholars who argue eloquently for the Aristotelian, not the Platonizing character even of the dialogues. One of them, Professor Düring of Göteborg, argues that in fact some of Plato's own dialogues may have been partly directed against the young thinker who had come so brilliantly to oppose him, to oppose him while accepting and re-interpreting in a very different sense the heart of his doctrine. This is a fascinating hypothesis, confirming once more, as Düring explicitly recognizes, the paucity of evidence and scope of theorizing allowed by such speculations. But even putting this tempting view aside, if we suppose that Aristotle *did* develop along something resembling the Jaeger line of growth, when did this development take place?

Immediately after Plato's death, Aristotle left Athens for Assos and Lesbos, where he spent three years. Now, D'Arcy Thompson has pointed out that many of the fauna mentioned in Aristotle's biological writings are forms that he would have found during his stay in the North Aegean, and we can reasonably guess that much of his biological research took place during this time. Except for the fragments of the dialogues, however, the whole set of Aristotelian writings as we have them presumably bear some relation to the course of lectures which he gave as head of the Lyceum, long after his stay at Assos and Mitylene, in the years 334–322 B.C. One need not attach much credit to the quaint theory that these are students' lecture notes, but that they represent a lecturer's teaching programme seems very plausible indeed. The consistent cross-references, the pursuit of difficulties 'dealt with in our course on . . .' give us a sense of an infinitely careful and systematic pedagogue. Thus, whenever Aristotle in fact wrote the several parts of the Corpus, we may take it that these works formed the skeleton at least of a carefully articulated curriculum which he elaborated *after* his years of devoted and brilliant biological research. In other words, D'Arcy Thompson was amply justified in his remark that Aristotle's biology may have provided the cornerstone for his metaphysics and his logic—for all his philosophy, in fact—which was elaborated in teaching form years after the sojourn in Assos and Lesbos. This thesis has been touched on by many critics but not so far as I can find systematically elaborated, and what I want to do in this book is to keep it in mind as a guiding thread for the study of Aristotle's thought.

Admittedly, in a way this thesis complements rather than contradicts that of the genetic school. Jaeger himself, in fact, has to push Aristotle's crucial development far back in time to the Academic period, so that the 'development' is long since over in the texts as we have them. But to draw the sort of conclusions Jaeger draws we have to suppose that Aristotle simply incorporated into his lectures a hodge-podge of inconsistent bits from earlier days. And this for two reasons seems to me an unreasonable thing to do. For one thing, the most obvious characteristic of Aristotle, on the face of his writings, is neatness. However tattered the manuscripts became during their long, mouldering stay in that damp basement in Skepsis, or if there were other copies, however much they were edited in the Lyceum, there was certainly enough left of the original to show us the immense, the appalling tidiness of their author's mind. Such a master of orderliness would not, could not throw together all sorts of inconsistent oddments and cover them over with a thin veil of cross-reference and programmatic outline— like a slovenly housewife who shoves all the litter out of sight in the cupboard when visitors ring the bell. The Aristotelian Corpus must have, in its main outline, something like the order it says it has. Secondly, even if scholars can ferret out earlier lines of organization, the Corpus as we have it does, as I have just said, represent, in most subjects at least, the lecture course of the Lyceum as Aristotle conceived it after the definitive period of biological research. And so we are entitled to study it as such, whatever its genesis.

Take one example of the situation here. Düring has made a painstaking study of the biological works and has analysed out three great lecture courses in biology that, as he sees it, Aristotle developed. But the final and crowning one consists in the whole of the biological corpus as we have it; and this represents Aristotle's coherent and mature view. It is this coherent and mature view that we are studying here, not primarily in the biological writings themselves so much as in the logic, physics and metaphysics, that is, in the core of what we should describe as Aristotle's philosophy (as distinct from his scientific opinions) with special reference to the question, what role his deep and inspired biological interest may have had in shaping his philosophical beliefs. 'Philosophy,' Whitehead has said, 'is the attempt to clarify those fundamental beliefs which finally determine the emphasis of attention that lies at the base of character.' What distinguishes Aristotle's 'emphasis of attention' from Plato's or Descartes's or any other philosopher's, I shall argue, is closely related to a certain kind of field naturalist's passion for the minute observation of the structures and life histories of living things. This is a passion which antedates, and helps to determine, the whole of the Corpus as we have it, that is, it bears essentially and deeply on Aristotle himself, on the mind of the most neatly and elaborately systematic of Western thinkers as from his own writings we can and do know him.

5. *Resolution of genetic problems*

So much for the *pros* and *cons* of the genetic interpretation. We must not abandon the contradictions this method seems to resolve, however, without a hint of the way in which a more philosophically oriented interpretation can accomplish the same end.

First, as to the organizational problems, and in particular the problem of the *Metaphysics*. Here the analysis of Father Joseph Owens gives us the thread to guide us out of the labyrinth. The major portions of the *Metaphysics*, he suggests, were a series of school texts or λόγοι, which Aristotle used as the basis for his lectures. Each could be worked through independently, yet each presupposed the preceding stage in the course through which the students of the Lyceum were moving, step by careful step, from their logical and physical studies to the acquisition of Wisdom. First: introduction; then knots to be untied, i.e. major difficulties in the way of further progress; next, discussion of the role of axioms, which must come at the head of every science but present a special stumbling block here; then, the assertion that despite all difficulties there *is* a first philosophy. Then, based on the philosophical dictionary, the study of sensible substance, potentiality and actuality, and unity. Then essays attacking the problem of non-sensible substance, the rejection of Forms and mathematicals, and the assertion of the unmoved mover: the climax at which the previous dialectical approaches have all been aimed. For the study of being *qua* being is, it turns out, the study of the primary instance of being, and toward that study the whole of the previous argument has been directed. In the last analysis, therefore, first philosophy as theology and first philosophy as the study of being are one and the same.

Next, the difficulties about soul. Since there is still in the treatise *On the Soul*, as in other biological works, the concession of immortality to one part of soul, the rational, one might argue that even here Aristotle was Aristotle from the start. Nevertheless, the Platonizing argument of the *Eudemus* and the functionalism of the *De Anima* do seem in tone and emphasis far apart, and perhaps it is right, therefore, to take some passages in other works as representing a transitional stage between the two. This may be true of the passage from *Youth and Old Age* quoted above. On the whole, however, the account of the *Parts of Animals* seems to me to differ from the *De Anima* at least as much in its context as in its philosophical purport. The question of the mechanism of soul in running the body may raise problems which call for special treatment, a treatment irrelevant and inappropriate to the psychology but not necessarily flatly contradicting it. Witness, for example, the references forward from the *Parts* to the *Generation of Animals*, the former presumably belonging to the middle and the latter to the final period. Plainly, in Aristotle's view these two texts at least belonged together in a rational order; and the same may be true of the *De Anima*. What is more, apparent contradictions also persist between works both admittedly of one period, or within a single such work itself. Compare, for example, the general theory of soul common to the central parts of the *De Anima* and to the *Generation of Animals* with the discussion in the latter work of the 'cognate pneuma' which carries soul in the process of reproduction. In dealing with a given individual one may stress as much as one likes that the soul is simply the form of the body, its organizing principle(s). But in the *Generation of Animals* Aristotle has to transfer the principle of life in the process of reproduction, from one body, the male parent, to another, the child. Soul is, in his language, the actuality of the body, not just what it may become, but what it is, and it is an axiom for him that actuality must always precede potentiality. The chicken (strictly speaking, the cock) must precede the egg, for only the organizational principle of chickenhood can make a small white and yellow blob become a full-grown bird. In the crucial transition from one individual to its offspring, therefore, we must ask: how does soul, inseparable as it is from its body, move? How does it get from the chicken to the egg? The carrier of soul is the semen, the 'residue' of the male parent, but semen, again, cannot be soul *purely*, for it is material and soul is form. What is it? Or what is in it that enables it to act as the carrier of life? In a puzzling passage in the *Generation of Animals*, Aristotle describes semen as made up of a special subtle stuff called 'cognate pneuma' in which soul has already been implanted, and he speaks of pneuma almost as if it *were* soul, or a very special sort of vehicle of soul, the sort of semi-detached something that is supposed to be characteristic of the earlier, transitional period. This sounds, in other words, more like the doctrine of the *Parts of Animals* than the *De Anima*, although geneticists place the *Generation of Animals* wholeheartedly in the latest, *De Anima* period. Moreover, in the *Generation of Animals* the heart is still referred to as the principle of life: again, the characteristic doctrine of the 'middle' period, and in referring to this view Aristotle remarks: 'As I have said many times over . . .' (741 b 16–17). He, at any rate, seems unaware that he has changed his mind. Yet both views are there; and so we could if we liked break down the *Generation of Animals* itself into earlier and later pieces. This suggests that perhaps in other cases also it is in fact the difference in the question asked, rather than in the period of composition, that produces the difference in the answer.

The central philosophical problem, finally, of the relation between the individuality of the real and the universality of knowledge lends itself readily, also, to a philosophical rather than historico-critical solution. In fact, this is just the crucial point at which, I believe, we shall find Aristotle's biological interests so relevant and illuminating. The practising field naturalist is too much preoccupied with the panorama of life before him to turn his eyes upward to the Platonic heaven of Forms. Yet what he is examining in his pools and rivers is not just individuals for their own sake as the historian or the politician examines them. What he is observing is the type *in* the individual, this frog as this *frog*, this octopus as this *octopus*, this man as this *man*. He is observing both the individuals, which, as he well knows, are the only things there *are*, and the universals *in* them, which are what, as a scientist, he knows. The particular shape of the particular spots on this particular frog are accidental and irrelevant, the structure and life history of *the* frog are all-important. Yet these exist only in the frogs that do exist and have existed and will exist, now and, for Aristotle, in all time past and all time to come forevermore.

Once we see the relation between individual and universal in this way, as every practising field biologist in fact sees it, moreover, we can also solve the problem of the apparent contradiction of the *Categories* and the *Metaphysics*. For everything depends on separating out our subject-matters and asking the right questions about each kind of thing in the appropriate way. It is again a question of context, in scholastic terminology, of the difference between the order of logic and the order of being. Once we have Aristotle's starting-point clearly in mind, these two 'orders' of inquiry will be seen, I hope, to complement, not to contradict one another. Meantime, let us at least hold in abeyance the genetic solution, which is philosophically a counsel of despair, until or unless we find that all else fails.

II
Aristotle and Plato

1. *Introduction*

'The facts of today are the fictions of tomorrow,' says a science lecturer. 'Never, never take a theory as a creed,' says another. All knowledge is tentative, the more tentative the better, so we seem to believe today. There were Greeks who thought so too: notably, for example, the successors of Plato collectively called the Middle Academy. But this was decidedly not the belief of Plato or Aristotle. They were supremely confident, both of them, that knowledge, to be knowledge, must be certain, once for all, eternal—and to be so, it must be *of* an object that is equally secure from the corrosion of time and decay. Moreover, knowledge, if it is knowledge, must be wholly and directly intelligible, not murky or mysterious but luminously clear; and so it must be directed to a reality that is delimited, all of a piece, the kind of reality a rational mind can truly comprehend. Thus knowledge for both Plato and Aristotle is primarily the knowledge of form. In contrast to our more sceptical attitude, therefore, Plato and Aristotle had a great deal in common in their conception of the mind and of the world that is there for it to know. And small wonder: for Aristotle after all spent nearly twenty years in the Academy under Plato's leadership, and left it in fact only after Plato's death. If they have much in common, then, how do they differ? The answer to this question will determine in large part our attitude toward the Aristotelian treatises themselves.

There are three possible, and actual, lines of answer. Those who are steeped in the dialectic of the Platonic dialogues, for whom western thought is a 'series of footnotes to Plato', see in Aristotle a pupil who misconstrued his master. Aristotelian form is Platonic form surreptitiously tucked away in the visible world. For Plato, the Ideas can be known only by a painful and profound conversion; the philosopher must climb laboriously out of the cave to the sun above. Aristotle denied this necessity, and was left with the dilemma we have already noticed, i.e. the contradiction between the denial of real universals and the assertion of the universality of real knowledge. Among recent writers, Léon Robin is perhaps the most outstanding exponent of this view.

Those more interested in the development of logic, on the other hand, are inclined to see in Plato's work a first adumbration of a correct logic, brought to full flower by his most brilliant pupil, and so for them Plato is but a halting Aristotle. This kind of interpretation, in fact, reaches back even to the Presocratic texts. For the generation of Parmenides, it was notoriously a problem, how non-being could be expressed. Parmenides cut the Gordian knot with his doctrine that only being is and is expressible, non-being is not and cannot be said. In the *Theaetetus* and *Sophist* of Plato this issue was still a vexed one. The Sophists, those acrobats of argument, had played ducks and drakes with the question, and it was still a serious philosophical problem for Plato to seek its solution. When we know, we know what is real, and that is what, in true statements, we express. But what are we at when we assert what we do *not* know, and what, in fact, is not the case? What is false opinion? The *Theaetetus* offers us several abortive answers and only the abstruse metaphysical speculations of the *Sophist* provide a solution of a sort. Yet we know perfectly well that we can and do make false statements. We can say, to use the example of the *Sophist*, 'Theaetetus flies', when we know that in fact he is doing no such thing, but is sitting here with us discussing philosophy. Why all the fuss? Because, say these logicizing historians, it was only Aristotle who worked out a correct theory of the logic of statements. Plato was still confused, even though not so thoroughly as Parmenides had been. The fact is that the statement 'Theaetetus is (exists)' and the statement 'Theaetetus is snub-nosed' or 'Theaetetus sits (or flies)', use the concept 'to be' in two different senses. Only the second is a *predicative* rather than an *existential* 'is'. Now, of course, Parmenides, living long before Aristotle and logic, had no notion of this difference. He thought that to say 'Theaetetus is snub-nosed' was the same sort of business as to say 'Theaetetus is'. And Plato, with his self-confessed respect for Father Parmenides, was still to some extent embroiled in this confusion of two meanings of 'to be'. Aristotle, on the other hand, repeatedly tells us that the Parmenidean problem is antiquated. As the discoverer of logic he knew what predication is. He knew the difference between a thing (a sensible substance) and the qualities or relations or positions or what-not that can be predicated of it. He knew, and expressed in the *Posterior Analytics*, the difference between the question 'Is it?' and the question 'What is it?' So he could establish in the treatise *On Interpretation* a systematic analysis of the truth and falsity of propositions in terms of what has since been referred to as the 'correspondence theory of truth'. As Wolff put it in the eighteenth century and Tarski in the twentieth, 'The proposition "Snow is white" is true, if and only if snow is white', and false if this is not the case. The metaphysical tangle has at last been abstracted from the logic of propositions and we are clear of the whole dilemma. Plato had made some steps in this direction in the *Sophist*. He had even, the adherents of this view believe, abandoned in his old age those delusive Forms and become, as it were, a crypto-Aristotle, a nearly-logician, more interested in concepts and how we use them than in the rarefied really-reals of recollection which had absorbed him in his youth and middle age.

Each of these views boasts doughty supporters, especially, in contemporary English-speaking philosophy, the second.[1] But the latter position is as unfair to Plato as the former is to Aristotle, and there are also, scattered through the literature,

[1] See Bibliographical Note, p. 253.

proponents of a third view, which respects equally both master and pupil, but sees in the relation between them neither essential decline nor essential progress, but two deeply divergent attitudes to experience, to man and the world. It is this view, represented for Platonic scholarship by the late F. M. Cornford and for Aristotle by Joseph Owens, which, it seems to me, the texts at our disposal plainly support, and which I propose to follow here. Let us, as Owens suggests, read as best we can Plato from the dialogues and Aristotle from the Aristotelian Corpus, and see where we find they stand.

2. Aristotle and Plato's problems

If we do this, we discover, I believe, not so much typically Platonic as against typically Aristotelian answers to the same philosophical problems as different questions, different starting-points altogether. Despite the beliefs they share, to which we shall return hereafter, what is most striking in the two philosophers is the oppositeness of their interests, of the problems that really deeply concern them. To put it rather one-sidedly: *Plato's problems are not problems for Aristotle* at all. He may indeed remark on the obsoleteness of the Parmenidean dilemma, but the dilemma of his teacher's generation he does not even recognize as a dilemma. He passes it by as if, far from being outmoded, it had never been.

It is difficult to justify this statement both simply and correctly. For one thing, Plato was essentially a thinker with *one* question, while Aristotle was a man of many. In fact, this comes close to being the most fundamental difference between them. So a neat table of one to one correspondences would falsify the situation from the start. But perhaps I may risk suggesting the direction of Plato's overriding philosophical concern, shall we say at four levels, or at any rate under four headings, and notice the stand Aristotle takes, or fails to take, on each of them.

First, consider the problem of perception. What do our senses tell us about reality? According to Plato, very little.

'Sensible things are always in flux and there is no knowledge of them.' This is Aristotle's statement of the flux-philosophy as, he tells us, the Platonists understood it. It was this fact, this scepticism about sensory evidence, that drove them to postulate their world of separately existing Forms. For knowledge, we saw, must be of something stable. If therefore sensible things keep changing, then either there is *no* knowledge or there is some *non*-sensible reality that we can know. That was the situation as Aristotle reports it and it is entirely borne out by the text of the dialogues themselves.

To the reader of the *Phaedo* or the *Republic* or the *Gorgias* it may seem that Plato merely despised sensation. The soul is a prisoner in the body, the philosopher practises dying, separating his mind, in his pure, heaven-directed thoughts, from the distracting welter of sounds and colours and textures and pleasures and pains. There was indeed a natural puritan in Plato; and there were influences which combined to strengthen in him this ascetic bent. There was the Pythagorean tradition of identifying the mathematical with reality, Parmenides with his insistence on the superiority of the One to the deceptive panorama of sense, Socrates with his search for universal definitions. Above all, there was the noble yet grotesque, almost comic saintliness of Socrates himself as Plato portrays him, for example, in the speech of Alcibiades in the *Symposium*. The guests at the banquet have been praising Love; Alcibiades, drunk as usual, breaks in and insists on praising Socrates (which comes to the same thing, for philosophical love, the love of wisdom, has its incarnation in Socrates). After praising him for his discourses, more ravishing than the Sirens' music, his strange powers of concentration, his bravery, and above all, his continence, his power of resistance to the charms of Alcibiades himself, he concludes his eulogy:

'. . . there is a point I omitted when I began—how his talk most of all resembles the Silenuses that are made to open. If you chose to listen to Socrates' discourses you would feel them at first to be quite ridiculous; on the outside they are clothed with such absurd words and phrases—all, of course, the hide of a mocking satyr. His talk is

of pack-asses, smiths, cobblers, and tanners, and he seems always
to be using the same terms for the same things; so that any one in-
expert and thoughtless might laugh his speeches to scorn. But when
these are opened, and you obtain a fresh view of them by getting
inside, first of all you will discover that they are the only speeches
which have any sense in them; and secondly, that none are so divine,
so rich in images of virtue, so largely—nay, so completely—intent
on all things proper for the study of such as would attain both grace
and worth.

This, gentlemen, is the praise I give to Socrates: at the same
time, I have seasoned it with a little fault-finding, and have told you
his rude behaviour towards me. However, I am not the only person
he has treated thus: there are Charmides, son of Glaucon, Euthydemus,
son of Diocles, and any number of others who have found his way of
loving so deceitful that he might rather be their favourite than their
lover . . .' (221 E–222 B)

Alcibiades concludes with raillery, as he began, and at the close
of the banquet there is Socrates, the imperturbable philosopher,
still discoursing until all the other guests have fallen wearily
asleep.

When Socrates had seen them comfortable, he rose and went
away . . . ; on arriving at the Lyceum, he washed himself, and then
spent the rest of the day in his ordinary fashion; and so, when the
day was done, he went home for the evening and reposed. (223 D)

The sage superior to sense: Parmenides, Pythagoras, and
above all Socrates are welded into one ideal of wisdom, detached and remote.

Yet Plato did not only turn away from the kaleidoscope of
sounds and tastes and visual patterns. He met its challenge
face to face. Confronting the manifold and insistent instability
of sensory evidence, he developed in the *Theaetetus* his own
theory of perception, and demonstrated that on this theory
perception cannot even be the doorway to knowledge, let
alone knowledge itself. Knowledge must be both infallible
and real. Now perception, he makes Socrates argue in the
Theaetetus, is indeed infallible, for on the sensory level each
man, as Protagoras rightly taught, is the measure of the things

that are that they are, and of the things that are not, that they are not. If the wine tastes sweet to a man in health and sour to a sick man, so it is, to each one in each case as it appears. His taste is the taste that it is at the moment when he is experiencing it; there can be no question about that. Around this Protagorean maxim Plato proceeds to build a cosmology of flux: a world of flowing things and flowing organisms meeting one another in an everlasting relativity. Admittedly, such a world meets the demand of infallibility clearly enough. There can be no error here. But can there be truth? In *pure* perception, devoid of every hint of judgment, there is indeed no missing of the mark, because indeed there is no mark to miss. Of such purely flowing things and selves, in fact, we cannot even say they *are*. For existence, we must admit, is not known by any sense at all. It is neither a sight nor a sound, a taste nor a tangible feeling; it is one of those somethings, like the truths of mathematics, which the mind must grasp, itself by itself, in independence of any particular perception offered it by sense. In contrast, the processes of sense, happenings that just happen but cannot say of themselves or of their objects that they *are*, cannot qualify for the name of knowledge. They may be infallible, in a rather Pickwickian sense, but they are not directed to the *real*. Perception is just the ongoing happening that it is; as a blind, unintelligent process unaware of being, it is not knowledge.

Now although in our time we have abandoned the Platonic— and the Aristotelian—search for guaranteed, logically certain knowledge of the real world, Plato's argument is strikingly apposite for our own philosophical problems, and this in two ways. First, the cinematic theory of perception, the changing organism in its interaction with the changing object, has itself a modern ring, which makes us suspect that the philosophical problem Plato draws from it may have important truth for us too. And secondly, there is in fact such philosophic relevance, for Plato is stating here a truth about the logical structure of all real knowledge which every philosopher since Hume has had to face. Experience, taken purely as passive and

44

sensory, is impotent to interpret itself. Sense data are disconnected fragments, no one of which ever entails any other. But knowledge consists in the awareness of connections between the items of experience. Therefore, between the raw data and the mind's grasp of coherent pattern, between experience and knowledge, there is and must always be a leap. The central problem of epistemology arises from the necessity to explain this gap. What are we as minds doing when we interpret the flow of sense? In the last analysis, Hume could go no further than a bundle-of-perceptions theory of mind, which he himself admits to be inadequate. It is inadequate, not only as a conception of mind itself, but as the basis for a theory of our knowledge of the world. Hume's own confession in the Appendix to his *Treatise* makes this plain:

In short there are two principles, which I cannot render consistent; nor is it in my power to renounce either of them, viz. *that all our distinct perceptions are distinct existences*, and *that the mind never perceives any real connection among distinct existences*. Did our perceptions either inhere in something simple and individual, or did the mind perceive some real connection among them, there would be no difficulty in the case. For my part, I must plead the privilege of a sceptic, and confess, that this difficulty is too hard for my understanding.

If this is the outcome of Hume's *Treatise*, so had it been of Plato's argument on knowledge as perception in the *Theaetetus*. Trué, Plato takes the question one stage deeper than Hume, on his limited principles, can do. Imbedding Protagoras's relativism in a flux metaphysic, he is able to put the question of the interaction of percipient and perceived, which lies wholly beyond the range of Hume's inquiry. If the object of knowledge is but the ephemeral flash into existence of the impact of a changing world on a changing person, what is *there* to be known? This is a question which Hume, starting with perceptions only, is unable to ask. But it entails the Protagorean question, which is Hume's, and which constitutes, it seems to me, the core of our modern epistemological problem. That my experience is only mine, and in terms of pure sense-data not even *mine* but only the blooming buzz it is, and that we nevertheless build on this foundation of sheer thisness a beautifully articulated, precise and workable structure of knowledge: that is the miracle we have to explain. For it *is* a miracle: a miracle inherent in all knowledge, most dramatically displayed for our generation perhaps in the achievements of mathematical physics, where the wildest abstractions, the most remote formalisms, utterly detached from anybody's manipulations of metal or glass or protoplasm or any sensible stuff, prove *true*. Perception is a mere unintelligible flow, yet we have, through the power of our minds, knowledge of the real, knowledge not of perceptions but of something remote from them that, independently of us and our thoughts and our equations and our matrices, *exists*.

What does Aristotle make of this puzzle: the puzzle of perception and reality, which underlies the Humean problem of induction? or the modern problem of the reality and relevance of the knowledge of pure mathematical form? He never saw it. Twenty years, almost, at Plato's feet, and he never saw it. His own report, summarizing the master's starting-point with Aristotelian pithiness and clarity: 'Sensible things are always changing, and there is no knowledge of them'. Yet he never saw it. Perception, he agreed, is not knowledge, but it is, obviously, commonsensically, the first step to knowledge. Who would puzzle his head with something as clear on the face of it as this? 'Are there real things in this sensible world at all?' 'What meeting ground is there, or can there be, between our vision of form and the stream of sense?' For Plato, for post-Humean philosophers, these are serious, even distressing questions. Aristotle never so much as asks them. We shall not inquire, he says in the *Physics*, whether there are natural objects, for that would be to explain *the obvious by the non-obvious*, and only a fool would do that. I shall return to Aristotle's own doctrine of perception in the next chapter. It is, as we shall see, very much a naturalist's doctrine. All I want to do here is to emphasize the absence from it of the Platonic problem, of the Platonic urgency. The dissolution of the visible world

46

into a puzzling something-nothing, the very root of Platonic, as of modern, epistemology. Aristotle reports as a piece of history, but it does not concern him. That corrosive dialectic, and the philosophic problems born of it, for him are dead and gone. Knowledge is infallible and real, agreed; this double demand will present for Aristotle its own problems; but the flux of the sensible world, with its cognate questions, is not among them.

It was through Cratylus, the disciple of Heraclitus, Aristotle tells us, that Plato became convinced of the flux-philosophy as applied to the sensible world. The dialogue of that name is concerned with the problem of naming, and there is indeed a close connection between the two themes. The problem of naming, therefore, may give us a second line of approach to Plato's central philosophical theme.

Names, to name effectively, must stand still, and so must the entities they name. Both our meanings and what they refer to must have a minimal stability if we are to talk at all. There may indeed be some alteration in the things we talk about from one occasion to the next, and our language must be sufficiently flexible to adjust itself to this changing situation. But if we let the change on either side proceed to an extreme, things as well as language, the articulation of our world and our articulateness about it, become jointly impossible. The way in which the persistence of change may threaten to dissolve the possibility of rational discourse is well stated in Michael Polanyi's discussion of the re-interpretation of language:

In this changing world, our anticipatory powers have always to deal with a somewhat unprecedented situation, and they can do so in general only by undergoing some measure of adaptation. More particularly: since every occasion on which a word is used is in some degree different from every previous occasion, we should expect that the meaning of a word will be modified in some degree on every such occasion. For example, since no owl is exactly like any other, to say 'This is an owl', a statement which ostensibly says something about the bird in front of us, also says something new about the term 'owl', that is, about owls in general.

47

This raises an awkward question. Can we safely sanction the practice of adapting the meaning of words so that what we say shall be true? If we can say of an unprecedented owl, belonging perhaps to a new species: 'This is an owl', using this designation in an appropriately modified sense, why should we not equally well say of an owl: 'This is a sparrow', meaning a new kind of sparrow, not known so far by that name? Indeed, why should we ever say one thing rather than another, and not pick our descriptive terms at random? Or alternatively, if our terms are to be defined by conformity to their present applications, would any statement say more than 'this is this', which is clearly useless? (76, 110–11)

The instability of the experienced world necessitates the flexibility of speech; but where then shall we find the limit, the check to change that will enable us to speak at all? Even to say 'This is this' we must know at least two meanings, one of them that elusive 'is' which, Plato argues in the *Theaetetus*, sense for itself could never lead us to enunciate or to understand. Of course we do speak, and speak rationally, but the point is: grasping for the stable and significant out of, or against, the flowing world of sense, we are faced with a task of monstrous difficulty, a task we may never solve. Or if we do so, what we can say will still be only a sign of our solution, never unambiguously and definitively the solution itself. A final and complete fitting of word to thing, of language to event, is beyond the power of human speech. Both words and the world, at least our ordinary experienced world, are too slippery for that.

Plato, looking back in his old age on his own career, has told us himself of the incommensurability of language and the real, not sensible reality only, but the eternal objects to which alone, as he sees it, the knowing mind must turn for its true nourishment. In the so-called 'philosophical digression' of the *Seventh Letter* he declares that he has never written down his philosophy and never could. Written speech is second-rate, as he says also in the *Phaedrus*, because the true soil of philosophy is in the living mind; in fact, what the philosopher is aiming at in his conversation with himself or with like-minded seekers after wisdom is an insight that lies beyond language altogether. The philosopher does indeed operate *with* language. He starts with a name (e.g. in the *Republic*, 'justice'), and asks for a definition of it (e.g. 'giving to every man his due'). Then he tests the definition against 'images', i.e. against remembered experience (the representative here of the sensible world) to see if it fits: here, in the *Republic*, comes the madman who wants his sword back and the like, to show us that the current definition falls short of the mark. So we try again. How do we know when at last our definition is correct? As far as verbalization can take us, we never do. Language is inevitably selective and abstract, and so we may have hit on a definition which no experience shows us to be wrong and which nevertheless names only some mere quality of the object, not in fact its essence. Or if the philosopher is fortunate enough, and gifted enough, to reach beyond all these three elements, names, definitions, images, and achieve a true knowledge of the thing itself, this occurs not in speech any longer but in a happening in his mind which Plato likens to a 'flash of fire'. Suddenly he sees, and is no longer the man he was. But language itself can neither generate nor in any direct or literal form describe this vision. Hence, on the one hand, Plato's writings do not state Plato's philosophy, and, on the other hand, what they hint at they hint at in myth and metaphor, characterization and dramatic setting as much as argument. In fact for Plato all speech, all interesting speech, is metaphorical. And hence, further, dialectic, the attempt to move through disciplined and reasoned argument to know-ledge of the really-real, remains a task: problematic, to be pursued again and again, now from one perspective, now another, but never to be finished and done with and set down, black on white, for him who runs to read.

In short, Plato, supreme artist of speech, is humbled and puzzled before the mystery of speech. Aristotle, with his terse enunciations, beautiful indeed in their precision of thought but strangely cramped in their linguistic form, seems to feel no such humility and no such puzzlement. He is as confident that men *can* delimit in speech the essential attributes of kinds of things as Plato is of the precise opposite. True, Aristotle does not take his view for granted. He argues in the *Posterior Analytics* for the possibility of 'unequivocal essential predication', that is, of real definitions, for he knows extremely well that the possibility of science as he conceives it depends essentially on the existence of such definitions. What he is chiefly arguing against, however, is not a general sceptical conception of the powers of language as such, but, e.g. the failure to distinguish between definition and proof, which would lead to an infinite regress, and hence to the impossibility of knowledge; or the failure to separate the proper subject-matter of each inquiry, since as he sees it the possibility of literal, exact definition depends on just such separation. Nevertheless, the path to literal, exact statement of essence lies open before him. The first treatise in the logic opens with the distinction between unambiguously and ambiguously designated things; that there *can* be some of the former sort, that logic treats of unequivocal statements, is taken as the groundwork of the whole endeavour. Aristotle does not solve differently from Plato the problem of naming, defining, concept-making; it is not in the same sense a problem for him at all. Thus immediately after the distinction just referred to, he proceeds with a classification of things in relation to predication, then moves on smoothly to the logic of propositions and arguments, supremely confident that the language of the scientist is in fact suited to deal with the nature of the real. For if there were no literal statement of essence there would be no scientific knowledge in his sense. And there is such knowledge; he has it, securely and indubitably. The elusive, unending pursuit of exactitude that now in one form, now in another, marks Plato's dialectic, Aristotle has left behind.

Consider Plato's central problem, thirdly, from another point of view. How, he is always asking, can we reach behind the illusory film of seeming and lay hold upon the really-real, the being which alone lends to appearances such dim adumbration of reality as they can claim? The philosopher's calling is to seek, in his life and his thought, to bridge the deep gulf between what truly is and what merely seems to be: to interpret the shadows, which are forever shadows, in relation to the real light of the sun to which they and the objects and the fire and the prisoners all owe their existence even in the cave. The gulf is never bridged systematically and happily once for all: we feel it in the later as in the earlier dialogues, but nowhere more intensely than in Plato's attacks on the younger and extremer Sophists. It is the failure of Callicles or Thrasymachus to distinguish properly between the real and the seeming good that forms in the one case the climax, in the other the effective starting-point of Plato's argument. Even the more austere epistemological argument of the *Theaetetus* is given its meaning and purpose in the 'digression' on the two forms of life, which contrasts the orator, who makes the worse appear the better reason, with the philosopher, whose attention is turned away from the flurry of case-winning to truth itself. And again, in directing one of his major 'metaphysical' investigations ostensibly to the definition of the Sophist, that maker of images, Plato seems to be expressing the same preoccupation.

What does Aristotle make of this contrast? If perception presents no problem for him, neither, *a fortiori*, does the search for reality behind appearance provide a major theme for his thought. He does, however, touch lightly in the *Ethics* on the problem of real versus apparent good, and here again the contrast with Plato is a striking one. For Plato the struggle to rise beyond the merely apparent to the real was unending; for ethical discourse it was a central, almost the only theme. Aristotle treats it in a paragraph, almost an aside, in Book III of the *Nicomachean Ethics*, and passes on. His chief concern here is with the structure of voluntary action, the role of deliberation, and so on. The end of an action, he has already established, is what we wish for; it is about the means that we deliberate. These distinctions will be fundamental to the analysis of the practical virtues, to which Aristotle will shortly proceed. But what is this end, the object of wish?

That wish is for the end has already been stated; some think it is for the good, others for the apparent good. Now those who say that the good is the object of wish must admit in consequence that that which the man who does not choose aright wishes for is not an object of wish (for if it is to be so, it must also be good; but it was, if it so happened, bad); while those who say the apparent good is the object of wish must admit that there is no natural object of wish, but only what seems good to each man. Now different things appear good to different people, and, if it so happens, even contrary things.

If these consequences are unpleasing, are we to say that absolutely and in truth the good is the object of wish, but for each person the apparent good; that that which is in truth an object of wish is an object of wish to the good man, while any chance thing may be so to the bad man, as in the case of bodies also the things that are in truth wholesome are wholesome for bodies which are in good condition, while for those that are diseased other things are wholesome—or bitter or sweet or hot or heavy, and so on; since the good man judges each class of things rightly, and in each the truth appears to him? For each state of character has its own ideas of the noble and the pleasant, and perhaps the good man differs from others most by seeing the truth in each class of things, being as it were the norm and measure of them. (1113 a 15-b, Oxf.)

Put this alongside the *Gorgias*, with its passionate rhetorical attack on rhetoric, the profession directed to mastery of the apparent and neglect of the real good. The force of rootless persuasion, the lure of greed and power, the paradoxes of punishment: what has become of all these? Put it alongside the *Republic*, with the dilemma posed by Thrasymachus in Book I answered at last in the myth of the tenth book. Thrasymachus may pour his speech like a bathman round our ears, but it takes the whole intervening argument—the Gyges story of the seemingly just but wholly unjust man, the city of pigs and its transformation into the luxurious city, the cave and the Good, the degenerate states and their corresponding souls— to give body and foundation to the theme of real as against apparent justice, the really as against the seemingly good life. Aristotle will deal, of course, in the *Politics*, with many of Plato's political themes; but the poignancy, the passion, the life of Plato's political inquiry, Aristotle can sweep aside in two brief paragraphs. 'Different things appear good to different people. . . . Perhaps the good man differs from others most by seeing the truth in each class of things, being as it were the norm and measure of them.' What good man, measure and norm for whom? For the problem of the real and apparent good is at bottom the problem of the relativity of moral standards. 'Different things seem good to different people.' Plato knew the urgency of this problem, knew the lengths to which the mind must reach in search of its solution—as we too know it in our way. But in Aristotle's neat, circular argument the crisis of Sophism, the collapse of an unstable humanism, is as if it had never been at all.

There we come, fourthly and finally, to the heart of the contrast. Perception, language, appearances all puzzle Plato because he is obsessed first and last by the need to refute the relativism of the Sophists, to overcome the distinction between nature and convention, to find an adequate basis for morality. His search is for standards, for norms that will hold against the shifting judgments of men. However theoretical his interest may seem to have become in later years (and it was never wholly so) it was this centrally moral preoccupation that drove him to philosophize. We have Plato's own account of the disappointments of his youth. First, disillusionment with his upper-class kinsmen under the Thirty, then worse disillusionment with the restored democracy: Socrates confronted by his accusers, the noblest and wisest and best man of all in his time put to death by his fellow-citizens, as foolish as he was wise, as crooked as he was straight. It is from this root that the thought of Plato grows. And in morals and politics, as we again in the twentieth century have come to know, there is no literal, unambiguous solution ready to hand. Standards, though we must live by them, must be forever justified afresh. Recent discussions of Plato's Forms have likened them to standards of measurement. This is an apt comparison, but of course no more. The standard pound weight is somewhere, we might go to look at it, and come away unchanged. The way to the Just, the Good is much more arduous, and in a sense transforms wholly the man who achieves it—although in another sense, for Plato, such a man only makes explicit what his nature already holds, recalls what he already knew. The vision of the Just or the Good is indescribable, their relevance to our daily problems never possible to specify with accuracy. Is it 'participation', 'imitation'? No account Plato could give was wholly consistent and satisfactory. Moral standards are like that. They are not rules to be counted and enunciated like the axioms of a geometry. They both shape and are shaped in relation to such rules; they both determine and are determined by our actions, our preferences, our dispositions. We may, like Plato, invoke recollection, immortality and the Forms to secure their real existence, or we may muddle through with an 'ethic of ambiguity', whether in a mood of hope or of despair. But if it is moral passion that moves us, and we are honest, there is no once-and-for-all way out. For Plato, again, it was first and foremost the confrontation of Socrates and the Sophists that set this problem. For us no one set of individuals or groups, but the very nature of our age, everywhere on the earth, seems to raise the same issue. Man systematically annihilating man, worse yet, systematically annihilating the minds and the dignity of men: it is the same conflict on a nightmarish, Brobdingnagian scale, coextensive with the surface of this globe.

Again, the problem Plato faced, the root problem of the human situation as it once more appears today, was no concern of Aristotle's. He is at pains to refute the theory of Forms, but Plato's preoccupation, his obsession as it sometimes seems, with the Sophists and their challenge to morality: this leaves him so unaffected that he scarcely needs to argue it. True, the vogue of Sophism, the turbulent times of the fifth century were over. The power as well as the conflicts of the Athenian empire were past and gone. But Aristotle was interested in history. His account of Athenian constitutional history is a major source for modern knowledge of that story. And at the same time Aristotle was surely a man of philosophical genius, whose mind was to shape the thought of western men for centuries to come. Yet the philosophical problem inherent in political life, and most dramatically in the political life of Athens in the late fifth century, passed by him altogether. The Sophists for him are purveyors of eristic, of fallacious argument—nothing more.

Is it not strange that Plato's greatest pupil, 'the mind of the Academy', should be so blind to the overriding issues that had formed his teacher's thought? The answer lies, however, not in Aristotle's blindness but in his own vision. His deepest interest lay in such an utterly different place: in an area where standards are not hazardously to be reached for but are present on the very face of experience itself: that is, in the structures and life-histories of living things, of animals, primarily of animals other than men, but men too, *as* animals, which are to the field biologist so plainly representative each of its kind. The animals went in two by two: for morphology as much as for reproduction there is no need for more. The trueness to type of each does indeed entail conformity to a standard, somewhat as the wisdom of Socrates did. But how much less problematically! True, once started on a Cratylean dialectic, we may doubt even our right to call a sparrow a sparrow or an owl an owl. But only a modern thinker, whose mind has been shaped by the influence of evolution and genetics, relativity and quantum mechanics, would push the very naming of biological kinds to such an extreme of scepticism. For Aristotle, as for any common-sense pre-Darwinian biologist, there was no problem in this kind of standard at all. A thing's nature is its form, and its growth is the path to its nature as form. Moreover, its form is its own form, as this frog or this octopus. There is no 'frog' or 'octopus' as such. Yet it is the form of this individual which we, as knowers, universalize, so that we understand not this particular specimen, which we perceive and do not wholly know, but the universal inherent in the particular, the potential universal which in our minds we actualize. What we know is the specific form, *a* frog, *an* octopus, what it is to be a frog, what it is to be an octopus. If this is the primary kind of standard, the first and best example of a

standard, how much more relaxed even our account of morals!
For when we think of form as the proper object of knowledge,
we think first and foremost of these forms, these essential
natures, so clearly present to us in each minute and loving
piece of biological research. 'Here, too,' says Aristotle, 'there
is beauty.' Here first, for him, there is intelligibility and form.
And so the heartbreaking duality of moral conflict fades away
before the comforting presence of self-completed, self-consistent,
this-worldly 'norms and measures', as the Father of Biology
met them and as every schoolboy doing his first dissection
meets them again. Aristotle was not present at the trial of
Socrates. Plato, one may be sure, never watched enthralled
the first visible palpitation of a tiny speck of blood in a developing chick. For Socrates, as Plato pictures him in the *Phaedrus*,
the scene beyond the city held no appeal. He was concerned
with one question only: who am I? What is it to be a man?
The whole sweep of Plato's cosmological speculations springs
from and returns to this humanistic root. For Aristotle, on the
other hand, man though the finest animal is but one among
many, and what most absorbs him everywhere is the careful,
exact distinction between those many kinds, or the many but
clearly separable aspects of some kinds. Plato's 'nature' is
nine-tenths myth, a moralist's 'likely story', meant to educate,
not to inform. Aristotle's ethic, on the other hand, is a naturalist's ethic, put in its due, second place to pure knowledge.
The *Ethics* is informative, indeed, about the society Aristotle
knows and has so sharply observed, but no passage in the
Ethics, it seems to this reader, is so moving, or displays so
poignantly the intellectual passion of the philosopher himself
as the apology for the study of the humbler parts of nature in
his introduction to the Great Course on Biology. He has
lectured already elsewhere, he says, on the eternal things of
the heavens; now we come to the corruptible, to plants and
animals. Each branch has admittedly its charm:

Having already treated of the celestial world, as far as our conjectures could reach, we proceed to treat of animals, without omitting,

to the best of our ability, any member of the kingdom, however ignoble. For if some have no graces to charm the sense, yet even these, by disclosing to intellectual perception the artistic spirit that designed them, give immense pleasure to all who can trace links of causation, and are inclined to philosophy. Indeed, it would be strange if mimic representations of them were attractive, because they disclose the mimetic skill of the painter or sculptor, and the original realities themselves were not more interesting, to all at any rate who have eyes to discern the reasons that determined their formation. We therefore must not recoil with childish aversion from the examination of the humbler animals. Every realm of nature is marvellous: and as Heraclitus, when the strangers who came to visit him found him warming himself at the furnace in the kitchen and hesitated to go in, is reported to have bidden them not to be afraid to enter, as even in that kitchen divinities were present, so we should venture on the study of every kind of animal without distaste; for each and all will reveal to us something natural and something beautiful. Absence of haphazard and conduciveness of everything to an end are to be found in nature's works in the highest degree, and the resultant end of her generations and combinations is a form of the beautiful. If any person thinks the examination of the rest of the animal kingdom an unworthy task, he must hold in like disesteem the study of man. For no one can look at the primordia of the human frame—blood, flesh, bones, vessels, and the like without much repugnance. Moreover, when any one of the parts or structures, be it which it may, is under discussion, it must not be supposed that it is its material composition to which attention is being directed or which is the object of the discussion, but the relation of such part to the total form. Similarly, the true object of architecture is not bricks, mortar, or timber, but the house; and so the principal object of natural philosophy is not the material elements, but their composition, and the totality of the form, independently of which they have no existence. (*De Part. An.* 645 a 4–37; Oxf.)

In confirmation of D'Arcy Thompson's thesis, we find here, it seems to me, not Aristotle's disavowal of metaphysics, but the very cornerstone of his conception of substance, of its nature and of our means of knowing it. Platonic Forms he has no need of, but his own doctrine of substance as form, as the form of and in the composite, is nowhere more expressly stated than here and in the whole Introduction to Biology that forms Book I of the treatise *On the Parts of Animals*. 'Here, too, there are divinities.' This is not Aristotle the empiricist turning against first philosophy, but Aristotle the scientist, on whom Aristotle the metaphysician will turn to reflect. And in another respect also Aristotle the logician, the methodologist of science, is setting out, in the *Organon*, the ideal for his own work as natural historian, or in the *Physics* laying down the general principles which govern all the study of nature, including this. In fact, what I propose to do here is in a way to put this passage at the head of the methodological, physical and metaphysical treatises and consider Aristotle the methodologist reflecting on the procedure of Aristotle the biologist, Aristotle the physicist of qualitative change, of growth, and of birth and death, generalizing from biology to 'nature' as such, Aristotle the metaphysician of life, working carefully through the difficult dialectical progression from what are plainly, visibly, substances—plants and animals, and the celestial spheres—to separate substance and the necessarily unchanged principle of all change.

3. *Illustrations*

A comparison of three pairs of Platonic and Aristotelian passages may clarify the contrast I have been describing. In a paper on 'The Problem of Life in Aristotle and Hegel', Erich Frank stresses the circularity of natural processes in these two philosophies. While the individual dies, the species goes on, oak tree eternally producing acorn, and acorn oak tree, in an unending cycle. This circle of generation in Aristotle, Frank likens to the account of immortality of the wise woman Diotima in the *Symposium*, when she speaks of the longing of all living things to reproduce their kind. But in fact Diotima's account set alongside Aristotle's statement in the treatise *On Generation and Corruption* illustrates much more emphatically the contrariety than the likeness of master and pupil.

Socrates has been reporting how Diotima instructed him in

love-matters, and how she explained that since love loves the good to be one's own forever, love is necessarily of immortality. This is true of all living things:

> For you must have observed the strange state into which all the animals are thrown, whether going on earth or winging the air, when they desire to beget: they are all sick and amorously disposed, first to have union with one another, and next to find food for the new-born; in whose behalf they are ready to fight hard battles, even the weakest against the strongest, and to sacrifice their lives; to be racked with starvation themselves if they can but nurture their young, and be put to any sort of shift. (207 A–B)

And men, too, seek immortality, first by begetting offspring, but equally and better by seeking 'immortal excellence' whether in deeds of valour or learning or legislation, for such people are pregnant in soul rather than in body, and the children they leave are 'fairer and more immortal'. So after the proper stages of initiation into these mysteries, Diotima at last explains to Socrates how a man may ascend the ladder of love, in search of the truest immortality:

> Beginning from obvious beauties he must for the sake of that highest beauty be ever climbing aloft, as on the rungs of a ladder, from one to two, and from two to all beautiful bodies; from personal beauty he proceeds to beautiful observances, from observances to beautiful learning, and from learning at last to that particular study which is concerned with the beautiful itself and that alone; so that in the end he comes to know the very essence of beauty. (211 C)

It is in this state of life above all others, Diotima continues, that a man finds it worthwhile to live:

> Do but consider . . . that there only will it befall him, as he sees the beautiful through that which makes it visible, to breed not illusions but true examples of virtue, since his contact is not with illusion but with truth. So when he has begotten a true virtue and reared it up he is destined to win the friendship of Heaven; he, above all men is immortal. (212 A)

Set beside this Aristotle's account of the cycle of generation. The incorruptible spheres, carrying the stars and planets with them, rotate eternally. Under the moon, in the corruptible world, natural motion imitates this circularity and is caused by it, since 'it is far more reasonable that what is should cause the coming-to-be of what is not, than that what is not should cause the being of what is'. (336 a 20–22) In the case of the four simple bodies, fire, air, earth and water, their mutual transformation is clearly an imitation of the celestial rotation; the seasons too revolve in consequence of the sun's motion, 'and so in their turn do the things whose coming-to-be the seasons initiate'. (338 b 4–5; Oxf.) But the history of living things seems to present a problem here:

. . . why do some things manifestly come-to-be in this cyclical fashion (as, e.g. showers and air, so that it must rain if there is to be a cloud and, conversely, there must be a cloud if it is to rain), while men and animals do not 'return upon themselves' so that the same individual comes-to-be a second time (for though your coming-to-be presupposes your father's, his coming-to-be does not pre-suppose yours)? Why, on the contrary, does this coming-to-be seem to constitute a rectilinear sequence? (338 b 6–11; Oxf.)

The answer is plain:

In discussing this new problem, we must begin by inquiring whether all things 'return upon themselves' in a uniform manner; or whether, on the contrary, though in some sequences what recurs is *numerically* the same, in other cases it is the same *only in species*. In consequence of this distinction, it is evident that those things, whose 'substance'— that which is undergoing the process—is imperishable, will be numeri-cally, as well as specifically, the same in their recurrence: for the character of the process is determined by the character of that which undergoes it. Those things, on the other hand, whose 'substance' is perishable (not imperishable) must 'return upon themselves' in the sense that what recurs, though specifically the same, is not the same numerically. (338 b 11–17; Oxf.)

Or as Aristotle puts it in the *Generation of Animals*:

These are the causes on account of which the generation of animals takes place, because since the nature of a class of this sort is unable to be eternal, that which comes into being is eternal in the manner that is open to it. Now it is impossible for it to be so *numerically*, since the 'being'[1] of things is to be found in the particular, and if it really were so, then it would be eternal; it is, however, open to it to be so *specifically*. That is why there is always a *class*[2] of men, of animals, of plants. (731 b 32ff.)

Man begets man and oak tree succeeds oak tree. That is the plain fact. Could two interpretations be more opposite in tenor and in context? For Plato, the drives of individual living things, their mating and paternal behaviour, appear as the humblest symptom of a universal striving, a striving which if rightly directed can lead its possessor up and away from this illusory world toward the vision of truth, of the beautiful, itself by itself, eternal and unalloyed. Admittedly, in Aristotle's account as for Plato there is an eternally existent, an immortal which is superior to and in some sense the cause of the mortal. It is not clear in what sense the Forms are causal (that is one of Aristotle's objections to them); but certainly in Aristotle's cosmology the eternal revolutions of the heavenly spheres are the cause of all motions in the sublunar world. But even though the corruptible imitates the incorruptible, it is not, except indirectly, through the striving for immortality, the ἔρως of individual mortals, that this comes about. Aristotle's emphasis is not on the desire to bring forth, the pangs of begetting, the joy of leaving an offspring, of flesh or spirit, to live after one, but on the smoothly flowing circle of life and death which in its self-containment and continuity copies the eternal rotation of the spheres:

Coming-to-be and passing away will . . . always be continuous and will never fail . . . And this continuity has a sufficient reason on our theory. For in all things, as we affirm, nature always strives after 'the better'. Now 'being' . . . is better than 'not-being': but not all things can possess 'being', since they are too far removed from the 'originative source'. God therefore adopted the remaining alternative, and fulfilled the perfection of the universe by making coming to be uninterrupted: for the greatest possible coherence would thus be

[1] οὐσία: substance.
[2] γένος: genus.

61

secured to existence, because that 'coming to be should itself come to be perpetually' is the closest approximation to eternal being. (336 b 25ff.; Oxf.)

There is no longing here, there are no steps of initiation into mysteries, no contrasts of illusory and real, but a circle within circles in a serenely perfected, an eternally articulated world.

My second comparison is suggested by Owens' analysis of one of the 'knots' (ἀπόριαι) of *Metaphysics* Beta. 'If, on the one hand,' Aristotle asks,

there is nothing apart from individual things, and the individuals are infinite in number, how then is it possible to get knowledge of the infinite individuals? For all things that we come to know, we come to know in so far as they have some unity and identity, and in so far as some attribute belongs to them universally. But if this is necessary, and there must be something apart from the individuals, it will be necessary that the genera exist apart from the individuals, —either the lowest or the highest genera; but we found by discussion just now that this is impossible. (999 a 25–31; Oxf.)

This way of putting the question, Owens remarks, is reminiscent of the passage in the *Philebus* where Plato distinguishes the classes of one and many, or finite and infinite, and explains that the art of understanding a subject matter consists in proceeding from the finite to the infinite in the proper way and at the proper pace. So to understand music, for example, we need to understand not just sound, but the particular number and kinds of sound that constitute harmony.

The gods, then, as I said, handed down to us this mode of investigating, learning, and teaching one another; but the wise men of the present day make the one and the many too quickly or too slowly, in haphazard fashion, and they put infinity immediately after unity; they disregard all that lies between them, and this it is which distinguishes between the dialectic and the disputatious methods of discussion. (16 E–17 A)

Now if it was the problem raised here that Aristotle had in mind, it was characteristic, Owens points out, that he approached it in the opposite direction from Plato. Plato proceeded from the finite and intelligible to the infinite and sensible, whereas when Aristotle came to put the problem that arose for his first philosophy from this duality, he moved from the infinite individuals to the question how, if there were nothing but these, we could know them, since what we know are the classes, the unities, into which they fit. Must these be thought to have an existence independent of the individuals? This is indeed characteristic. Plato starts with an intelligible One and subdivides it; Aristotle starts with the existence of individuals and asks how we can acquire universal knowledge about these empirically experienced individual things. But there is more to the comparison too. A little later in the *Philebus* Plato returns to his distinction between finite and infinite and defines these two classes. The infinite is whatever admits of indefinite fluctuations of degree, like hot and cold, pleasure and pain. The finite is what does not admit of such fluctuation, the equal, double, and 'everything that puts an end to differences and makes them harmonious by the introduction of number'. (25 D–E) Out of the union of these two arise the 'mixtures' which are the ordinary objects of our experience. Now the infinite in this sense, be it noticed, is not just the *many* but the flux: that stream of sensible things which are always changing 'so that there is no knowledge of them', and it is upon this indefinite flux of qualities that the finitude of order must be imposed. Aristotle in *Metaphysics* Beta, on the other hand, speaks not of the indefinite in this sense, but of infinite individuals, that is, the numerically infinite, the indefinite number of members of a class in whose defining character they somehow share. If individuals are infinite in number, they are still *definite* individuals, not fluctuating more-or-lesses like Plato's ἄπειρον. Thus in going from infinite to finite instead of from finite to infinite, Aristotle has not only reversed the order specified by Plato for dialectic; he has transformed the infinite itself. And the difference in the direction of his thought is possible only through this transformation. Plato's infinite, the indefinitely fluctuating, is in itself the utterly opaque, the sheer unintelligible; it could be understood only through the prior imposition

63

of some order upon it. Aristotle's infinite individuals are the many sensible substances, the cabbages and kings, which we meet in sense-perception as he understands it, before, in the order of our learning, we have explicitly understood the universals, the defining formulae, which they exemplify. Such individuals are definite enough; there are just a great many of them. The problem is, how we sort them into classes, and what these classes *are*, if it is the individuals, not the species and genera, that are real. In other words, Aristotle has not simply met the same problem with an opposite approach; he has re-read the problem itself in a new sense—a new sense which will make possible an Aristotelian answer.

Lastly, two brief statements from Plato's *Timaeus* and from Aristotle's *Generation of Animals* bring the central contrast into sharp relief. Timaeus at the beginning of his cosmology makes a distinction which underlies his whole account of creation. He asks:

> What . . . is that which always is, and has no becoming? And what is that which is always becoming and never is? (27 E–28 A)

However his interests and his methods shifted, this dichotomy was fundamental to Plato's thought from first to last. In the *Generation of Animals*, on the other hand, Aristotle writes:

> It is as if nature were a runner covering a double course there and back, and retracing her steps toward the starting-point from which she set out. For becoming (generation) starts from non-being and advances till it reaches being; and decay goes back again from being to non-being. (741 b 22–4; MG)

For Plato, an unbridgeable gap; for Aristotle, a smooth transition. For Plato, form forever transcending process; for Aristotle, form achieved *in* process, in the eternal recurrence of birth and death, growth and decay.

4. *Aristotle's Platonism*

Are we to conclude, then, that putting aside the exoteric writings (which in part at least are usually, though not always, interpreted as Platonizing), we may take the Aristotle of the Corpus as one who had wholly turned his back on the philosophical issues that interested the Academy? We must beware, after all, of too sweeping an answer, and stress in conclusion the sense in which Aristotle did remain a Platonist. What I have been arguing here is that the *problems* that engaged Plato were for Aristotle no problems; his interests followed a different bent. And of course the core of Plato's doctrine: the Forms, recollection, the dualism of soul and body, Aristotle was at pains to refute. Yet the criteria of knowledge and of being were the same for both of them. Knowledge to be knowledge must have certainty; this it can have only if its object is permanent. That is, being, the proper object of knowledge, must contain nothing of flux, nothing indeterminate. It must be finite. Infinite being, whether of God or the world, would be for Plato or for Aristotle inconceivable. 'All determination,' wrote Spinoza, 'is negation.' For Plato and Aristotle, on the contrary, it is *in*determinateness that would negate the stability and fixity of being. To say that being is determinate, however, is to say that it is form: somehow or other, wherever they are and however related to sensible things, it is forms that the knowing mind properly and rightly knows. Further, form is causal, it is the reason why things are what they are and the reason why our minds can know them. Further still, form is the source of unity: it is one as against the multiplicity of the informed, or of the unformed. Moreover, the mind in knowing form is somehow like it, at one with it. All this is common ground. But Aristotle found form, intelligibility, definiteness, where Plato had never found it: in the limited, recurrent but orderly processes of nature itself. And from this discovery, of orderly becoming, of perishable but recurrent structures, he built a cosmos such as Plato and the Platonists had never known.

III

The Tools of Philosophy

1. *Logic and method*

Whenever and however 'the scientific revolution' happened, it was in some sense founded on the rejection of an Aristotelian cosmology. In this we may take Galileo's *Two New Sciences* as typical. Whoever and however significant were his forerunners, Galileo did express and apply there for the first time the technique that came to characterize classical mechanics: a way of handling problems by constructing artificial situations such that nature can be asked pertinent questions permitting quantitative, progressively improvable answers. Of the three interlocutors, one represents Galileo, the practitioner of the New Sciences, another an admirer enthusiastic for the application of mathematics to nature but lacking the instinct for doing it properly; and the third is Simplicio, the Aristotelian whose name suggests the naïveté and irrelevance of his thought. Aristotelian categories were outmoded. This was so, not only because Galileo was applying mathematics to physical problems, as the Aristotelians had not done, or had done only peripherally, stressing the difference, not the similarity, between these two branches of theoretical science. Others, notably Pythagorean and Platonizing astronomers, had used mathematics for the solution of problems about the real world. True, these were celestial, not terrestrial problems. But apart from the equation of the celestial and the terrestrial as fit subjects for mathematical treatment, what chiefly characterized Galileo's new technique was his use of measurement: that is, the kind of quantification which instead of getting out *the* answer produces a rough approximation which can be progressively improved. This was revolutionary; and it was a revolution, as Galileo himself believed and after him many more seventeenth-century thinkers agreed, against the finality and self-sufficiency of the Aristotelian universe.

Yet whatever modernity makes us deny in the once-for-all Aristotelian cosmology, there is one solid achievement we must concede to Aristotle, and that is the discovery of logic. In the Platonic dialogues there is no disentangling matter and method. It was Aristotle who for the first time separated out the study of terms, and of valid and invalid forms of inference, both mediate and immediate, from the inquiry into the nature of the world, of the being, to the knowledge of which rational discourse is directed. Logic has expanded in the last hundred years far beyond its traditional syllogistic form, and even the traditional syllogism was elaborated, or at least embroidered, through the centuries, into a body of rules which are not to be found as such in the text of Aristotle's *Analytics*. The fact remains, however, that it was Aristotle who began it; and the doctrine of the syllogism can be perfectly assimilated, say, to the logic of *Principia Mathematica* as a limited branch of the logic of propositions. Formal logic so expanded is in turn a branch of mathematics—or if you prefer to see it the other way around, mathematics is an extension of formal logic. Thus Aristotle takes a unique place in the history of logic, and therefore of the foundations of mathematics. In fact, we may say that despite his many scattered contributions to biology in detailed observation, his major contribution to theoretical knowledge was in the field of logic.

If we look at Aristotle's own division of the sciences, however, we find that logic has no place in it. Apart from the practical sciences (household management, ethics, politics) and the productive sciences (the principles of the arts, both fine and useful), there are three branches of theoretical science: physics, or second philosophy, mathematics, and first philosophy (our 'metaphysics'). Of these, physics deals with those things which exist separately but are subject to change of some

67

kind: that is, in Aristotle's terminology, they have matter, for matter is just precisely the possibility of change. Mathematics, at least in part, deals with things which do not change but do not exist separately either, i.e. it abstracts from naturally existing bodies their quantitative (spatial or numerical) aspect and thus studies not groups of substances but limited and dependent aspects of substances. It studies a certain aspect of the form of bodies, but an aspect which is dependent, since it is abstracted from the complete essential form of the body itself. An ox, for example, should have broad shoulders and a good straight back; it is said of a good beef beast that you should be able to put a box over it. The geometer might measure the box for you, and even give you a topology to suit, like D'Arcy Thompson's patterns in *Of Growth and Form*. But, essentially, being a bullock is not the same, and never could be the same, as being a box, or being of the quantity to fit in a box. Thus for Aristotle the study of shape and number, though 'formal', is not the study of *essential* form. First philosophy, finally, studies objects which both exist independently and do not change, that is, are not en-mattered. It studies (in some sense which we have yet to consider) pure form existing independently and in itself. Neither in the *Metaphysics* nor in the *Nichomachean Ethics* nor in the *Parts of Animals*, where Aristotle sets out these distinctions, is logic included in this list.[1]

This is as it should be. For the logical works, the *Analytics* and *Topics* as Aristotle calls them, are not a branch of scientific knowledge, but the instruments of science, an *Organon*, as the ancient editors entitled them. They tell us how we ought to proceed in the arguments and expositions of the several branches of knowledge, but do not themselves constitute the knowledge of anything. That Aristotle himself understood his logical treatises in relation to the method of science and not as pure exercises in logic is plain, moreover, from the

---

[1] The classification in the *Parts of Animals* does not contradict the other two, as both the Oxford and the Loeb translations suggest that it does. This was pointed out to me by Professor Charles Kahn.

introduction to the *Prior Analytics*, which sets forth the nature of syllogistic reasoning:

> We must first state what our inquiry is about and to what it pertains: that it is about demonstration and pertains to demonstrative science. (24 a 10–11; MG)

Syllogism as such, as Aristotle proceeds to explain, is wider than demonstration. There are valid syllogisms which are not founded on scientific premises and are therefore not demonstrative, but dialectical. Nevertheless, the study of the syllogism is announced as part of the subject 'demonstration' and as having to do with ἐπιστήμη ἀποδεικτική, the scientific knowledge produced by demonstration. Thus the wider, purely formal subject (in the modern, not the Aristotelian sense of 'form') is explicitly introduced as ancillary to the narrower subject of scientific methodology.

We may, therefore, legitimately consider Aristotelian logic not as the first adumbration of a formal system but as a discipline enabling the student to acquire scientific knowledge. This does not mean that logic provides a set of psychological or rhetorical exercises, like the Port Royal Logic or modern books on 'straight and crooked thinking'. What it was meant to provide was a set of general rules for scientists (as Aristotle understood science) working each in his appropriate material. The rules are rules of validity, not psychological rules, but the reference to the material is also relevant. True, it is not explicitly relevant in the *Prior Analytics*, which deal with syllogism in general. Nor is it directly relevant in the *Topics*, which deal with dialectical reasoning, that is, reasoning not tied down to a base of appropriate scientific first principles. But as the passage quoted above indicates, Aristotle thought of the *Prior Analytics* as a more general treatment *preliminary* to the *Posterior Analytics*, which was to be fundamental to would-be possessors of ἐπιστήμη or scientific knowledge; and the *Topics* developed explicitly a second best type of syllogism, useful in all the areas—and they are many—where demonstration and therefore true scientific knowledge are in the nature of the case not to be had. From the point of view of Aristotle's purpose in the logical works as a whole, it is the *Posterior Analytics* that are the keystone of the structure. For the *Posterior Analytics* will tell us how we can shape our propositions and arguments about things in such a way as to achieve proper scientific knowledge of them. The foundation of the whole, on the other hand, has been laid down in the first treatise of the *Organon*, the *Categories*. As we shall see, the *Categories* tell us what *things* are like to enable us to speak scientifically about them.

What I want to do here, therefore, is not to consider Aristotle's logic as logic, but to look at some of the *methodological* aspects of the *Organon*, and in particular three parts of it: the opening distinctions of the *Categories*, the discussion of the constituents of a science, and the account of the process by which our minds come to develop such sciences. Once we have each of these matters clearly in view, we can consider what bearing Aristotle's experience as a practising biologist might have had on his conception of the nature and method of science as such.

2. *The Categories*

It has sometimes been doubted whether Aristotle himself wrote the first treatise in the *Organon*. I am taking it, however, on good authority that he did in fact write at least the first nine chapters; if he did not, these chapters in any case present sound Aristotelian doctrine, and are fundamental to the entire undertaking of the remaining treatises.

The first chapter, as I have already mentioned, distinguishes between things in so far as they are univocally, equivocally or derivatively named:

Things are equivocally named, when they have the name only in common, the definition (or statement of essence[1]) corresponding with the name being different. For instance, while a man and a portrait can properly both be called 'animals', these are equivocally named. For they have the name only in common, the definitions (or statements

70

THE TOOLS OF PHILOSOPHY

of essence[1]) corresponding with the name being different. For if you are asked to define what the being an animal means in the case of the man and the portrait, you give in either case a definition[2] appropriate to that case alone.

Things are univocally named, when not only they bear the same name but the name means the same in each case—has the same definition[2] corresponding. Thus a man and an ox are called 'animals'. The name is the same in both cases; so also the statement of essence. For if you are asked what is meant by their both of them being called 'animals', you give that particular name in both cases the same definition.

Things are 'derivatively' named that derive their own name from some other, that is given a new verbal form, as for instance, 'grammarian' from 'grammar', from 'heroism', 'hero', and the like. (1 a 1–15)

It has been rightly pointed out that Aristotle is dealing in the logic with terms, propositions (certain arrangements of pairs of terms), arguments (certain arrangements of three or more terms), not, as in the *Metaphysics*, with reality. But, as I have already said and must emphasize here again, Aristotle's logic is not a pure logic, a system valid for 'all possible worlds', like the formal systems envisaged by Leibniz. It is an analysis of the kind of discourse valid for expressing man's knowledge of this one, unique universe. It begins, therefore, not with a distinction between kinds of words, or terms detached from any semantic reference, but with the fundamental classification of *things* essential to the elaboration of scientific language. And what is essential to the possibility of scientific knowledge is that there should be some things at least that can be named *univocally*. If there were no literal use of language there would be no Aristotelian science. True, the highest branch of science, first philosophy, must be constructed through the use of a certain, precisely delineated type of equivocal language. We shall see later why and how this must be done. But in principle, sciences are sets of propositions in which certain essential

[1] λόγος τῆς οὐσίας: 'formula of the substance'.
[2] λόγος: 'formula' or 'statement'.

71

characteristics are unambiguously predicated of certain classes of things. (In speaking of science I am here and henceforward referring to episteme, Aristotelian science; the difference between such 'scientific knowledge' and modern science should become clear as we proceed.) To assert that there are things amenable to univocal naming, that there are some things whose definitions stay put, is the first task of logic. Univocality is therefore, as we saw in the last chapter, not a problem for Aristotle but a starting-point. He refers to it later (e.g. 97 b) as a *sine qua non* of scientific definition; but as such it is an accepted fact, not a goal to be reached or missed. It is a fact in the *world*, which the knower's discourse reflects.

The second chapter establishes another basic classification of *things* which is equally fundamental to the possibility of science. The chapter is once more a brief one; I shall quote it almost in full and comment on it. After distinguishing between combined and uncombined words (i.e. between propositions and terms), Aristotle proceeds:

But as for the things that are meant, when we thus speak of uncombined words, you can predicate some of a subject, but they are never present in one. You can predicate 'man', for example, of this or that man as the subject, but man is not found in a subject. By 'in', 'present', 'found in a subject' I do not mean present or found as its parts are contained in a whole; I mean that it cannot exist apart from the subject referred to. And then there is that class of things which are present or found in a subject, although they cannot be asserted of any known subject whatever. Again, a particular whiteness is present or found in a body (all colour implies some such basis as what we intend by 'a body') but cannot itself be asserted of any known subject whatever. We find there are some things, moreover, not only affirmed of a subject but present also in a subject. Thus knowledge, for instance, while present in this or that mind as a subject, is also asserted of grammar. There is, finally, that class of things which can neither be found in a subject nor yet be asserted of one—this or that man or horse, for example. For nothing of that kind is in or is ever affirmed of a subject. More generally speaking, indeed, we can never affirm of a subject what is in its nature individual and also numerically one. Yet in some cases nothing prevents its being present or found in a subject. Thus a piece of grammatical knowledge is present, as we said, in a mind. (1 a 20–b 8.)

What is this chapter about? We have started on our investigation of the use of language in getting to know things, and in particular such things as can be known unambiguously. In the next treatise, *On Interpretation*, Aristotle will be dealing with two terms combined into propositions, next with triads of terms forming syllogisms, and so on. Thus he would seem to be treating here of uncombined expressions, 'man', 'horse', 'knowledge', 'whiteness', to give his own examples. But he is not treating these as a grammarian, who deals with words simply as units of speech. On the contrary, he is dealing with the classification of *things* in so far as such uncombined terms can be used to designate them. He is classifying things as available for the primary units of scientific discourse. The simplest way to put this is to say that the *Categories* deals with things in so far as they properly evoke different sorts of answers to the question, What is it? Aristotle is showing us how to ask this question in an orderly way, in a way germane to the process of acquiring scientific knowledge. In a series beginning in each case with an individual something, we proceed in increasing circles of generality until we reach the last answer possible for that kind of something, and this last answer is the category in question.

Let us try to see just what this classification amounts to. First, we must be quite clear about the meanings of 'predicated of' and 'present in'. The word translated here as 'predicated' is simply 'said' or 'spoken' (λέγεται). Now clearly anything which can be *said* of something else as its subject must have some kind of generality. To say 'this frog is this', is not to *say* anything about it. To say 'this frog is green', or 'this frog is croaking', or 'this frog is funny', is to say of it something that could be said of other objects also. An adjective which could be used only on one unique occasion would not function as an adjective; and the something unique it designated would not be something sayable of a subject. Therefore all things

73

that are predicable of subjects are non-individual. Contrari-wise, whatever is not predicable of a subject is in some sense non-general, particular. Thus all things are cut by one cut: predicable of a subject/not predicable of a subject.

Secondly, 'present in'. Aristotle is not speaking here, he says emphatically, of the presence of parts in a whole, of the frog's heart, for example, in the frog. He is speaking of the sort of 'thing' which cannot exist independently of its subject: this particular case of spottiness, for instance, could not exist apart from this frog with its spotted skin. When, on the other hand, we say, 'this frog is spotted', we are referring in our predicate not only to the spots on this frog, but to spottiness in general, the sort of 'thing' ascribable equally to a frog or to a child with chicken-pox. This particular case of spottiness, however, we do not *ascribe* to anything; it is just *in*, is, in traditional language, an accident of this particular frog. The 'present-in' sort of thing, in other words, is essentially de-pendent; it is not to be met with anywhere except in something else. This gives us, therefore, another exhaustive cut between two classes: dependent things and independent things, things that do not exist by themselves and things that do, accidents and the concrete entities, or substances, of which they are accidents.

Putting these two dichotomies together, we get the four-fold classification Aristotle is describing: (1) predicated of, not present in; (2) present in, not predicated of; (3) both; (4) neither. Suppose I have a tame frog named Jumbo. (1) 'Jumbo is a frog.' 'Frog' is predicated of him, but not present in him. Although, admittedly, 'frog' is not anywhere in the world, independently of the existence of this or that frog, or of all frogs, neither is it in any particular one of them, as its particular spottedness is 'in' it. (2) The particular spottiness of Jumbo's skin is just this particular case of spottiness. If you ask me why I say Jumbo is spotted and I point to the blotches on his back I am pointing out just this accident of this frog. Of course I may say more generally that frogs are spotted, referring a particular class of accident to a particular class of

74

subjects. But the point here is that although neither frog as such nor spottedness as such exist independently, individual frogs do, whereas individual spots do not, not without frogs or leopards or chicken-poxy children to be the spots of. And the fundamental distinction between things-present-in and things-not-present-in is a distinction made between individuals, not between the more general 'things' that can be 'said' of subjects.

What of class 3? Being a class of things predicated, it must be general, and being a class of things present-in, it must be a class of dependent things, of accidents. It comprises, in fact, cases where a relation of greater or lesser generality holds between accidents. Thus, in Aristotle's example, knowledge is not an independently existing entity; it does not exist apart from a knower, but is either an activity or a habit of a person who knows. But knowledge as an intellectual habit in general is predicated of grammar, which is one kind of knowledge. In the case of my pet frog, I might say that spottiness is one kind of pigmentation, thus subsuming one sort of accident under a wider heading of similar accidents. Both are things of the present-in variety, but the more general can be ascribed to the less general within the same kind.

Only members of class 4, finally, are both individual and independently existent. This is, in our case, Jumbo, in Aristotle's examples, this man, this horse. These are what Aristotle terms *first substances*; and they are fundamental, he goes on to say, to all the other classes. For they are the ultimate subjects in which other things (individual accidents) are, or of which other things (predicates) are said. 'If there were no first substances,' says Aristotle, 'none of the other things could exist.' (2 b 5–6) The fourth class, therefore, is ontologically unique, and since knowing follows being, the development of knowledge will follow the distinction between the things that are in this primary sense, and everything else. The fundamental distinction is that between substance and the accidents of substance, or, as the *Categories* list them:

Each combined word or expression means one of the following: a substance, or how large, or of what sort, or related to what, or where,

75

or when, or in what attitude, or how circumstanced, or what doing, or what undergoing. (1 b 25–27)

As they came to be rendered, these are the categories on the one hand of substance and on the other of quantity, quality, relation, place, time, position, state, action, affection.

But there is a complication here. Class 1, man or horse, in Aristotle's example also belongs to the category of substance, but its members do not exist independently in the same way as do members of class 4. Frog, horse and man are not things in the same primary way as this frog, this horse or this man. The former are what Aristotle calls second substances, which are predicated of first substances but not present in them. In the *Metaphysics*, as we saw, such 'things' as these, species and genera (say, frog and oviparous animal), or universals in general, are denied the status of substance altogether. Here they are said to be substances, though in a secondary way. But the reason for this is plain. In the *Categories* we are asking the question 'What is it?', and the things we are asking about are, as we have just seen, divided in two directions: among individuals: independent/dependent, i.e. substance/accident; within substance or any given accidental category, between subject and predicate, i.e. between individual and general, or less and more general. So we have a situation which can be schematically represented as follows:

		this case of:				
individual	Jumbo	10″	spotted	leaping	in the back garden	etc.
species	frog	length	multi-coloured			
genus	amphibian	measurement	colour			
category	substance	quantity	quality	posture	place	etc.

In each category, if we ask, what is it?, the first answer points to the individual, then we generalize to species and genus, and the last answer is in terms of the category itself. So when we ask 'what is it?' and answer '*a* frog' or '*a* horse', we are still answering within the line of what-is-it questions that come under the category *substance*. 'Frog' is in fact our second answer to the question 'what is it?' under the heading *substance*; what it designates is therefore second substance. We could analogously call spottiness a case of second quality, as distinct from this instance of it, which is a first quality. That is why genus and species must be counted substances in the order of logic; they are second (or at any rate, other than first) answers to the series of what-is-it inquiries which will terminate with the most general answer 'substance'. The foundation for the denial of their substantial status in the order of *being*, however, is plainly laid down in the dictum just quoted (p. 75). All other things are either predicated of first substance or present in first substance and *if there were no first substances none of the others* (i.e. members of classes 1, 2 and 3) *could exist at all*. Thus if species and genus are not dependent in the same way as accidents, neither do they exist independently in the same way as first substance. They are kinds of first substances. There is no contradiction between this document and the *Metaphysics*, but the line of argument, the final cause of the discourse, is different, and the terminology, though not its import, is altered accordingly.

Nor could Aristotle have been content here with the distinction between substance and accident at the *individual* level alone, for knowledge depends wholly on the right application of *predicates*, which are general, to kinds of substances, which are also general. I may be interested in this particular frog if I want to catch him or feed him or do away with him because he is a nuisance, but as a scientist I could only be interested in, say, the skeleton or the circulation or the intelligence of *the* frog, and of this frog only as representative of the species frog. The propositions which constitute a science are univocal statements attributing certain characteristics to certain *kinds* of substances. The whole trick of establishing an Aristotelian science consists in selecting from some other categories the correct essential attributes to supply, as its starting-point, the definition of the kind of substance to be studied, and the terms

77

to be demonstrated of this kind of substance in its conclusions. Therefore the rising scale of generality is every bit as fundamental to the whole procedure as the division, at ground level, so to speak, between things-not-present-in and things-present-in. In order to establish a science of some subject matter, we must take a natural class of first substances, and elicit from some other category or categories, also at appropriately generalized levels, the right predicates for the characterization of its essence. But we should not, of course, describe this as a 'trick', for it is things themselves that sort themselves out, in this well-ordered cosmos, in such a way as to make such science possible.

That things do sort themselves out in some such way may seem on the face of it obvious. It is not hard for most people to know a hawk from a handsaw. Yet the sparrow-owl dialectic we noticed earlier, though not common sense, is philosophical sense, and was so to every generation of Greek philosophers who had preceded Aristotle. It was the changing face of nature, set free from mythological explanations, that started men philosophizing. Everywhere there is a rhythm of contrarieties, hot, cold, moist, dry, hard, soft. The philosopher must find a pattern in the rhythm, the order that somehow rises from the sheer contrariness. Things come from an indefinite and return to it, said Anaximander. Change is so unintelligible as to be totally unreal; only the One, eternal and fixed, has being, said Parmenides. It is the number in things, not the things themselves, that are real, said the Pythagoreans. 'By convention hot, by convention cold; by convention sweet, by convention bitter; only the atoms and the void are real', pronounced Democritus. Nothing is, said Gorgias, if it were, we could not know it, if we knew it, we could not express it. Aristotle knew all this, and lectured on it habitually in the Introductions to his courses. It was always: my predecessors agreed on this; they erred here, they were right there. And the Platonic dialectic of perception and the Forms he knew not only as history but at first hand. If the problem of Parmenides seemed to him antiquated and the problem of Cratylus even more irrelevant, this was not because he simply took things in a cabbages-and-kings way as any child might find them. It was because his experience included an aspect sufficiently striking and sufficiently massive to overcome the traditional dialectic of flux and permanence. Things as he saw them sorted themselves out in defiance of the philosophers. The Forms of the Platonists and the invisible atoms of Democritus were for him unnecessary. The Forms were verbiage, a superfluous addendum to the order inherent *in* the perceptible world. The atoms and void, though these concepts had indeed a scientific ring, were no proper explanation either, because they explained the rich world of changing qualities, of directed rhythms, in a purely quantitative and non-directive way.

What was this experience? Surely it was the experience of the practising biologist, who can tell a placental from an ordinary dogfish,[1] or the catfish now known as Parasilurus Aristotelis from other species, and specify the reason for his distinctions. He can tell, too, that a chicken will hatch out of a hen's egg, not only after the obvious twenty-one days, but after just these precise stages of development. The more detail one observes, the more precise does nature's order appear in structure and in process. Why all the fuss? Why explain the obvious by the non-obvious? The order *in* nature, the precedence of form over the formable, of the completed process over the steps that tend to it: these are facts visible enough, and precise enough, to carry all the distinctions of the philosophers and turn them from instruments of doubt and fumbling into precise intellectual tools of a well-catalogued, neatly inter-related body of definite and certain science. For this enterprise, the first distinction we need is that between the individual things that are, and the characteristics by which we identify them, the distinction necessary if we are to establish statements of their essential natures, statements which relate certain essential attributes to them as the subjects distinguished,

[1] See Johannes Müller, 'Über den glatten Hai des Aristoteles', *Abh. d. Kgl. Akad. d. Wiss.*, 1840, 187–257. W. Haberling, in 'Der glatte Hai des A.', *Arch. Gesch. Math. Naturw. u. Tech.* **10** (1927–8), 166–184, has published the letters relating to Müller's rediscovery of Aristotle's distinction between two closely similar, but reproductively divergent Mediterranean forms.

by this attribution, from everything else in all the universe. In his account of biological method at the start of the Great Course in Biology Aristotle remarks:

What kept our predecessors from arriving at this method of explanation was that the being-what-it-is and the definition of substance had not yet been achieved. (642 a 25; MG)

I shall return presently to Aristotle's strange phrase 'the being-what-it-is' and its importance for his methodology; for the moment I may clarify it by mentioning a similar usage also in the biological writings. In the treatise on the *Progression of Animals*, he speaks of nature as 'preserving the peculiar substance of each thing and what it is for that thing to be': the phrase is basically the same: τὸ τί ἦν αὐτῷ εἶναι. (708 a 11–12.)[1] We may for the moment perhaps join the two phrases linked in both passages, the being-what-it-is and the entity, and speak, loosely, of *the peculiar identity of each kind of thing*. This is what nature preserves, and what the scientist who has achieved the right method of knowing apprehends and respects. It is the ontological basis for this method, which depends on knowing the 'peculiar substance of each thing and what it is for that thing to be', that Aristotle has laid down in the first two chapters of the *Categories*.

3. *Aristotle's discovery*

In both the remarks I have quoted, Aristotle uses the phrase usually, though not satisfactorily, translated as 'essence', and which I have rendered 'being-what-it-is'.[2] This concept might be thought of as primarily metaphysical. Yet in the *Parts of Animals* Aristotle is not speaking about his predecessors' conception of being as such, but about their scientific methodology. It was the proper treatment of nature, and in particular of living things, for which, lacking the 'being-what-it-is' and the

[1] For an interesting conjecture about the origin of this phrase, especially in the form that includes the dative, see Miss Anscombe's recent essay (4, pp. 24–6.)

[2] See Bibliographical Note.

definition of substance, they were inadequately equipped. What has this seemingly metaphysical conception to do with the method of an Aristotelian science? Substance, so closely linked with it in both our biological passages, has, as we have just seen, been marked out at the very beginning of the *Organon* as different from and fundamental to all other things. It is the right application of the appropriate accidental categories to a set of substances that constitutes a scientific discourse. From the *Categories*, and the classification of things referred to by uncompounded terms, to the *Posterior Analytics* and the per-fection of science is a long road. In the course of it, in the treatise *On Interpretation* and the *Prior Analytics*, Aristotle has laid down the fundamental techniques of immediate and mediate inference as the scientist will need them. In the *Posterior Analytics*, finally, he comes to the *raison d'être* of the whole procedure: the specification of the constituents of a science; and here the concept of being-what-it-is, the being of each kind of thing which the defining formula aims at specifying, plays a major part. For the establishment of scientific know-ledge depends first and foremost on the possibility of stating *real definitions* of *limited kinds of things*. Substances fall naturally into classes in such a way that we can specify, in carefully chosen formulae, their essential natures. We can follow nature in keeping to *'the peculiar substance of each thing, and what it is to be that thing'*. That is what Aristotle's predecessors, Plato included, were unable to do, because they lacked the right instruments for doing it; this is, from his own point of view, Aristotle's major discovery.

It was a discovery which could only be stated in a very precise and delicate fashion. Aristotle is the first great master of technical philosophical language, and much depends here on the interrelations of three of his technical terms often translated interchangeably as 'essence': the two we have just found so closely linked in the biological passages: substance and being-what-it-is; and third, or, in a way, standing between these two, the τί ἔστι or 'what-is-it'. When οὐσία, substance, is rendered as essence, it is usually where Aristotle refers not

81

to substances, frogs, dogs, or men, but the 'substance' *of* something. This breadth of meaning is well rendered by Owens' translation of οὐσία in the *Metaphysics* as 'entity'. In general, οὐσία is the fundamental ontological real which all scientific knowledge has directly or indirectly for its object. Usually one speaks of *entities*, though one may speak of *the entities of things* without essentially altering the meaning of the term, though changing its reference somewhat. The τί ἐστι corresponds to the scientific question specified by Aristotle in *Posterior Analytics* II, in his list of four kinds of inquiries: that, why, whether it is, what it is. It is in general the *what it is* that science aims to know. Demonstrations, by demonstrating that certain attributes belong necessarily and uniquely to certain classes, exhibit their *what*, the essences of those things. Definitions are formulae stating the appropriate aspect of this 'what' as the starting-point of demonstration. Scientific discourse on the face of it articulates *whats*. Aristotle is here following in the steps of Socrates as well as Plato and refining further the technique of getting things under the right headings and grouping them in the right way. 'What is it?' was the question they were all three concerned to ask. But what of our remaining concept? There are substances, and we ask what they are, we seek their essences. Where does being-what-it-is come into it? This is precisely where, Aristotle has told us, his predecessors went astray; this is the concept they lacked. What is it and what does it accomplish in the structure of science?

In the *Metaphysics*, Owens explains, the 'being-what-it-is' refers to the form of substance, or to substance as form, while what-it-is may equally designate the matter or the composite of form and matter, which are not so exactly and fundamentally substance as form is. This is undoubtedly correct; but I should like to venture, very hesitantly, to add to this distinction another which seems to me to emerge both from the linking of being-what-it-is with definition in the *Parts of Animals* and from the occurrence of the term in the logical works. In talking of essential predication and the like, Aristotle regularly speaks of τί ἔστι, or of predicates 'contained in the τί ἔστι'; but when definition comes to be considered in detail in the *Posterior Analytics*, Aristotle regularly uses 'the being-what-it-is' alongside the other and commoner term. Previous to this discussion, also, it occurs in a reference to definition which provides another clue to its meaning:

> If definition is possible, that is, if the being-what-it-is is knowable . . . (82 b 38; MG)

Through definition, in other words, it is the thing's being-what-it-is that we know. This is the unique, inherent form of the thing, which Socrates and Plato, for all their search for 'whats', had failed to grasp. Without it they could not give a correct account of definition, and so they failed also to single out demonstration as distinct from dialectic as the correct method of science. In other words, the being-what-it-is, as the form of substance, *ties down the 'whats' of definitions to their objects*. There are, it seems to me, four closely integrated steps here. (1) A *definition* is a set of words specifying (2) the *what* which through understanding the mind can inspect. What thus proves knowable, however, is (3), the *being-what-it-is* of (4), the substance or class of substances that are the object of knowledge. Through a verbal formula the mind knows, has present to it, the what of a class of things. But how do we know that this is not just a dream of our own, that it is our conception of something that *is*? Because substances have, corresponding to our vision of essence, definable forms, proper ways of being, which are in shape and nature congruent with the essences our verbal formulae express. It was this truth about the things that are that 'our predecessors' lacked. There was for them no 'being-what-it-is' and so no definition of substance. They had not discovered the what of real things, they did not know that these were knowable and so for them real definitions of real things, the proper starting-points of science, were not possible. Definitions, in other words, had not been correctly linked to entities through form. Democritus, Aristotle remarks in the *Parts of Animals*, has come nearest to this discovery, blundering upon it despite himself. The atoms, in other words, were at least stable forms explicative of our perceptions of things, knowable yet *belonging to the things*. Things are not as Democritus thought they were, since their functioning, their principle of organization is not just their shape; their qualitative natures and the direction of their development must be comprehended in the knowledge of their being. Yet the assertion that there are knowable forms *in* things was at least a step in the right direction. Nobody before him, however, Aristotle is confident, had discovered the full character of the being-what-it-is of each kind of thing and so made scientific knowledge possible.

It is instructive to consider this situation alongside Plato's account of method in the *Seventh Letter* (341 B ff.). Plato lists five elements in the search for knowledge: (1) name, (2) definition, (3) image, (4) knowledge, (5) object. The difference between Plato and Aristotle in the conception of 'images' (i.e. experience) we have already discussed, and it will become clearer when we consider Aristotle's own theory of perception. Leaving perception aside, we have in Aristotle's method: defining formula, what it is, being-what-it-is, substance or object. Defining formula embraces name and definition, Plato's first two. For Plato, however, these strings of words are always tentative. There is no assured bridge from words to object. Between formulation and knowledge of the thing there is a leap. For Aristotle, on the other hand, definition, that is, successful definition, is possible, because 'the being-what-it-is is knowable'. What makes the difference is not only that the things are this-worldly, concrete things. This might be so, and we might still have the indefinite groping of guesswork, inspired or uninspired, as our intellectual destiny: that is, indeed, the 'philosophy of ambiguity' which may be for us the only honest attitude in an eternally unstable world. But this was not the case for Aristotle, because he had discovered definable form, the being-what-it-is of things, the fixity, intelligibility, certainty *in* things. That is what enables us, in schematizing his achievement, to insert a fifth in our previous list of four, a fifth corresponding to Plato's fourth element, that is, the knowledge which, in Aristotle's case, links the essence as formulated with the form as knowable form of the thing. So instead of Plato's

name ←→ definition/?   knowledge ←→ object,

we have

defining formula ←→ what is it ←→ knowledge ←→ being-what-it-is ←→ object.

This is Platonic knowledge in that it is finite and of the finite, intellectual and of the intelligible, certain and of the certain, real and of the real, eternal and of the eternal, universal and of the universal (of classes of substances, not individuals), of form, not of the flux. All this is pure Platonism, yet transformed into its opposite through Aristotle's discovery of the being-what-it-is of things. Things in the natural world present themselves to our minds, whose nature it is to be capable of receiving such presentation, as *definable*; the *what* verbalized in definition is linked through an unbreakable bond to the definable essence of the thing.

I need not stress here again that this discovery, while the moralist's despair, is the biologist's daily stock in trade. That is what Aristotle himself has said in so many words in the Introduction to Biology, and in the *Posterior Analytics* he has carried out with inimitable precision the implications of his discovery for the procedures of scientific argument and scientific knowledge.

4. *The constituents of science*

I do not propose to follow here in detail the knotty arguments of the *Posterior Analytics*, but to look in the light of the preceding exegetical remarks at the outline of Aristotle's view of the constituents of science. For this purpose I may formulate my thesis as a commentary on one of Aristotle's brief enumerations of these constituents:

Every demonstrative science is concerned with three things: the subjects which it posits (i.e., the genus whose essential attributes it studies), the so-called common axioms upon which the demonstration is ultimately based, and thirdly the attributes whose several meanings it assumes. (76 b 11–16)

(a) The first necessary step in achieving scientific knowledge of a subject-matter is to separate the subject of study from the rest of existence. Some people, Aristotle says (97 a), think one should try to know the whole of existence; one thinks of the *Seventh Letter* and Plato's statement that the mind must range through the whole of existence in search of the knowledge one seeks: there are no limits on relevance and irrelevance. The arguments of the dialogues, with their expanding and many-levelled subject-matters, everywhere exemplify this belief. Aristotle's position is just the opposite. We can never *know* anything about anything, as distinct from having opinions about it, unless we cut out one limited subject-matter out of a wider range and restrict ourselves to it. Only in this way can we be certain of the precise application of our attributions to their subjects. Suppose, for instance, that we draw two perpendiculars to the same straight line and find that they never meet. We may suppose that it is because they are both perpendicular that they never meet, whereas it is parallels, not perpendiculars, that have this property. If, however, we examine as well other cases of parallel lines, not drawn perpendicular to a given straight line, we shall be able to specify correctly the properties of perpendiculars which belong to them *as* perpendiculars. Similarly, we know that parallels never meet because we have defined parallels as one class of pairs of lines distinct from pairs of lines not parallel, and so on. In each case it is a species within a genus, a genus within a wider genus that we know. Only in this way can we mark out precisely the subject-matter we are dealing with from everything else. If there were a *summum genus* it would not be knowable by demonstration and the 'knowledge' of it would not be scientific knowledge.

That is why it is mistaken, for example, to interpret Aristotle as a hesitant and partial forerunner of Linnaeus or other great classifiers. One can elicit from his works a kind of overall classification of animals; and, of course, there was the famous Tree of Porphyry, which was supposed to represent the hierarchy of nature as Aristotle saw it. But overall classification was not Aristotle's primary concern. There are ten categories listed in the *Categories*; elsewhere the list may run to six or eight; it depends what inquiry one is engaged in, which attributive classes are of interest for the particular discourse in hand. Similarly, the classification of animals may be undertaken differently in the context of different investigations. If we try to classify everything at once, we shall be back with the Platonic dilemma: sweeping through the universe in search of a precision we can never find. If, on the other hand, we confine each inquiry to its proper subject-matter, we may succeed, by the appropriate method, in eliciting its proper truth. Knowledge, Aristotle and Plato agree, is of the finite; only the determinate is intelligible. But Plato seeks finitude, definition, against a background of indefinite flux. On the contrary, the finite, the intelligible, Aristotle is convinced, must be sought in an area already bounded. It is all-important for the possibility of science that there are definite things characterized by definite structures and definite life-histories, things which group themselves naturally according to these structures and processes, so that the world, in itself, displays the finitude essential to knowledge, and knowledge mirrors the intelligibility of the world. Not only art but knowledge imitates nature; and what principally characterizes nature is the orderly realization of each kind of thing in its due place and its due time. The unambiguous predications of science are possible only because things sort themselves out naturally into kinds; knowledge results from the mind's response to such natural groupings. Transcend them and you transcend the limits of univocal speech, which are the bounds of science. You have strayed beyond the well-fenced limits of the being-what-it-is and are lost in the quicksands of dialectic once more.

The ideal instance of a proper subject-matter, for Aristotle, is a well-marked collection of substances, for, as we have seen, the demarcation of substance from its accidents underlies the whole procedure. Not all sciences, however, directly study substances. Mathematics, as in the case just referred to, abstracts from the qualitative aspect of first substances and studies their quantity alone. The mathematical study of astronomy or optics gives Aristotle some pause here: these sciences study really existing bodies, yet in their mathematical aspect, because they study peculiarly mathematicizable things. Mathematics as such, however, studies not fully real things as real, but only their quantitative aspect in abstraction from their full physical existence. The difference between 'concave' and 'snub' is Aristotle's favourite example of this difference. 'Concave' is a shape simply; 'snub' implies flesh and bone. Ethics, similarly, studies not men as men in their whole nature, but men solely as agents. Even in such cases, however, it is the concept of a subject-genus on which the procedure rests, and this conception in turn rests on its ideal case: the segregation of one natural kind of natural individuals.

(b) It is all-important, then, that the subject-matter of a demonstrative science be precisely delimited. Of such a subject-matter, Aristotle says, we know both that and what it is. Of the third constituent in our list, the attributes, we must know the meaning; it is their inherence in the subject-genus which we are going to demonstrate. In terms of the categories, again, these attributes will be drawn from the non-substantial categories, and of course we must choose them appropriately, and at exactly the same range of generality as the subject-genus itself. In the ideal case, where it is a particular group of substances we are studying, we mark out our subject-genus and then choose attributes exactly co-extensive with it, so that our conclusions will be, in Aristotle's terminology, 'commensurately universal' propositions. Thus we should be mistaken if we demonstrated of aquatic animals that they are oviparous, since some of them are not. Similarly, in the abstractive realm of geometry, we should be mistaken if we demonstrated of plane figures that they have the sum of their angles equal to two right angles, since some plane figures are rectangles, circles, etc. and do not possess this character. The attributes whose inherence we demonstrate must also be necessary, belonging to the essence of the subject-genus *qua* that subject-genus. If we demonstrate of man that he is risible, this will indeed be coextensive with mankind, but laughter for Aristotle is not an *essential* attribute of man, only a 'property' which in fact all men possess.

(c) So much for the attributes, which on the whole present no serious problems. The starting-points of demonstration, the propositions from which demonstration moves, are a different case. Aristotle describes them here as the 'so-called common axioms', and elsewhere mentions 'common axioms' as among the 'elements' of a science. They are common, however, only by analogy. The possibility of science for him depends on the uniqueness of the starting-points of demonstration appropriate to the particular subject-matter. Thus, for example, the axiom that the whole is greater than the part will be only by analogy common to arithmetic and geometry. In the one case it is stated as for discrete, in the other as for continuous quantity. What is essential in the structure of a science is the *peculiar* premises. Of these again, hypotheses (in the narrow geometrical sense at least), which are asserted to exist, and postulates, which are taken though not believed in, seem to be minor aids to knowledge. What is left as the central body of premises of science are a set of definitions stating the essential nature of the subject-genus in question:

Thus it is clear that of things that are essential (τῶν τί ἔστι) some are immediate, and are first principles, and both that they are and what they are have to be assumed or made plain in some other way. (This is what an arithmetician does; he assumes both what a unit is and that it is.) (93 b 21–25; MG)

This statement forms part of the conclusion of one stage in Aristotle's argument about definition and its relation to demonstration. The subject is a difficult one, but we may single out two points of special importance for discussion here.

First, there is the question why these unique starting-points of demonstration are necessary. Clearly, there is some knowledge by demonstration. Suppose, Aristotle says, that, as some people hold, there were no other kind. Then either (1) everything is demonstrated in terms of everything else, and we have a circular structure like that of a dictionary; or (2) we have no knowledge at all, since our demonstration has nowhere to begin: we have no prior and better knowledge from which to start.

The first alternative is clearly unsatisfactory, since it expresses one of two mistaken conceptions. (72 b ff.) First, what some of the advocates of circular demonstration are referring to is the apparent circle of induction and demonstration, not a genuine circularity in demonstration itself. Knowledge proceeds, Aristotle says, from things better known to us to things prior absolutely and back again, that is, from perception through induction to first principles and back to the conclusions from first principles. But this is not circular demonstration, since the first half of the procedure is not yet knowledge, for it is not universal, eternal, necessary. In short, induction is not demonstration, and so this is not a circular demonstration at all. Secondly, if we really take circular demonstration strictly, as some of its advocates do, such a theory 'simply amounts to this, that a thing is so if it is so':

That this is all that follows will be clearly seen if we take three terms; for it makes no difference whether we say that a circular proof is effected through many or few terms, provided that there are not fewer than two. For when if A is, B must be, and if B is, C must be, then if A is, C must be. Then if when A is, B must be, and when B is, A must be (this is what is meant by circular proof), let A represent C in the first proof. Then to say that when B is, A is, is equivalent to saying that when·B is, C is; and this is equivalent to saying that when A is, C is. But C is the same as A. Thus it follows that those who assert that demonstration is circular are merely maintaining that when A is, A is. (72 b 35–73 a 5)

'By this method,' Aristotle tartly remarks, 'it is easy to prove anything.' (73 a 6; MG) Thus logic and mathematics conceived as systems of tautologies would hold no interest for Aristotle. Again, for him as for Plato, purely formal knowledge would not be knowledge at all.

The other alternative may again be subdivided. Some people say that since demonstration is the only form of scientific knowledge we have to start from *unknown* premises. But since the principles of demonstration must be 'better known' than the conclusion, this will not be knowledge. We are reminded of Socrates' attempt in the *Theaetetus* to define knowledge as judgment in which unknowable units are combined into a knowable whole. Again, interestingly enough, in the form Aristotle gives it here, this view resembles the modern formalism of Hilbert, where one is meant to take arbitrary postulates composed of meaningless marks and prove the conclusions of one's system from them. For Aristotle, it is inconceivable that the known should rest on the ground of the unknown. The other sub-alternative on this view, moreover, would be equally fatal to the possibility of science, for it would involve an infinite regress. Whatever premises we may take for one 'demonstrative' argument will again serve as the conclusions for another, and so on ad infinitum. This is not knowledge but an endless pursuit of the illusion of knowledge. Were Aristotle to be given the choice that Lessing envisaged in his famous essay, he would unhesitatingly choose the other way: knowledge every time, not the striving for it. For, as we shall have occasion to emphasize as we proceed, Aristotle is entirely convinced that every process, including the search for knowledge, has its being and its significance through its relation to its own successful achievement. Nobody could be on the way to Egypt unless it were possible to be in Egypt. A preference for striving for its own sake would be a preference for obscurantist nonsense instead of plain good sense.

If there is demonstrative knowledge, then, there must be definite starting-points of knowledge, exactly coextensive with the subject-matter of each science. These will be primarily and chiefly definitions of the subject-matter of the science. The second question we must face in this connection is the question of the nature of such definitions. Are they conventional: decisions to use words in a certain way, or something more, and if so, what?

A scientific treatise may, of course, contain nominal definitions. The scientist may introduce technical terms which he proposes to use in a particular way. The view that all definitions are nominal, however, Aristotle emphatically rejects:

> Thus since in defining one exhibits either what the object is or what its name means, if definition is in no sense of the essence (τί ἔστι), it must be an expression meaning the same as a name. But this is absurd. (1) In the first place, there would be definition not only of non-substances, but also of non-existents; because even these can have a significant name. (2) All expressions would be definitions, because a name could be attached to any one of them; so we should all converse in formulae, and the *Iliad* would be a definition. (3) No demonstration can prove that a given name has a given meaning; therefore neither do definitions (in establishing the meaning of a term) furnish evidence also that the name has a given meaning. (92 b 26–34)

This is, once more, a clear anticipation and rejection of a common modern view of this matter. It is impossible that all definitions should be mere conventions about how to use certain words, because in that case any set of words strung together could be supposed as much as any other to designate a substance. A set of words strung together and named the 'Iliad' would have as good a claim to being the definition of a class of real, individual things as any other formula. Any mere sequence of words could be the starting-point of a science, and knowledge would be cut loose from its root in things, in the entities there *are*. It is toward these real natures that the formulae by which we lay down the proper starting-point of a science must be directed. In short, scientific definitions must be not nominal, but *real*. On this possibility, and the correct realization of it, all else depends.

Consider for a moment the implications of Aristotle's choice of an example. For this is not the only time he uses it; and the reference to the same example in the *Metaphysics* (1030 a 7ff.) may help to illuminate its significance here. If definitions were nominal, any string of words, the *Iliad*, for instance, might be a definition; that shows us, in the order of logic, where we must not go. If any set of words could designate substances any arbitrary unity, the *Iliad*, for instance, might be a substance; that shows us in the order of being *why* we must not go that way. For the artist, poems are creatures analogous to God's creatures. It is the poets who are our teachers, not because they describe or instruct but because they create, they fashion men and the world of men, and submitting to their spell we become as they would have us. That is why Plato, artist despite himself, feared art, and tried to demote it to an imitation at third remove. In its power to corrupt, to dethrone reason, to sway passion, the *Iliad* is more dangerously real than any mere particular object in the visible world. Not so for Aristotle. 'Imitation' in the *Poetics* is not a denigrative term, nor is the activity it designates dangerous. For the poet in his making is simply doing what every craftsman does. He is producing by the rules of his art an artificial object intended for a certain proper and limited use. Such production remains always within the bounds of an orderly, forever articulated world. Like every other habitual skill, it has its right place in the ordered existence of the animal, man, who practises it. Cobblers make shoes to protect our feet; poets make poems for our enjoyment and the purgation of our passions. To suppose that such a made thing, in the case of a poem, such a verbal thing, was a substance would be absurd. Nobody makes substances. They come into being and perish, in eternal recurrence; they are not made. Therefore to say that a string of words constituting such a made thing was a definition of a kind or genus of substance, the starting-point of a science, would be correspondingly absurd. Definition must state appropriately the essential *what* of a limited and specifiable kind of really existing individual substances, or of some limited and specifiable aspect of such a limited kind. This *what* has been firmly anchored, in the chapter preceding the one I have just quoted (II, 6; 92 a 7ff.), in the being-what-it-is of the object. It is this which no argument can demonstrate, and which the essential predicates contained in definitions are meant to designate. (Cf. 94 a 34–35, where 'what the formula means' is identified with the 'being-what-it-is'.) Otherwise science will lack the unique and definite, ontologically grounded starting-point from which alone it can proceed.

5. The finitude of scientific discourse

A science, then, demonstrates the inherence of essential attributes in a limited subject-genus, and does this by arguing from premises which include *real* definitions of its subject-genus. Before we go any further, we must stop and 'make a fresh start', as Aristotle so often says, to reflect on a matter of crucial importance from Aristotle's point of view, that is, the finite structure of scientific discourse. We have seen this already in the enumeration of the constituents of science, both in the limited nature of the subject genus, and in the denial of an infinite regress of premises for demonstration. But the point is central and will bear elaboration, as indeed Aristotle elaborates it in the argument of the *Posterior Analytics*. This argument has been discussed by Professor Raphael Demos in an illuminating paper on the structure of substance in Aristotle. (27) It is in fact the structure of science, not of substance, that Aristotle is discussing here, but of course Professor Demos is right in seeing an intimate connection between them. His discussion rests on Aristotle's fourfold concept of cause, which is specified in the *Organon*, and is also fundamental to the *Metaphysics*, but is most easily understood through its exposition in the *Physics*. There Aristotle will analyse causes of change in natural things.[1] A thing's nature (the originative source of change in it) is what it is *because* of the matter in which its form is embodied, *because* of the form

---

[1] Wicksteed calls them 'becauses', in order to stress the difference from the narrower modern conception of cause, but we may use the word 'cause' if we remember how varied is the Aristotelian meaning—more like our 'reasons'.

so ordering its material aspect, *because* of the starting-point of change, which triggers the process that constitutes the thing in question as a natural and therefore changing entity, and *because* of the end product, the achievement, at which the process aims. The four causes fall into two pairs; the structure of a substance at a moment is what it is by virtue of the relation of matter and form; through time it is what it becomes in virtue of the relation of the beginning of motion to its goal. These two pairs have an important bearing, Professor Demos points out, on two passages in the *Posterior Analytics*. In I, 19–23, Aristotle argues that demonstrative knowledge must be bounded in three directions. It must begin from fixed premises and move through a finite number of middle terms to precise and definite conclusions. A science is not infinitely expandible in any of these three directions, because what it exhibits is itself a finite structure, the essence of a natural group of individuals. Thus once more, science depends for its possibility on the fact that things have essences, *whats* stateable in definitions. The range of their exemplification in individuals, their existence as enmattered forms, must be closed through the specification of form if they are to be understood. This frog, this ox, this man would not be a subject for science unless the indefinite range of matter were cut into intelligible parts through the existence of the being-what-it-is of each kind: of frog, of ox, of man. Therefore in science it is the definition of such forms and the demonstration of their essential attributes on which it all depends. We come back once more to Aristotle's discovery: that there is the being-what-it-is of each thing and that substance is definable. The finitude of scientific discourse in all three directions reflects this priority of determinate form over the indeterminacy of matter in the real things of the natural world.

Intelligibility, therefore, depends on the possibility of defining essence, on the subordination of matter to form in the actual individuals that exist in this well-ordered world. But individuals change; and such change too must itself be ordered and finite if we are to have knowledge of it and of the individuals

95

whose nature it is to change. Substances changing through time are known in terms of the other pair of causes, the later state of affairs, which completes the series, giving us the *reason* for the earliest event, which starts it off. This pattern Aristotle considers in *Posterior Analytics* II, 12, when he discusses knowledge of the causes of past, present and future events. If at a moment substance is intelligible through form, through time it is intelligible through its end. Both these are essence, for the end of development is the fully developed individual of its kind toward which the process of development tends. The egg develops into a full-grown bird; it is the bird, not the egg, that is the primary reason for the process. This is not a limit to be asymptotically approached; it must *be*. If eggs only tried to be chickens but never succeeded they would be not 'eggs' but only blobs, and the 'process' of ontogenesis would not be a process. The steps in development are necessary to development, but it is the 'peculiar entity of each thing', its being-what-it-is, that is the reason for those necessary, earlier steps. The end of a man's development is not superman, but man. Finite structure and finite process are the two intelligibilities the mind can know, and it is because the world is an orderly assemblage of such structures and such processes that there is knowledge.[1]

[1] Some modern Aristotelians may object that I am overstressing the finitude of Aristotelian science. Admittedly, in considering the number of first principles, not just of one science, but of a range of sciences, Aristotle remarks: 'The principles are not much fewer in number than the conclusions . . . The conclusions are infinite in number, whereas the terms are finite.' (88 b 4–6.) This is part of a dialectical argument refuting the contention that all arguments have the same premises, and should not, perhaps, be taken as directly stating Aristotle's doctrine; yet it does suggest that there is no restriction on the conclusions to be drawn in an Aristotelian science. In other words, there would be ample room for expansion within the framework of a given discipline. We could never say, these are all the conclusions we shall ever draw about this. Nevertheless, the fact remains that Aristotle is explicit about the limited character of the subject-genus, the definiteness and uniqueness of the starting-points, the finite number of middle terms, and therefore the finite number of steps before any given conclusion. And knowledge reflects the known; all this bears out the thesis which the *Physics* and *Metaphysics* alike confirm, that things and the unique universe containing them are finite through and through.

THE TOOLS OF PHILOSOPHY

6. *An Aristotelian explanation*

Before we proceed to consider the process by which, in Aristotle's view, scientific knowledge is acquired, we may fill in the bare outline of our sketch of his method by looking at an example of its use. This is an inquiry into the efficient cause of a class of natural events: the reproduction of animals, but we find as always the complex of all four causes in the background, and in particular, we find well exemplified here, it seems to me, the peculiar determinateness and finality of Aristotelian explanation. With very little comment, we may let the passage speak for itself.

In the first chapter of Book II of the *Generation of Animals*, Aristotle considers the question, how the principle of life (which is the form of an individual) is transmitted, in reproduction, to another individual. Aristotle was convinced that the form of the offspring was contained in the semen, and that the maternal parent contributed only the matter. But form, soul, is not stuff, but function. How can it act as efficient cause, as the agent of motion? That is the first question. Further, Aristotle asks, in what order does the moving cause move? Are the parts of the embryo formed all at once, or in sequence, and in what sequence? The latter question became, in the seventeenth century, a centre of raging controversy, but for Aristotle (though he would have been on the winning side) it is only a part of the more important inquiry about the moving cause. Let us look at his argument.

First, we establish plainly *which* cause we are after: the efficient:

How, we ask, is any plant formed out of the seed, or any animal out of the semen? That which is formed by means of a process must of necessity be formed (a) out of something, (b) by something, (c) into something. 'Out of something.' This of course is the material or matter. Some animals have their primary matter within themselves, having derived it from the female parent, e.g. those animals which are produced not viviparously but out of larvae or eggs. Others derive it from the mother for a considerable time by being suckled.

97

These are the animals which are produced viviparously not exter-nally only but also internally. So then, that 'out of which' the parts are formed is material of this sort. The problem now before us, how-ever, is not Out of what, but By what, are they formed? (733 b 24ff.)

Why not, we may ask, the question 'into what', which was also mentioned? Presumably because in ontogenesis this is obvious: into the new animal. It is the 'out of' and the 'by' that need elaboration. Moreover, the fourth cause, the what, the form, will be identified with the 'into what', for it is the new adult, which instantiates the specific form, for the sake of which generation has taken place. The problem here, however, as we shall see presently, is to get the form (soul) *into* generation, into the moving cause, since as we know, it must be there somehow, as specific form, all along. But how?

We are asking, then, 'by what' are the new animals formed. This involves two further questions:

Either something external fashions them, or else something present in the semen or seminal fluid; and this is either some part of Soul, or Soul, or something which possesses Soul. (734 a 1.)

Take the first of these:

Now it would appear unreasonable to suppose that anything ex-ternal fashions all the individual parts, whether they be the viscera or any others, because unless it is in contact it cannot set up any movement, and unless it sets up a movement no effect can be pro-duced upon anything by it. Hence it follows that there must be some-thing already present inside the fetation itself, which is either a part of it or separate from it. (734 a 2ff.)

Note how the argument moves, by sub-division, to the precise answer: external or internal; not external; therefore internal; and either part of the semen, or separate. But, as we see now, not separate:

To suppose it is some other thing, and separate from it, is not reasonable. If it were, the question arises: When the animal's genera-tion is completed, does this something disappear, or does it remain within the animal? We cannot detect any such thing, something which

98

is in the plant or the animal and yet is no part of the organism as a whole. (734 a 6ff.)

Notice also that Aristotle has the actual observation of the ontogenetic process always in mind—and before the minds of his students. This is no lecture course without practicals! The argument continues:

And again, to say that it fashions all the parts or some parts of the organism and then disappears is ridiculous. If it fashions only some of the parts, what will fashion the rest? Supposing it fashions the heart, and then disappears, and the heart fashions some other part: to be consistent we must say that either all the parts disappear or all the parts remain. It must, then, persist. And therefore it must be a part of the whole, existing in the semen from the outset. (734 a 9ff.)

This concludes, or appears to conclude, the answer to the first question. The moving cause is something internal to the semen, and existing in it from the outset. The second question is briefly answered:

. . . if it is true that there is no part of the Soul which is not in some part of the body, then it must also be a part which contains Soul from the outset. (734 a 14ff.)

Now we come to the question of sequence, and this produces a dilemma. Somehow, the moving cause of embryogenesis resides in the semen, and contains soul, the actuality of anything that is alive; so in a sense the offspring is already there in the semen. Yet at the same time the offspring, or the parts of the offspring *cannot* be contained in the semen. For if they were, all sorts of absurd consequences would arise:

How, then, are the other parts formed? Either they are all formed simultaneously—heart, lung, liver, eye, and the rest of them—or successively, as we read in the poems ascribed to Orpheus, where he says that the process by which an animal is formed resembles the plaiting of a net. As for simultaneous formation of the parts, our senses tell us plainly that this does not happen: some of the parts are clearly to be seen present in the embryo while others are not. And our failure to see them is not because they are too small; this is

99

certain, because although the lung is larger in size than the heart it makes its appearance later in the original process of formation. Since one part, then, comes earlier and another later, is it the case that A fashions B and that it is there on account of B which is next to it, or is it rather the case that B is formed after A? I mean, for instance, not that the heart, once it is formed, fashions the liver, and then the liver fashions something else; but that the one is formed after the other [just as a man is formed after a child], not by it. The reason of this is that, so far as the things formed by nature or by human art are concerned, the formation of that which is *potentially* is brought about by that which is *in actuality*; so that the Form, or conformation, of B would have to be contained in A, e.g., the Form of the liver would have to be in the heart—which is absurd. And there are other ways too in which the theory is absurd and fondly invented. But besides, for any part of the animal or plant to be present from the outset ready formed within the semen or seed, whether it has the power to fashion the other parts or not—even this is impossible if everything is formed out of semen or seed; because it is plain that it was formed by that which fashioned the semen if it is present within the semen from the outset; but semen must be formed before (any part), and that is the business of the parent. Therefore no part can be present within the semen. Therefore it does not contain in itself that which fashions the parts. And yet this cannot be external to the semen either: and it must be either external to it or inside it. (734 a 16–b 4)

So, having demonstrated that the moving cause cannot be external to the semen, and so must be internal, we demonstrate that it cannot be internal either—yet it must be one or the other. We can evade this dilemma by moving between the horns; this Aristotle does by elaborating the distinction already mentioned between actual and potential:

Well, we must endeavour to solve this difficulty. Maybe there is some statement of ours, made without qualification, which ought to be qualified: e.g. if we ask, *in what sense* exactly is it impossible for the parts to be formed by something external? we see that in one sense it is possible, though in another it is not. Now it makes no difference whether we say 'the semen' or 'that from which the semen comes', in so far as the semen has within itself the movement which the generator set going. And it is possible that A should move B, and B move C, and that the process should be like that of the 'miraculous' automatic puppets: the parts of these automatons, even while at rest, have in them somehow or other a *potentiality*, and when some external agency sets the first part in movement, then immediately the adjacent part comes to be *in actuality*. The cases then are parallel: just as with the automaton (1) in one way it is the external agency which is causing the thing's movement—viz. not by being in contact with it anywhere now, but by having at one time been in contact with it, so too that from which the semen originally came, or that which fashioned the semen (causes the embryo's movement)—viz. not by being in contact with it still, but by having once been in contact with it at some point; (2) in another way, just as the activity of building causes the house to get built.

It is clear by now that there is something which fashions the parts of the embryo, but that this agent is not by way of being a definite individual thing, nor is it present in the semen as something already perfected to begin with. (734 b 5–19)

The mechanical model is dear to the hearts of modern embryologists; but remember that for Aristotle the model itself is not the explanation, but a pointer to the explanation: which resides in the relation, in a series of events, between potentiality and actuality. This becomes clear in the next paragraph:

To answer the question, How exactly is each of the parts formed? we must take first of all as our starting-point this principle. Whatever is formed either by Nature or by human Art, say X, is formed by something which is X *in actuality* out of something which is X *potentially*. Now semen, and the movement and principle which it contains, are such that, as the movement ceases each one of the parts gets formed and acquires Soul. (I add 'acquires Soul', because there is no such thing as face, or flesh either, without Soul in it; and though they are still said to be 'face' and 'flesh' after they are dead, these terms will be names merely ('homonyms'), just as if the things were to turn into stone or wooden ones.) And the formation of the 'uniform' parts and of the instrumental parts goes on simultaneously. And as in speaking of an axe or any other instrument, we should not say that it was made solely by fire, so we should not say this about a foot or a hand (in the embryo), nor, similarly, of flesh either, because this too is an instrument with a function to perform. As for

101

hardness, softness, toughness, brittleness and the rest of such qualities which belong to the parts that have Soul in them—heat and cold may very well produce these, but they certainly do not produce the λόγος in direct consequence of which one thing is flesh and another bone; this is done by the movement which derives from the generating parent, who is *in actuality* what the material out of which the off-spring is formed is *potentially*. Exactly the same happens with things formed by the processes of the arts. Heat and cold soften and harden the iron, but they do not produce the sword; this is done by the movement of the instruments employed, which contains the λόγος of the Art; since the Art is both the principle and Form of the thing which is produced; but it is located elsewhere than in that thing, whereas Nature's movement is located in the thing itself which is produced, and it is derived from another natural organism which possesses the Form *in actuality*. As for the question whether the semen possesses Soul or not, the same argument holds as for the parts of the body, viz. (a) no Soul will be present elsewhere than in that of which it is the Soul; (b) no part of the body will be such in more than name unless it has some Soul in it (e.g. the eye of a dead person). Hence it is clear both that semen possesses Soul, and that it is Soul, *potentially*. And there are varying degrees in which it may be *potentially* that which it is capable of being—it may be nearer to it or further removed from it (just as a sleeping geometer is at a further remove than one who is awake, and a walking one than one who is busy at his studies). (734 b 20–735 a 11)

It is the distinction between grades of potentiality and actuality, applied to the nature of efficient cause, that has provided the solution. The father, an actual man, produces semen, a potential man, yet, as possessing soul of a sort, an *actually* potential man, actual enough to contain the potentiality of the first part, the heart, which in turn is sufficiently upgraded to trigger the production of the next part, and so on. This, not the mechanical model, *is* the explanation. We have a determinate sequence of steps, starting, after all, with an external agent, who is actual, and who produces the next moving cause, which is potentially actual, and so on in sequence, the most pervasively necessary part first, then each in order:

So then, the cause of this process of formation is not any part of the body, but the external agent which first set the movement going—for of course nothing generates itself, though as soon as it has been formed a thing makes itself grow. That is why one part is formed first, not all the parts simultaneously. And the part which must of necessity be formed first is the one which possesses the principle of growth: be they plants or animals, this, the nutritive, faculty is present in all of them alike (this also is the faculty of generating another creature like itself, since this is a function which belongs to every animal and plant that is perfect in its nature). The reason why this must of necessity be so is that once a thing has been formed, it must of necessity grow. And though it was generated by another thing bearing the same name (e.g. a man is generated by a man), it grows by means of itself. So then, since it makes itself grow, it *is* something: and if indeed it is some *one* thing, and if it is this first of all, then this must of necessity be formed first. Thus, if the heart is formed first in certain animals (or the part analogous to the heart, in those animals which have no heart), we may suppose that it is the heart (or its analogue) which supplies the principle. (735 a 11–26)

Now, Aristotle says, the difficulty is solved:

The queries raised earlier have now been dealt with. We have answered the question, What is the cause (in the sense of principle) of the generation of each individual—what is that which first sets it in movement and fashions it? (735 a 27–9)

So we have 'explained' the moving cause of the organism, the transference of form from one generation to the next. But in fact all four causes are involved: the end, which is the form; what-it-is-to-be-a-man; the matter, supplied by the mother, which the moving cause, the potential-actual semen informs or activates. All four together, determinate principles ordering a determinate set of entities, give us the framework, bounded and self-sufficient, within which Aristotelian explanation can take place.

7. *The knowledge of the starting-points*

If the finite structure of knowledge mirrors in its appropriate way the finite structure of what is, the knowing mind itself

103

must also be equipped for such reflection. So, indeed, in Aristotle's view, it is.

Demonstration consists in the technique of drawing inferences from appropriate premises, and the knowledge so derived is scientific knowledge. But scientific knowledge, or the premises for it, must be acquired, like all knowledge, on the basis of some pre-existent knowledge. Then we must know before we can know. Are we caught in another vicious circle here? If we are not to be so, both the road to the knowledge of the starting-points of demonstration and the nature of our state of knowledge of them when we know them must be distinguished from scientific knowledge itself. Aristotle carries through these distinctions in the closing chapter of the *Posterior Analytics*.

First, as to the way in which we acquire our knowledge of first principles: we might ask, he says,

whether we develop cognitive faculties which we did not possess before, or have always possessed these faculties without knowing it. It seems paradoxical that we should have possessed them always, because then it follows that we possess, without knowing it, powers of apprehension which are more accurate than demonstration. If on the other hand we acquire them, not having possessed them before, how can we gain knowledge and learn without some pre-existent power of apprehension? It is an impossibility, just as we said in the case of demonstration. Thus it is evident both that we cannot always have possessed them and that we cannot acquire them if we are completely ignorant and have no positive capacity. We must, then, have some faculty, but not such as to be superior in accuracy to those mentioned above. Clearly this is a property of all animals. They have an innate faculty of discrimination, which we call sense-perception. All animals have it, but in some the perception persists, while in others it does not. Where it does not, there is either no cognition at all outside the act of perception, or no cognition of those objects of which the perception does not persist. Where perception does persist, after the act of perception is over the percipients can still retain the perception in the soul. If this happens repeatedly, a distinction immediately arises between those animals which derive a coherent impression from the persistence and those which do not. Thus sense-

104

THE TOOLS OF PHILOSOPHY

perception gives rise to memory, as we hold; and repeated memories of the same thing give rise to experience; because the memories, though numerically many, constitute a single experience. And experience, that is, the universal when established as a whole in the soul—the One that corresponds to the Many, the unity that is identically present in them all—provides the starting-point of art and science: art in the world of process and science in the world of facts. Thus these faculties are neither innate as determinate and fully developed, nor derived from other developed faculties on a higher plane of knowledge; they arise from sense-perception, just as, when a retreat has occurred in battle, if one man halts so does another, and then another, until the original position is restored. The soul is so constituted that it is capable of the same sort of process. (99 b 25–100 a 14)

So we move from sense-perception, that which is prior relative to us, to the starting-points of demonstration, which are prior in nature. And notice that this is possible because sense-perception already contains in rudimentary, or, as the *Physics* puts it, in a vague and general form, the universals which experience will develop and stabilize. Aristotle emphasizes this in the continuation of the same passage:

Let us re-state what we said just now with insufficient precision. As soon as one individual percept 'has come to a halt' in the soul, this is the first beginning of the presence there of a universal (because although it is the particular we perceive, the act of perception involves the universal, e.g. 'man', not 'a man, Callias'). Then other 'halts' occur among these (proximate) universals, until the indivisible genera or (ultimate) universals are established. E.g. a particular species of animal leads to the genus 'animal', and so on. Clearly then it must be by induction that we acquire knowledge of the primary premises, because this is also the way in which sense-perception provides us with universals. (100 a 15–b 5)[1]

'Sense-perception provides us with universals': sense-perception may seem on its surface fleeting, like a rout in battle, but

[1] The 'induction from sense-perception' Aristotle is referring to here leads to the most universal concepts: the categories; but it provides an analogy to scientific induction, which leads to the first principles of an appropriate subject-genus.

it carries within itself the source for the beginning of a restoration of order, the series of halts that are the progressive stabilization of universals in the soul. The path to first principles is inductive; Aristotelian and modern accounts of science have this name in common. But it is not much more than a name, for the processes it designates in the two cases are very different. Aristotelian induction takes its character from the character of Aristotelian sense-perception and its inborn capacity for providing the material for experience and for the systematization of universals in the soul. Induction, for Aristotle, never needs the imagination of genius; it never has to take off *from* perception to pursue some inspired guess. It is rooted from start to finish in the potential intelligibility of the perceptible world and the power of sense to grasp the first empirical beginnings of that intelligibility. Aristotelian science should need no men of genius, whether heroes of science or its martyrs. It is the natural, systematic development, through the natural stages of sense-perception, memory and experience, of the cognitive powers of man.

It has often been said that Aristotle failed as a physical scientist because he was *too* empirical, because he stayed too close to the everyday world of common sense. Duhem, in his *Système du Monde* (I, 1 and 4–5; in a passage quoted by Ross in the Commentary on the *Physics*) said of Aristotle's dynamics:

This dynamics seems, indeed, so admirably suited to everyday observations, that it could not fail, at the beginning, to win the acceptance of those who first speculated about forces and motions.

At the Piraeus, Aristotle observes a group of haulers; their bodies bent forward, they pull with all their might on a rope attached to the prow of a ship. Slowly, the boat approaches the shore with what appears to be a constant speed. Other haulers arrive and take hold of the rope in addition to the first group; the vessel now cuts the water more rapidly than it had before. But suddenly it stops. The keel has struck the sand. The men who were sufficient in number and strength to counteract the resistance of the water cannot overcome the friction of the keel on the sand. To pull the boat up on the shore they need new reinforcements. Are not these the observations which Aristotle has been trying to translate into mathematical language?

Before physicists could succeed in rejecting Aristotelian, and constructing modern dynamics, they had to understand that the facts which they witnessed every day were by no means the simple elementary facts to which the fundamental laws of dynamics immediately apply; that the progress of the boat pulled by haulers, or of a carriage being drawn along a road, must be regarded as movements of extreme complexity, that resistances from which really simple phenomena must be entirely free play, in these cases, a very important part; in a word, that in order to formulate the principles of the science of movement, one must consider, by an abstraction, a body moving under the action of a unique force in a void. From his dynamics, on the other hand, Aristotle rightly concludes that such motion is inconceivable. (**87**, 31–2)

Duhem's critique does put its finger on an important point. We have only to put any part of Aristotle's account of local motion beside any Galilean experiment to see the gulf that separates them. Galileo constructs highly imaginative experimental situations in order to get out just those factors in them that he wants to work on; the rest is irrelevant. Aristotle wants to elaborate and make precise the order in nature as it is, not to analyse it away into a few measurable quantities. His explanations remain *within* the thing or process they explain, rather than breaking away from it to devise and invent experimental techniques and return with approximations only to the real world. He never leaves that world. It was Galileo, too, who, first in modern times, distinguished what came to be called primary from secondary qualities; if we read such seventeenth-century writers as Boyle, we see how pervasively this distinction influenced the development of modern science at its start. Aristotelian perception, on the other hand, is full, common-sense, *Gestalt*-like perception, the presence to us through the normal functioning of our sense-organs of solid, visible, audible, odorous, tasteable, *things*: these we start from and these we stay with, elucidating and making

THE TOOLS OF PHILOSOPHY

precise and explicit the universals they themselves contain.[1]

There is more to Aristotle's account of perception, however, than his failure to abstract from all but a few aspects of reality. There is no need for such abstractive devices for him, not only because of what he lacks, but because of what he has, and what he has is the field naturalist's confidence that his specimens are *specimens*. If each natural individual differs from every other of the same species, it is only in its 'matter', in irrelevant detail, that it differs. But it contains within itself, and perception of it already grasps, *in posse*, its being-what-it-is, its peculiar entity, which the intellect in full possession of knowledge will apprehend with directness and certainty. Thus the study of nature is a process of refining perception, not of turning away from it. To the student of philosophy turning to inspect the evidence of sense, whether Cartesian or Heraclitean-Platonic, such a theory of perception may appear naïve. But the experience of the field naturalist must here be given its due weight. Pre-Aristotelian scepticism of sense was tied to a belief that if there is intelligibility it is finite. And Aristotle found that finitude where every natural historian finds it, in the things of perception themselves. The biologist actually *sees* more, or sees more systematically than the person ignorant of biology. His knowledge consists in a systematic refinement of perception, which elucidates and transforms the perceptible world, but never leaves it. For him, the relevance of fact to theory is more intimate, their togetherness closer, than for the modern physical scientist. He is learning to be at home *in* the world, not to impose abstractions upon it. And he can do this because his perceptible world, the world of nature, contains within it its own intelligibility.

Consider, for example, a novice and an expert looking at a flower. In a way they perceive the same flower and in another way they do not. The expert's expertise consists in the fact,

---

[1] Admittedly, this interpretation of Aristotle's theory of perception may seem hard to reconcile with some passages in the *De Anima*. My view resembles that of I. Block as stated in a recent article in the *Philosophical Quarterly* (11); the interpretation of Hamlyn (41) is more sympathetic to the geneticists' approach.

not simply that he has mastered a strange nomenclature, but that he has developed his perceptions themselves to a fine point. He sees in the flower the specific and generic characters which the novice has not learned to distinguish with precision in the object they are both looking at. If one knows e.g. that white clover belongs to the Leguminosae, one sees the characteristic sunbonnet-shapes in every tiny bloom on the little white head. Before one knows this, has one 'seen' the same thing? For the naturalist, what he sees already *contains* what he will learn; he learns to see it better. Newton did not *see* either the heavens or falling bodies better than his predecessors; but Vesalius *saw* the structure of the muscles better than Galen had. Copernicus did not see the sunrise differently from the common man, or from Aristotle himself. His new knowledge may be metaphorically described as 'vision' (or 'theory', which is the same thing), but it did not, one supposes, transform the actual content of his visual field. But in biological knowledge of the pre-analytical sort learning stays in large part within perception, and alters it. The biologist actually sees more and sees more systematically than the person ignorant of biology. That is surely what Aristotle was referring to when he said in the first chapter of the *Physics* that learning moves from the general, the thing perceived with its universals grasped only roughly and in outline, to the particular, i.e. the particular in the sense of the exact, the detailed articulation of this nature as distinct from that.

So much for the path from perception to first principles. What of the developed knowledge of first principles when we do achieve it? How is it to be distinguished from scientific knowledge? According to Aristotle, we must know first principles with certainty and accuracy—and with even greater certainty and accuracy than scientific knowledge itself, since the premises must be prior to and better known than the conclusion. Now there are only two powers, Aristotle says, by which we can know anything with certainty: scientific knowledge (ἐπιστήμη) and intuition (νοῦς). But scientific knowledge, we have seen, must start from some higher and truer

109

knowledge, the knowledge of the appropriate premises of demonstration, and therefore:

since nothing can be more infallible[1] than scientific knowledge except intuition, it must be intuition that apprehends the first principles. This is evident not only from the foregoing considerations but also because the starting-point of demonstration is not itself demonstration, and so the starting-point of scientific knowledge is not itself scientific knowledge. Therefore, since we possess no other infallible faculty besides scientific knowledge, the source from which such knowledge starts must be intuition. Thus it will be the primary source of scientific knowledge that apprehends the first principles, while scientific knowledge as a whole is similarly related to the whole world of facts. (100 b 12–17)

These two arguments, on induction and on intuition, are parallel yet significantly different. First, Aristotle has argued that 'we must possess a capacity of some sort' inferior to scientific knowledge but allowing us to set out in the direction of acquiring it, or rather, of acquiring knowledge of its starting-points. And he has found in perception, memory and experience just the powers we need. He has found them spread, in their lower reaches, far over the animal world, reaching their culmination in the best of animals, man. So observation of the facts bears out the theoretical necessity. What about νοῦς? The necessity is the same: if we have not *some* power by which to apprehend the premises of science, the first step in the finite sequence of terms to our conclusions cannot be taken. Therefore, if there is scientific knowledge there must be intuition at its head. But where is the observation to confirm this? Syllogizing as such need not be so rooted; it *could* be all dialectical, argument tied only to common opinion and common experience. But then it could achieve only the lesser accuracy of a practical or a productive science, not the exactitude of theory. How do we know this is not the case? The only fact that confirms Aristotle's theoretical conclusion here is the fact that scientific knowledge does exist. Yet 'it is hard', he himself has admitted, 'to know for sure whether one knows

[1] *Lit.* 'truer'.

110

THE TOOLS OF PHILOSOPHY

or not'. (76 a 26.) Perhaps then we only think we know. ἐπιστήμη and νοῦς, Aristotle argues, are the two certainty-bearing powers of the mind, and so since we cannot grasp the truth of first principles by the one, we must do so by the other. Yet there are the people who believe there is no demonstration, and against them, in the last analysis, Aristotle can only affirm his own belief that there is—and if there is, there must be νοῦς on which to ground it. In short, this is one of those rarities in Aristotle, an *a priori* argument. It is needed to save the very possibility of knowledge in his sense: to save the finite structure of science, rooted in the finite structure of the real.

It is, on the face of it, a most unconvincing argument. How do we know there is knowledge of conclusions? Because there is knowledge of premises. How do we know there is knowledge of premises? There must be, if there is to be knowledge of conclusions. And *if* there are two sources of certainty, νοῦς and ἐπιστήμη, and one of these is the source of inferential certainty, then the other must be the source of the certainty of the starting-points of inference. But how do we know there are two such sources? Presumably because if there were not, there could not be the whole premise-inference-conclusion structure we have been describing. To the student of Kant there is perhaps nothing alarming here. Circular arguments are permissible if they exhibit the ground of the possibility of something we actually do have. But to claim with Kant that we have experience and to claim with Aristotle that we have the very special thing that he calls scientific knowledge are two very different claims. The existence of νοῦς seems to be hung simply and solely on the demand that, to have Aristotelian science, we must have it, and so we do. The comforting continuum of life which allows us, in the previous argument, to climb from rudimentary sensation to the developed process of induction is here missing entirely. In other words, this seems to be apriorism pure and simple; yet for all Aristotle's empiricism his whole system depends on this one argument. Without νοῦς, no ἐπιστήμη; without ἐπιστήμη, no science.

111

Is it as arbitrary as this? Aristotle is confident, both here and in the *Ethics*, that there are these two sources of intellectual certainty. The certainty of inference, of the mind in movement, he knew as master of formal logic; he if anyone knew a valid from an invalid syllogism; he knew it also from the demonstrations of geometers, his favourite examples in the *Analytics*. To yield knowledge, however, inference must start from true premises, and, Aristotle insists, premises not only true but truer than the conclusion, commensurately universal, the cause of the conclusion, etc. Such premises are first and foremost statements about the essences of things; and that, again, is just what Aristotle's experience as a biologist told him it was possible to achieve. The refinement of perception to make explicit the universal *in* the individual, the species in the specimen: this is the experience that underlies Aristotle's confidence about νοῦς. Starting with the definition of substance in the *Categories*, rising to the critique of definition itself in the *Posterior Analytics*, this is the point, in the direct confrontation of the mind with the *what* of a group of substances, at which the exposition of Aristotle's methodology once more comes to rest. For the third cornerstone of its foundation in being is here completed. The first resides in individual things, substances as distinct from their accidents. The second is the being-what-it-is of each kind of substance, the ground of the essential attributes which defining formulae state. And the third is the mind's confrontation with these same essential natures, the apprehension of *universalia in re*. True, there is still to come, in the treatises as we have them, the massive account of dialectic in the *Topics*; but dialectic for Aristotle is the second best procedure, to be used in introductions to science, in the interstices of scientific argument, or in the less accurate disciplines which are modelled on theoretical science but cannot in the nature of things achieve its level of accuracy. The heart of Aristotle's method lies in the great bridge from the definition of substance at the opening of the *Organon* to the account of real definition, and finally of νοῦς, in Book II of the *Posterior Analytics*.

IV

Second Philosophy

---

1. *The subject-matter of Aristotelian physics*

Every science (and again I mean, of course, every Aristotelian science) has three constituents: its proper subject-matter, its proper starting-points, and a proper set of attributes which its demonstrative arguments *prove* to inhere essentially and uniquely in its subject. The treatise referred to by Aristotle under the title *On Nature* is no exception to this rule. Let us look at some features of it under these headings, keeping in mind our principal thesis, and this in two respects. First, as we watch Aristotle putting his method into practice, we shall be confirming once more our hypothesis that it is in fact a field naturalist's method, which aims at discovering, and respects above all else, the 'peculiar entity of each kind of thing and what it is to be that thing'. Secondly, in the study of nature, we shall be exhibiting at the same time the field naturalist's peculiar subject-genus, the matter to match the method.

In the treatise *On Nature* (Books I to IV of our *Physics*), Aristotle distinguishes the subject-matter of the physical treatises as a whole from the subjects studied by other disciplines. In the whole range of treatises that fall under 'physical science'—including what we call biological and psychological subject-matters—we have to do with all those things that exist 'by nature':

> Some things exist, or come into existence, by nature; and some otherwise. Animals and their organs, plants, and the elementary bodies (such as earth and fire and air and water)—these and their likes we say exist by nature. For all these seem distinguishable from those that are not constituted by nature; and the common feature

113

that characterises them all seems to be that they have within themselves a principle of movement (or change) and rest—in some cases
local only, in other quantitive, as in growth and shrinkage, and in
others again qualitive, in the way of modification. But a bedstead
or a garment or the like, in the capacity which is signified by its
name and in so far as it is craft-work, has within itself no such inherent trend towards change though owing to the fact of its being
composed of earth or stone or some mixture, it incidentally has within
it such a principle derived from these and in so far as it is composed
of them. For nature (or a nature) is the (a?) principle and cause of
motion and rest to those things, and those things only, in which it
inheres primarily, as distinct from incidentally. (192 b 8–22)

This gives us our subject-matter, segregated in a straight-
forward and common-sense way from other subject-matters.
We cannot, and need not, *demonstrate* the existence of our
subject-genus. As Aristotle will say shortly, it is obvious that
there are things existing naturally. To deny it indicates a want
of the right sense for what is knowable in itself and what is not.
To assert it needs only the simplest and plainest induction.
This seems to be the sort of thing Aristotle has had in mind
at the opening of the treatise when he has told us that knowledge, including the knowledge of nature, must begin with
what is more luminous to us and proceed to what is more
luminous in itself. The former, he says there, consists in our
general grasp of the individual sensible thing, and the latter
results from a more discriminating analysis of its constituents.
Thus to see that there *are* things existing by nature is the first
step in our science; definition and demonstration will articulate more precisely the essential structure of such things.

But the description of 'nature' just quoted comes at the
beginning of the second book. The first book, as is usual in
Aristotelian treatises, has been concerned with the successes
and failures of his predecessors. We know from the *Organon*,
and Aristotle's students knew, that neither the subject-matter
nor the premises of a science were open to the techniques of
demonstration. So they must be approached by some other
route. The two reasonable paths are by induction from com-

mon experience, and, through dialectical reasoning, from the efforts of previous philosophers. As we have just seen, the first of these, in the case of nature, is short and simple; the second, the argument of Book I, is more circuitous. In at least two important respects, however, it appears to be indispensable. First, as Owens has pointed out in connection with the *Metaphysics*, Aristotle's hearers in the Lyceum, acquainted with the current conceptions of nature and of the problems of philosophy, would be hindered in their scientific progress by some of these traditional ideas and modes of argument. Both the problems, and the solutions, of older thinkers, must be wrestled with before the proper, Aristotelian approach to a given subject can be successfully undertaken.

What I want to emphasize here, however, is another point about this introductory dialectic, in the *Physics* in particular. Like the *Categories*, the opening of the works on logic, *Physics* I fulfils the task of tying down the subject-matter, in this case, the subject-genus Nature, firmly to its foundation in *substance*. Here, once more, we are to be guided to Aristotle's great discovery of the being-what-it-is of each kind of thing and the definability, and hence knowability, of each kind of substance. It was this insight which his predecessors lacked and which he must firmly establish before nature could be known. For the argument of *Physics* I comes down to the contention that change is always change from one form to another, or from the want of form to its presence, *in a subject*. It is nature as subject ἡ ὑποκειμένη φύσις, which earlier thinkers had missed. But we shall learn in the *Metaphysics* that 'subject', what underlies, is one sense, and the pre-eminently 'natural' sense, of substance. In the *Categories*, too, first substance is that which is neither present in nor predicated of a subject, because it *is* a subject, this man, this horse, in which particular accidents inhere and of which generals are predicated. In the order of knowing and of being, and between the two in the order of natural beings there to be known, the relation between (logical) subject and (real) substance or concrete entity must be kept firmly in mind.

115

The earlier investigators of nature, Aristotle argues in Book I, had sought the principle of change in the balance of contraries, or, alternatively, in their search for a unity underlying change, they had denied contrariety and therewith change itself. But they had failed to understand the character of the underlying unity, and of the relation of the contrariety to that unity. A contrary cannot change into its contrary, hot into cold, or white into black or blue or yellow; but a thing, a subject of accidents, can change from possessing one quality to the possession of another. A tree now bare becomes leafy, a man now sleeping can awake. The non-leafy tree becomes leafy, the unconscious man conscious. Once the two opposites are fettered to their substrate, the alteration becomes intelligible. At the range of classes, the kind of thing that is present in a subject is predicated of a class of subjects; and we see that this predication is true now, but was not so earlier. Tadpoles grow legs and lungs and become adult frogs. This is change, the kind of change of which first substances are uniquely capable.

What of the origin of such substances, however, the origin of an oak from an acorn or of a man from semen? The analogy of subject-predicate change allows us to make this situation too intelligible. There is an underlying subject, the acorn or the semen, which though not yet in fact imbued with the full form of which it is capable, *is* capable of such endowment. There is still a subject, which wants a form, the form of being an oak tree, or of being a man, and is capable of acquiring it. So, Aristotle is able to say, there are in one sense two principles of natural things: matter and form, and in another, three: subject, shortage of form, and form. Again, as in the *Posterior Analytics*, we see that things are held within intelligible limits, at a moment, through the subordination of matter to its form, and, during a time span, through the transition in a subject from the want of a given, appropriate form to its existence: from the starting-point of an ontogeny to its proper goal.

Aristotle is at pains, at the opening of the *Physics*, to establish this trio of subject, form and privation, which, as I have said, ties the whole inquiry firmly to its root in the character

116

of substance as the subject of change. Only substances, Aristotle will say shortly, have natures or exist by nature. If this connection of nature with substance, if the *underlying* nature, had shown herself to them, he has concluded in Book I, his predecessors could have overcome their ignorance. It was the knowledge of change as rooted in a subject that they lacked.[1]

2. *Aristotelian physics and the Categories*

Aristotelian physics, then, is in the first place substance-accident physics. As such it is especially suited, secondly, to the treatment of living things: individual concrete entities falling into natural classes. Thanks both to its substance-accident and to its biological orientation, thirdly, Aristotelian physics differs profoundly in its scope from physics in its modern sense. Let us consider these three points before proceeding to the second constituent of our science.

[1] A parenthetical point here on the occurrence of the term 'shortage' or 'privation'. If this argument is so fundamental, we must explain why, in the succeeding books of the treatises *On Nature* and *On Motion*, Aristotle seems to drop almost altogether the distinction he has made here, simply reserving 'shortage', in II, 1, for 'later treatment'. He uses the term 'shortage' or 'privation' in special contexts, in discussing the infinite and the void, or in Book V (6) when he speaks of rest as a 'shortage' of motion; but the concept is not stressed as it is in Book I. Is this again, one might ask, a separate treatise, earlier or later than what follows? On the contrary, the triad of subject, privation and form, and especially the singling out of privation as the contrary of form, is necessary in order to include in the original outline of the principles of nature the basis of *substantial* change. When a substance comes into being, what takes place is not the change of subject from one quality to another and contrary quality, but the coming into existence of matter-informed-by-such-and-such-a-form from matter not so informed, that is, from the privation of form. The principal books of the *Physics* deal first with the concepts fundamental to the study of nature as such, and with disputed concepts like the infinite and the void, which must be dealt with if nature is to be properly understood. Then, as we shall see, Aristotle undertakes the study of motion, especially local motion, first generally, then, in the treatise *On the Heavens*, in the celestial spheres, next qualitative change, then growth (*De Gen. et Corr.* I), and only in the second book 'On Generation and Corruption' does he return to substantial change and the general foundation laid down in *Physics* I for its eventual treatment. This is just what he had said he would do. But the argument which establishes the whole range of the subject-matter must cover the entire field, and just the field, to be considered in the whole series of analyses.

The dependence of the subject-matter of physics on the concept of substance, and in particular on the subject-accident distinction of the *Categories*, emerges very clearly from Aristotle's account of the kinds of motion in the opening chapters of the treatise *On Motion* (*Physics* V to VIII), and it is these chapters that I want to examine here.

The concept of substance and the distinction between substance and accident are pervasive for all Aristotelian thought. Whatever is not a substance and therefore a subject of accidents is an accident and therefore a modification of a substance. The latter is the case for nature, the subject-matter of physics, and *a fortiori* for change, the mark of things that are 'by nature'. Change is not a substance, a subject of accidents; therefore it must be an accident of subjects, something that happens *to* them. There are, as Aristotle sees it, four types of change. There is, first, generation and decay, the change *of* substances, and then there are three types of change *in* substances: change of *quality*, change of *quantity* (i.e. growth), and change of *place*, the last three being grouped together under the comprehensive name of *motion*. In other words we have:

Things that are by *nature* (or have natures)
    which contain an internal source of *change*

                a. *substantial*

                   or

                b. *accidental* (*motion*)

                   1. qualitative

                   2. quantitative

                   3. local

Note that local motion, motion in the modern sense, is only one of the four types of change, or one of the three types of motion. All four, moreover, are directly dependent on the doctrine of the *Categories*.

Substantial change, to begin with, is change *of* substances, where a substance is actually generated, as, in Aristotle's favourite example, a man from a man. It is a change of contradictories, from what is not man (but the seed of a man) to what is a man, and back to what is not. Socrates does not exist, he is born, drinks hemlock and dies. The primary instances of substantial change are reproduction, where change is from the non-being to the being of a substantial entity, and death, which is its cessation.

What about the three other kinds of change, change of quality, quantity and place, all three comprising Aristotelian 'motion'? These three are not changes *of* substance, but changes *in* substances, still tightly tethered to the concrete entity to which they happen. A man is born or dies; but between the two extremes of birth and death he is confident or afraid, fat or thin, here or there. But why, we may ask, have we these types only? What of the other categories? In the opening chapters *On Motion* Aristotle eliminates the other categories as possible sources of types of motion.

There can be no change in the category of relation, he explains, because often the particular case of a relation changes although nothing happens at all to one of the terms of the relation, and nothing happens to either term *qua* term, but only incidentally. For instance, if a child's father dies, Aristotle would say, the man has died, the child has not changed. He may become sad, and so suffer a change of quality; but it is not his relation of child to father that has altered. Nor has his father, in dying, ceased to be his father, except incidentally; what has happened to him essentially is that he has died. Now we may argue that some relations are not like that. When a man's wife dies he ceases to be a husband and becomes a widower. Is this not relational change? It would be so for Aristotle only incidentally, in reference to the substances, in this case the man and woman, involved. The wife dies. The man changes in quality: in his condition of wife-possessing and the habits that go with it. Or when the American people acquire a new president, they do not change; nor does the newly inaugurated president change *qua* himself by assuming a new relation to them. He, the same man, the same subject of accidents, has acquired new powers; that is all. In other words, for Aristotle, relations are simply links between things;

when the things change, the links may break but are not themselves altered. Nor when the links break does this necessitate
a change in the things. There is therefore no motion in this
category. Substance, in other words, is fundamental; relation
is a mere addition to it.

Nor, Aristotle goes on to say, can there be motion in the
category of action and passion. This seems at first sight sur-
prising. If I am stroking the cat and stop stroking the cat,
surely this is a change of action on my part and of affection on
the cat's part. Thus this would seem to be a clear case of change
in the category of action and passion. But the trouble is that
this category can be widened to *mean* agent and patient in
general, i.e. in fact, mover and moved. So if there were essentially changes *of* action as such, there would be movements
of movement, change of change. This Aristotle cannot permit.
Why not? we may ask. This would be like the situation envisaged by Plato for perception: a slowly changing agent, a
slowly changing patient, a slowly changing action of one on
the other. Surely this is what the world is like: a flowing
sequence of becomings which never really are. Not Aristotle's
world, however. As there are things first, and relations added
to them, so there must be things first, and actions of or on
things thereafter. Being must control becoming. What there
is, is first, substances and the rhythm of their generation, the
cycle of nature out of non-being to being and back again.
This is the cycle of generation and decay which forms for
Aristotle a special problem, because it is not a change in a
subject, but a change of subjects. Secondly, within the range
of beings, of concrete natural things within the natural span
of their allotted times from birth to death, there are changes
from contrary to contrary, from disease to health, from ignorant to learned, from 'in Athens' to 'in Egypt'. All these,
however, happen unequivocally *to* such concrete things. The
rootedness of change in its subject is fundamental to and
presupposed in the Aristotelian account from first to last. A
regressive motion of motion which would destroy the fixity
of the subject as well would be unthinkable.

Aristotle specifies a number of reasons why there cannot be motion of motion, change of change, and they all reflect his confidence that change is tied to the nature of substance and its accidents. First, he asks, what could a motion of motion, a change of change *mean*? One of two things. Either the change itself is the subject of change. But this is clearly not the case, since change *is* not subject but is *of* or *in* a subject. Or could it be then, secondly, that there is a change of change relatively to some other subject? Again, this could not happen except incidentally, since movement must be the transformation, Aristotle says, *from one form to another*, from one point of fixity, one intelligible what, to another such point of fixity, another such intelligible what, as for instance from health to sickness or sickness to health. To deny this would be absurd, for:

we are to suppose, then, that the subject changes from health to sick-ness and at the same time changes out of this change into some other. Now it is obvious enough that when he has actually become sick, he may start upon any other change or cease to change at all; but this is one change succeeding (or not) another, it is not one change changing into another. And each successive change must always be along a definite line, though it might be along any one of all the possible lines, including the direct opposite of the one it succeeds— in this case the change from sickness to health. But naturally the subject of change may incidentally carry with him his change of one kind into a change of another kind that he enters while the first change is going on; for instance, he may shift from the process of recollecting something and so arriving at knowledge to the process of forgetting it and so arriving at ignorance. (225 b 28–33)

Such a process does not change the change; it introduces one change following on another. Change to mean anything must *be* the change it is, one substance changing in a definite manner from one characteristic quality, quantity or place *into* another. 'Change of change' is meaningless.

Or again, if we allowed the generation of generation, the change of change, Aristotle argues further, we should be embarked on an infinite regress and have banished change itself along with that of which we conceived it to be the change. This is clearest in the most fundamental type of change, generation, which, though not explicitly in question here, is the source of the coming into being of the substances of which other changes are the changes, and so is at the bottom of all other change. But if generation were generated, nothing, Aristotle maintains, could come to be at all:

> . . . if genesis is to have a genesis, and there is to be change of change, then we must go back *ad infinitum*. The consequent necessarily presupposes the antecedent, so that if the ultimate genesis was once in the course of being generated, the ultimate generand was at best only in process of being generated and was not in itself there, even though the subject that was in course of becoming the generand was. And again, taking the ultimate genesis as itself a generand, *its* genesis was once in process of generation, so that it was not itself yet generated, and so forth. And since there is no first link of our infinitely receding chain, neither is there the next or any following link; so it would be impossible that anything should ever come into existence, or move, or change. (225 b 35–226 a 6)

Or, to put it another way, for any case of change, Aristotle points out, there must be both a starting-point from which and a goal toward which. Learning, for instance, leads to knowledge, not, he insists, to the coming-into-being of knowledge. If to the latter, then there will *be* no knowledge at all, but merely a perpetual becoming, an unintelligible flux. Again, no one could go to Egypt if it were not possible to be in Egypt. Every change is the change that it is in the light of the goal toward which it changes. It is a kind of change appropriate to the being-what-it-is of the kind of substance in which it occurs. It is part of an ontogenesis, a natural development, not an indefinite ongoing to issue one knows not where.

3. *Aristotelian physics and biology*

Aristotelian physics, it should now be plain, deals with change of or in substances. Substances are concrete entities, and, as is plain from Aristotle's list of the things that are by nature ('animals and their organs, plants, and the elementary bodies'), living things are pre-eminent among them. In Aristotle's account of change therefore, secondly, biological change plays a leading part. Of the four kinds of change themselves, two are plainly first and foremost biological in origin. Generation is generation: man begetting man. Increase is growth, a characteristic of living things. Neither stones, mountains nor Democritean atoms grow. Nor can growth be studied, like rectilinear motion and the like, in terms of a set of quantities abstracted from a living system, but only as the growth of this or that type of plant or animal.

Qualitative change, on the other hand, is not, for Aristotle, uniquely characteristic of living things. In fact, the inanimate world consists fundamentally in such changes: basically through the round of the four elements which are simply pairs of contraries, hot, cold, moist, dry. Thus, fire is hot and dry, air hot and moist, water cold and moist, earth cold and dry; and these four pairs of qualities, which are basic to all others, cyclically yield place to one another in the informing of prime matter. This is a very general, not simply a biological cycle. On the other hand, the basic pairs of contraries and their changes from one to another, if not derived from biology, do play a very central part in Aristotle's biological thinking. So pervasive are they that it is hard to single out a few examples to illustrate their use. But we may cite as a general reference Aristotle's statement in Book II of the *Parts of Animals* about the need to sort out clearly the meanings of hot and cold, solid and fluid:

There ought . . . to be some clear understanding as to the sense in which natural substances are to be termed hot or cold, solid or fluid. For it appears manifest that these are properties on which even life and death are largely dependent, and that they are, moreover, the causes of sleep and waking, of maturity and old age, of health and disease; while no similar influence belongs to roughness and smoothness, to heaviness and lightness, nor, in short, to any other such properties of matter. That this should be so is but in accordance with rational expectation. For hot and cold, solid and fluid, as was stated in a former treatise, are the foundations of the natural elements. (648 b 2–11; Oxf.)

123

Aristotle accepted the common identification of life with heat, allied to the equation (universal in his time) of digestion with a kind of cooking:

> Now since everything that grows must take nourishment, and nutriment in all cases consists of fluid and solid substances, and since it is by the force of heat that these are concocted and changed, it follows that all living things, animals and plants alike, must on this account, if on no other, have a natural source of heat. (650 a 3–8; Oxf.)

In sanguineous animals, blood is the source of this essential heat; and the main storehouse and centre of blood, and therefore of animal heat, is the heart. The heart is also the seat of sensitivity, since

> of all substances there is none so suitable for ministering to the operations of the soul as that which is possessed of heat. For nutrition and the imparting of motion are offices of the soul, and it is by heat that these are most readily effected. (652 b 10–13; Oxf.)

The brain, on the other hand, is merely a cooling agent, which 'tempers the heat and seething of the heart'. (652 b 27–28) For the brain is cold and bloodless; it is composed of the cold elements earth and water. This is no *a priori* dictum on Aristotle's part: the brain is cold even to the touch, he says, and it is clear that it is made of earth and water because of

> what occurs when it is boiled. For, when so treated, it turns hard and solid, inasmuch as the water is evaporated by the heat, and leaves the earthy part behind. Just the same occurs when pulse and other fruits are boiled. For these also are hardened by the process, because the water which enters into their composition is driven off and leaves the earth, which is their main constituent, behind. (653 a 22ff.; Oxf.)

The brain, then, is cold, and rightly so, since some balance of cold against heat to effect due moderation is necessary for the rational functioning of the whole.

Such qualitative explanations are universal in the biological writings; I must not stay to illustrate them further here. The point I want to make is this: even for qualitative change, although it is not restricted to and may not be derived from

124

the study of life, still the widespread application of this phenomenon in biological contexts gives it a biological rather than,
in modern terms, a purely 'physical' interest. Local motion, the
one kind of change indifferently apparent in living and non-
living things, the one kind of change simple enough to serve
for the initiation of the experimental and quantitative techniques of modern science, is but one facet of this total, much
more organic than 'physical' picture of the structure of the
natural world. Admittedly, local motion even for Aristotle is
the highest motion, for it is the purely local motion of the
heavenly spheres which forever escape the sources of decay.
It is, in fact, Aristotle argues, the celestial motion that causes
the nether motions of corruptible things: the sun's double
coming and going provides the heat on which all life depends.
Yet we must not confound the 'highest' with 'all', nor try to
fit explanations appropriate in the sphere of eternal things on to
the many diverse phenomena of nature, which though less
'fine' than the heavens, lie closer to us, and are knowable in
greater detail and with other intellectual instruments to the
student of nature who seeks to know in the right way and with
appropriate precision and relevant argument each nook and
cranny of this uniquely ordered universe.

The biological slant of Aristotelian physics also explains
why, in contradistinction to our conception of motion, Aristotle
is inclined to speak jointly, as he often does, not of motion
only, but of 'motion and rest'. It seems quaintly naïve to
physicists that 'rest' should appear as a positive contrary to
'motion'. But if one is thinking of patterns like sleep and
waking, living and dying, or even purely local motion in the
case of animals, this is a simple empirical necessity. Only the
more abstract thought of a Democritus or a Heraclitus would
conceive of a world in which everything, always, is in motion,
and rest is conceived of, if at all, as the absence of this one
positive kind of ongoing. True, plants and animals too are
always growing, always taking and concocting nourishment.
But especially for animals, times of quiescence just as clearly
exist: human infants rest more of the time than they move,

125

sleep more than they wake. Projectiles, too, and all things moving, come to rest. Why dissolve this clearly seen, and readily intelligible phenomenon into a flux both hypothetical and alien to the delimiting, defining power of mind? For the motion of thought, too, has its proper rhythm: mind, too, moving between right premises and right conclusions, is moving, like all things natural, from rest to rest.

4. The scope of the Aristotelian physical treatises

Aristotelian physics, then, is wholly rooted in the distinction between substance and accident and, studying the changes of and in substances, is interested at least as much in biological as in inorganic change. Thus Aristotle's inquiry into the principles of natural science is set in another context altogether from the Galilean or Newtonian; it is both wider, less concentrated on an isolated aspect, and narrower, fixed, in its reference to substances, within strict canons of relevance which from an Aristotelian point of view modern physics fatally neglects.

The very organization of Aristotle's writings on nature clearly exhibits this contrast. For we have to deal here, not with the *Physics* alone, but with a whole series of treatises, the sum total of which cover the subject-matter in question. These are:

> On Nature
> On Motion
> On the Heavens
> On Generation and Corruption,

then the *Meteorology* and all the biological (including the 'psychological') works. Now with all this before us, to begin with, the title 'Physics' for our traditional treatise of that name is misleading. 'Lectures on Nature', the traditional Greek title, is better, but even so, our present work comprises what for Aristotle were two treatises: *On Nature* (*Physics* I–IV) and *On Motion* (probably *Physics* V, VI and VIII, with VII another version since interpolated). The subjects dealt with are roughly as follows. The treatise *On Nature* deals in the most general way with the principles of nature as such, that is, with the originative source of change in all things possessing internally such a source of change. This is, as we have seen, what nature is. Now change, we have also seen, is either substantial, from non-being to being and back again, from the birth of Socrates and back to his death; or it is the change *in* an existing substance from one characteristic to another, from here to there, from such to some other such, from smaller to larger, that is, local, qualitative or quantitative change. The treatise *On Motion*, as Aristotle calls it, Books V to VIII of our *Physics*, deals with motion in general in these three senses (and to some extent also with local motion in particular) and then with the first cause of motion, the unmoved mover. Next in the sequence of physical treatises Aristotle considers that portion of the world where motion is local only, the celestial spheres, then the qualitative changes characteristic of the sublunar world, the elements fire, air, earth and water, and their cyclical transformation into one another. These two subjects comprise the treatise *On the Heavens*, which comes after the *Physics*. Then in the treatise *On Generation and Corruption* Aristotle completes his account of qualitative change, considers growth, and finally discusses the change of the subjects themselves, which has been postponed until the treatment of the lesser forms of change, i.e. change of contraries *in* subjects, has been concluded. This last raises special problems of its own. The sequence is thus:

1. general principles of nature   *On Nature*
2. motion in general, singling out   *On Motion*
    local motion
3. pure local (celestial) motion   *On the Heavens* I
4. qualitative motion   *On the Heavens* II
                                          On Generation and Corruption I (in part)
5. quantitative motion   *On Generation and Corruption* I (in part)
6. substantial change   *On Generation and Corruption*

So at the close of the last treatise in this series the whole range of the natural world has been covered in a general way, and it is now time to proceed to consider the sciences of the sublunar world in its particular parts. This further enterprise, still part of physical science, will comprise all the branches of both biology and what we call psychology, all dealing with things that *have natures* and are *by nature*. In the whole undertaking, local motion and its causes, that is, the subject matter of modern mechanics and dynamics, take a well-catalogued but subsidiary place.

5. *The starting-point of physical science*

My argument so far has been concerned altogether with the first constituent of a science, its subject-genus, and I have mentioned the two paths—the dialectical and the inductive—of fixing the subject-matter. Next among the constituents of a science, we have seen in discussing the *Posterior Analytics*, are the definition or definitions of its fundamental concepts. What I want to consider in the case of the *Physics* is the definition of nature and the implications of this definition for Aristotle's view of the natural world.

The distinction of things that are by nature and those that are not leads Aristotle to a first rough statement of a definition of nature. Animals and plants have in themselves an inherent source of change; a bedstead or a garment or the like has not:

. . . nature is the principle and cause of motion and rest to those things, and those things only, in which it inheres primarily, as distinct from incidentally. (192 b 21–3)

Aristotle explains, again by means of an example, what he means by 'not incidentally':

What I mean by 'as distinct from incidentally' is like this: If a man were a physician and prescribed successfully for himself, the patient would cure himself; but it would not be *qua* patient that he possessed the healing art, though in this particular case it happened that the physician's personality coincided with that of the patient, which is not always the case. And so it is with all manufactured or 'made' things: none of them has within itself the principle of its own making. Generally this principle resides in some external agent, as in the case of the house and its builder, and so with all hand-made things. In other cases, such as that of the physician-patient, though the patient does indeed contain in himself the principle of action, yet he does so only incidentally, for it is not *qua* subject acted on that he has in himself the causative principle of the action. (192 b 23–32)

It follows, then, that those things 'have a nature' which possess inherently such a principle as Aristotle has just described. 'Nature' is not just something in general but a principle of change belonging to certain kinds of things, and in fact, as I have already mentioned, to substances only:

and all such things are substances; for each of them is a subject, and nature is always in a subject. (192 b 33; MG)

Here we have, in a few words, the essential fastening down of natures to substances on which the whole framework of the Aristotelian cosmology depends. It is this necessary relevance of a thing's nature to itself as concrete entity that the earlier physicists had missed. The Platonists too in making the perceptible world an amorphous more-and-less had failed to seize on the only reasonable basis for scientific knowledge: the basis which presents itself on the face of things themselves through their revelation to us of their distinctive characters. We need not turn from nature to the Forms, because the nature of things themselves as substances gives us the unique and necessary starting-point for scientific knowledge of the world of change. Those who fail to stand on this necessary starting-point, and are driven to argue about *whether* there are natures, and events happening 'naturally', are reasoning 'like a man born colour-blind'. Such people's discourse

amounts to reasoning about names with no corresponding concept in the mind. (193 a 8–9; MG)

Nature in this general sense, however—as the inherent principle of change in such substances as possess such a principle —has more than one meaning, and these alternative meanings

129

hold within themselves the fourfold character of Aristotelian explanation. I have already spoken of the four causes in the previous chapter; Aristotle will expound them at length later, in *Physics II*, but he elicits them here from the very definition of nature itself, and refines that definition accordingly. Let us reconsider them now in this connection. First, he discusses the material cause, so much beloved of earlier philosophers:

> Now some hold that the nature and the substance of things that are by nature consists in its proximate unformed constituent, on the analogy of the wood of a bedstead or the bronze of a statue . . . And in like manner, it is thought, if the materials themselves bear to yet others the same relation which the manufactured articles bear to them—if for instance, bronze and gold are so related to water, or bone and timber to earth—then it is in the water or earth that we must look for the nature and substance of the gold and so forth. And this is why some have said that it was earth that constituted the nature of things, some fire, some air, some water, and some several and some all of these. For whatever each thinker took in this way, whether one or many, he regarded this as constituting the substance of all things in general, all else being mere modifications, states and dispositions of them. Any such ultimate or ultimates they regarded as eternal—for they did not admit the transformation of elements into one another—while they held that all else passed into existence and out of it endlessly.
>
> This then is one way of regarding 'nature'—as the ultimately underlying material of all things that have in themselves the principle of movement and change. (193 a 10–32)

This is nature as the material ground of change, the 'matter' emphasized by pre-Socratic students of nature or later by the atomists. More fundamental for Aristotle, however, is nature as form, as the defining principle, the *order* in things:

> . . . from another point of view we may think of the nature of a thing as residing rather in its form, that is to say in the 'kind' of thing it is by definition. For as we give the name of 'art' to a thing which is the product of art and is itself artistic, so we give the name of 'nature' to the products of nature which themselves are 'natural'.

130

And as, in the case of art, we should not allow that what was only potentially a bedstead and had not yet received the form of bed had in it as yet any art-formed element, or could be called 'art', so in the case of natural products; what is potentially flesh or bone has not yet the 'nature' of flesh until it actually assumes the form indicated by the definition that constitutes it the thing in question, nor is this potential flesh or bone as yet a product of nature. (193 a 30–b 3)

From these considerations we may obtain a more accurate definition:

Nature is the distinctive form (μορφή) or quality (εἶδος) of such things as have within themselves a principle of motion, such form or character not being separable from the things themselves, save conceptually. (193 b 4–5)

This is a preferable definition, Aristotle believes, to one that emphasizes matter alone, for matter is the mere potency of a thing, as the seed to the man, the acorn to the oak. Its form, on the other hand, is its *actuality*, which is most properly what it *is*, its 'en-tel-echy', that which has its end in itself, the what that contains the goal toward which its development has tended. Thus the nature of a man resides more truly in the defining form of man than in the characteristic stuff that constitutes a human organism. His soul, which is for Aristotle the way he functions as a man, is more properly man than his body. As he says (e.g. *De Part. An.* 640 b 34–36), a cadaver is not a man, but only the remains of what *was* a man; nor is the semen man, but only potentially so. Nor, he remarks here, is the concrete individual, the compound of form and matter, Socrates or Callias, 'a nature', but a thing that comes to be *by* nature. A man is a substance which *has* a nature (whether this be regarded as matter or, preferably, as form) and which is generated 'by nature', that is, through the principle of change inherent alike in the generating parent and in the generated offspring.

Natural things, moreover, are changing things, and we may consider their natures, therefore, in respect to the *terminus*

131

a quo and the *terminus ad quem* of such change. So Aristotle continues:

> Again men propagate men, but bedsteads do not propagate bedsteads; and that is why they say that the natural factor in a bedstead is not its shape but the wood—to wit, because wood and not bedstead would come up if it germinated. If then, it is this (incapacity of reproduction) that makes a thing art and not nature, then the form (of natural things) will be their nature, as in the parallel case of art; for what is generated by a man is a man. (193 b 8–12)

Aristotle is here clearly referring to the originating motion which will be described at greater length in the treatment of 'efficient' or 'moving' cause. This is man, not simply as form of man, but as generator of another man, as 'that from which' an ontogeny proceeds. It is identifiable with form, but in its operation distinguishable from it. And correlative with this is 'final cause', the end-point of generation:

> Again, *na-ture* is etymologically equivalent to *gene-sis* and (in Greek) is actually used as a synonym for it; *nature, then, qua genesis is the path to nature*. Now, it is true that healing is so called, not because it is the path to the healing art, but because it is the path to health, for of necessity healing proceeds *from* the healing art, not *to* the healing art itself; but this is not the relation of nature to nature, for that which is born starts as something and advances or grows toward something. Toward what, then, does it grow? Not toward that from which it came, but toward that to which it advances. (193 b 14–19) [*My ital.*]

Once more, Aristotle concludes, 'it is the form that is nature', but this time form as final cause, as goal.[1]

Note that here again the externality of art is contrasted with the internality of nature. In art the principle or effective starting-point must be contained in the skill (medicine) which is external to what it produces (health). In the case of a *nature*, on the other hand, we have a process which starts from some-

---

[1] It is at the close of this paragraph that Aristotle brackets the problem of 'shortage' as quasi-form for later treatment. He will, from this on, be concerned principally with non-substantial change, change between contraries, and only much later, at the proper place in his systematic analysis of natural things, will he return to this aspect of his theme.

thing (which already has a nature) to something which again has its own, the same, nature and growing (nature) is precisely this transition from one substance of the same kind to another, a transition self-contained, eternally recurrent, needing no agent beyond itself. Nature is thus from the start more self-contained and perfect than art; art is an imitation of nature, not the other way around. On the contrary, when Aristotle likens nature to art, it is for the sake of explication, not because he thinks of nature (as Paley thought of God) as a super-craftsman, but because he conceives of craftsmanship as something within our power, and therefore better known to us, that is in certain respects parallel to and like the processes of nature itself.

The definition of nature, then, already contains within itself the doctrine of the four causes which dominate the inquiries of Aristotle both here and in other disciplines. They are founded in the double character of natural entities: as enformed, that is, ensouled bodies and as life-histories from birth to death. It is, as we have already seen in discussing the methodology of science, the determinate character of these two pairs of concepts, the matter/form and the from-what/to-what relation, that makes the real world, including the world of natures, knowable.

Three subjects call for further comment here, all connected, in particular, with the most misunderstood of the four causes, final cause. First, we must be careful to keep in mind the character of Aristotelian teleology. Further, we must consider the role of necessity for Aristotle, in contrast to finality; and finally, the meaning for him of luck and chance, which are also contrasted with final cause.

6. *Aristotelian teleology*

With the conception of final cause, even more clearly than with the conception of substance, we are close to the biological source of Aristotle's thinking. For his expression 'that for the sake of which' corresponds closely to the biological concept of function. Aristotelian 'that for the sake of which' is not, in itself, a concept of purpose. Aristotle himself makes this quite plain. Purposive action, as he explains in the *Ethics*, is action involving deliberative choice. Nature, on the other hand, does not deliberate. The ends of nature are forms internal to the natural entities whose forms they are. Many expressions used by Aristotle, unfortunately, suggest a less sophisticated teleology: 'Nature does nothing in vain'; 'nature has chosen the best possible course in the circumstances,' and so on. But his explicit analysis of the meaning of 'nature' and 'final cause' must stand as definitive against these misleading maxims. Things, the things we meet in the world, oak trees and octopuses, are knowable because as *such* things, things of definite kinds, they contain in themselves determinate principles which make them the things they are and make them undergo the transformations they undergo. Nobody, no Olympian spirit, decides to turn a tadpole into a frog; but to *be* a tadpole is to be the offspring of a frog, in the course of becoming a new frog, according to the ontogenetic pattern that is 'frog'. There is no Nature, but each kind has *its* nature, which contains within bounds its material aspect and orders its changing states toward the achievement of the form appropriate to itself.

The Aristotelian conception of being, of knowledge, of man, all depend on the recognition of such inherent principles in natural kinds of things; and Aristotle's achievements in biology would be inconceivable, also, without this fundamental recognition of the forms and functions characteristic of living organisms. Some accounts of Aristotle's biology, Joseph Needham's, for example, balance against his genuine achievements, in particular, his detailed knowledge of chick embryology, his unfortunate lapses into teleology. This is to misunderstand altogether the character of his enterprise both as biologist and as philosopher; for it is precisely his grasp of the operational principles of organisms, of the coincidence of form and function, that makes him at once the philosopher and the biologist he is. Other writers, such as D'Arcy Thompson, E. S. Russell, or William E. Ritter, have explicitly acknowledged this conjunction. Thus Ritter says:

134

The teleology for which Aristotle is roundly condemned by many present-day biologists he was not at all or very slightly guilty of. On the other hand those who condemn the teleology which he did hold, that of completed wholeness as essential to the adequate interpretation of any phenomena of nature whatever, are in so far not only failing, themselves, in reaching such interpretation, but are tacitly denying the possibility of it. (**80**, 382.)

In short, it is the control of every step in a natural process by the character of the whole which serves as Aristotle's model for 'final cause'. Human, purposive action is but a limited case of such forward-directedness, with the super-added qualification of knowledge and deliberate choice. The directedness Aristotle is primarily interested in is the intrinsic directedness of organic development, not itself thinking or planned by thought, but, like thought, ordered and determinate and therefore an appropriate object for the thinker. It is here, in the finite and recurrent life-histories of animals and plants, and in the structures which develop accordingly, that he has found the model of intelligibility, of form-in-individuals, without which no single item of biological or any other knowledge for him would be knowledge at all. To detach efficient from final, or material from formal causes, as many modern biologists profess to do, would be, for Aristotle, to throw the intelligible back into the unintelligible, the principles of things into their mere conditions. It would be to turn knowledge into the vain search for knowledge, to make of man a useless passion, as some modern thinkers do and perhaps must do, but as Aristotle decidedly did not. We *do* have knowledge, Aristotle believes, not because we can take the development of the chicken to bits as if it were an artifact, not because we can reconstruct the whole out of its parts. We have knowledge because there *are* wholes, i.e. finite structures, developing as individuals, but eternal as species, which it is within the power of our finitude, our specific form as animals capable of memory, experience, insight and rational discourse, to discover by induction and elaborate in scientific argument. Without the directedness of nature there would be nothing, no *things*, for us to know. And

135

this directedness includes the directedness of our own existence, in which pure knowledge for its own sake is the highest and fittest goal. This is not a teleology which adds to some astute 'scientific' observations and predictions some other superstitious and ignorant remarks about nature's purposes. It is teleological science, that is functional science, the study of the rhythms of change characteristic of living things: rhythms which cannot be understood, any more than musical rhythms can be, as aggregates of isolated bits, but only as the *whole* patterns that they are. And in temporal patterns it is the outcome—the frog or the man, the rose-tree or the thistle—that governs the pattern that will have been. Not prediction of future from present, but of present from future is the essential time-scheme of Aristotelian nature:

> Thus matter and genesis must be first in time, but logically (τῷ λόγῳ) the substance and form of each thing is first. (*De Part. An.* 646 a 35–b 2)

Compare with this the statement of a twentieth-century embryologist who has been summarizing recent advances, undreamt of by Aristotle, in the biochemistry, micro-anatomy, micro-physiology of the fertilized egg:

> In large part the destiny of every man resides, though only potentially, in the germ cell from which he comes. In that organization, so hard to trace, everything is inscribed, even our power of thought, of appraisal, of preference. (**26.**)

In stressing patterns of development, then, Aristotle speaks as a student of living things, and his language is not so foreign to the modern biologist's, and in particular, to the embryologist's, as it may sometimes seem. At the same time, however, we must not forget substance, and the fact that knowledge, for Aristotle, is possible only because substances, concrete existing things, can be tied firmly into kinds. Aristotle's 'development', in contrast to modern phylogeny, is fettered securely to the eternity of species, the eternal round of becoming which, following forever its determinate and intelligible pattern, 'will never fail'. We can identify our attitude to living things with his only by a gigantic abstraction: by forgetting altogether the evolutionary character of our universe. I shall have more to say later of the contrast between Aristotle and Darwin. Suffice it here to notice that Aristotle's biology, and the philosophy founded on it, are radically non-evolutionary and anti-evolutionary. Our vision of species as a concretion of history, our belief that kinds are only snail-slow rhythms in a world forever in change, would be for Aristotle a betrayal of the very spirit of knowledge, of mind and of the real. We have cast out of our thoughts the all-important difference between things and their characters, and are trying out of the fragments left from this disaster to reconstruct a purely Heraclitean universe: so, surely, it would appear to Aristotle. There are, to be sure, passages in which he pictures a 'scale of nature' not, on the face of it, unlike an evolutionary summary of the ascent of life. He knows that there are 'transitional' forms between plant and animal, between land and water dwellers. On land and sea, in earth and sky, 'nature' has filled what evolutionists call every 'ecological niche' with some appropriate inhabitant. But it is entirely plain from his asseverations elsewhere that Aristotle—like Goethe long after him—thought of these 'transitions' morphologically and *not* historically. The round of nature imitates the round of the celestial spheres: so that while father generates son and not son father, man generates man, eternally. Only the fixity of each ontogenetic pattern through the eternity of species makes Aristotelian nature and Aristotelian knowledge possible.

7. *Necessity*

If, then, Aristotle's functionalism is close to the practice of naturalists or embryologists in any age, his emphasis on the permanence of kinds cuts him off sharply from the modern evolutionist's thought. In another aspect of modern biology, in fact, its tendency to mechanism, some of Aristotle's

SECOND PHILOSOPHY

predecessors, notably Empedocles and Democritus, had postulated
an origin of things conceptually much closer to a modern view.
And Aristotle is explicit in his rejection of their position.
Empedocles had developed a theory not unlike that of natural
selection, picturing, in one stage of his cyclical cosmology,
limbs, heads and other parts of animals coming together and
surviving when a viable organism happened to result. Democritus had developed a systematic atomic theory, such that
things were explained as the necessary result of the configura-
tion of their minute parts. The appeal of this theory to modern
minds scarcely needs comment. In fact, Democritean and
Aristotelian science have even been contrasted as the two
models of what knowledge should and should not be. What
Galileo did, on this view, was to bring the scientist back from
Aristotelian superstition to the pre-Aristotelian, rational out-
look. Aristotle himself, however, was acutely conscious of this
very contrast, and saw in his correction of Empedoclean and
Democritean mechanism the very core of his own method.
He is clearly aware, moreover, of the proper, if subordinate,
place of the mechanism of his predecessors with relation to his
own theory of inherent teleology. He makes this plain in
Book II of the *Physics* (ch. 9), and plainer still in the introduction
to the Great Biology Course in the *Parts of Animals*, as well
as elsewhere in the biological works.

Mechanistic biology seeks to elicit the complexities of organic
behaviour from an analytical account of the minute parts and
the antecedent conditions of living things. This presupposes
the thesis that the constituent parts necessarily produce the
whole, and that the antecedent state of those parts necessarily
produces the consequent functioning of their aggregate. Thus,
in Aristotle's terms, material and motive causes, taken apart
from their companion causes, form and end, are thought to
necessitate the living phenomena which we in fact observe.
That would be, in effect, to make necessity an independent
cause superior to form and end (or, we may say, to form
simply, since end, or that for the sake of which, is in fact the
form itself of each particular thing which is the *raison d'être*

138

of its development). Is it correct, however, to elevate necessity in the study of nature to this dominant role? Aristotle argues emphatically that it is not so, not because he rejects necessity in nature, but because he distinguishes its several roles, in relation to form or end, and applies them appropriately, as he believes, in their appropriate contexts.

Aristotle distinguishes two meanings of necessity, one of which is again divided into two very different kinds. The purest necessity there is, is the necessity of the things that are 'forever': the unmoved movers toward which as a fixed end of aspiration all other things move; the unending revolutions of the heavenly spheres; the kinds of natural beings which persist in their individual embodiments, even though each of the latter comes to be out of non-being and returns to it again. It is this simplest necessity, the things that are forever, that theoretical science studies: things the causes of which cannot be other than they are. The sciences of doing and making, in contrast, are less accurate, because they study things the principles of which may change. For as we have seen, Aristotle shares with Plato the belief not only that knowledge must be certain but that it can be so only if it reflects in its own serenity the stability of eternal *things*.

Distinguished from this *simple* necessity, is what Aristotle calls *hypothetical* necessity, necessity dependent on an end beyond itself. The nature of a thing is the internal source of change within it, i.e. the organizing principle which directs its development toward its particular end. Now if nature as form is prior to nature as matter, nature as that-toward-which, nature as end, is the characteristic biological manifestation of nature as form. Accordingly, what is first in nature is not what is forever, but what will be, the culmination of development, and this will-be, in nature, in turn controls natural necessity. What the physicist knows first and foremost is the *function* of each part and of each behaviour sequence of the organism he is studying; he knows what each organ and each activity are *for*, and the necessities he invokes are *conditional* on this end. This concept of necessity subordinate to end, of

139

hypothetical necessity, is a constant feature of Aristotle's biological writings. It is the concept which most sharply differentiates his method from that of Empedocles or Democritus. Necessity run wild is unintelligible; necessity harnessed to nature's ends is what the biologist is constantly seeking to understand. The function of the heart, as we have seen, e.g. is to preserve animal heat and to mediate the sensitivity of the organism to its environment. From this point of view it was 'best' that the heart be where and as it is, being as it were the hearth and sovereign of the body. At the same time, in relation to this end, it was necessary that the heart, unlike other organs, be of uniform composition, in order that it should be able to receive the reports of all the senses; that it should be made of blood, and hollow, to serve as a suitable receptacle for the blood, etc. Similarly for every organ and every activity the biologist asks why it is better so, i.e. why it is so and not otherwise, what its function is; *and* how, relatively to this function, the available conditions are used to achieve its effective realization.

Analysing the successive stages of ontogenesis in the *Generation of Animals*, Aristotle criticizes the theory of Democritus and summarizes his own method. This passage tells us better than any interpreter could do, just how Aristotle conceives the role of hypothetical necessity, which is, in effect, material and motive cause as subordinate to end. 'Some of the early physiologers,' Aristotle tells us, 'endeavoured to describe the order in which the various parts are formed, but they were none too well acquainted with what actually happens.' (742 a 17ff.) They failed to understand the dual character of 'priority':

As with everything else, so with the parts of the body: one is, by nature, prior to another. But the term 'prior' at once comprises a variety of meanings. E.g., take the difference between (a) that *for the sake of which* a thing is, and (b) that thing which is *for its sake*: of these one (b) is prior in point of formation, while the other (a) is prior in point of being (οὐσία). (742 a 18ff.)

This is the first and fundamental distinction. But what is for the sake of the end again has two divisions:

(i) that whence the movement is derived and (ii) that which is employed by the end ; or, in other words, (i) something which generates, and (ii) something which serves as an instrument for what is generated. Of the two, the productive factor must exist prior to the other: e.g. a teacher must exist prior to a learner, while pipes are posterior to the person who is learning to play them: it is superfluous for people who cannot play pipes to possess them. (742 a 24ff.)

In all, then, there are three things:

(1) the end, which we describe as being that for the sake of which; (2) the things which are for the sake of the end, viz. the activating and generative principle (second, because the existence of that which is productive and generative, *qua* such, is relative to what it produces and generates); (3) the things which are serviceable, which can be and are employed by the end. (742 a 27ff.)

That is, we have final cause, motive cause and material cause, in that order of importance, or ontological priority. Ontogenetically, however, in the history of the embryo, the order is different:

Thus, first of all there must of necessity exist some part in which the principle of movement resides (for of course this is part of the end, and the supreme controlling part of it); after that comes the animal as a whole, i.e. the end; third and last of all come the parts which serve these as instruments for various employments. (742 a 33–37)

Aristotle applies his distinction here to the difficult question of the order of formation of the parts of the growing embryo:

If it is true, then, that there is a part of this kind—a part which contains the first principle and the end of the animal's whole nature—which must of necessity be present in an animal, then this part must of necessity be formed first of all—formed first, *qua* activating, though formed along with the whole creature, *qua* being part of the end. Thus, those instrumental parts which are in their nature generative (of other parts) must always be there themselves prior to the rest,

141

because they are for the sake of something else, as being a first principle; those parts which, although they are for the sake of something else, are not generative, come later. That is why it is not easy to determine whether those parts are 'prior' which are for the sake of something else, or that part for whose sake these others are present. The activating parts intrude themselves into the picture, because in formation they are prior to the end; and it is not easy to determine between the activating and the instrumental parts. Still, .this is the line we must follow in trying to find out the order in which they are formed; for the end, though it comes after some of them, is prior to others. And on this account the part which contains the first principle is the first to be formed; then follows the upper portion of the body; and that is why in embryos we see that the parts around the head and eyes are the largest at the outset, while the parts below the umbilicus, for instance the legs, are small. The reason is that the lower portions are for the sake of the upper portion, and they are not parts of the end nor are they concerned in generating it. (742 a 37ff.)

So we have, first in time, the moving cause, which, however, exists for and in dependence on the end; then the 'animal as a whole', the major portion of the body, the head and trunk; and last the instrumental parts, serviceable to but not themselves carrying or producing the predominant principle.

Both the first and third of these are *hypothetically* necessary, necessary to the normal development of the organism for the sake of which they exist. But their necessity cannot stand alone as an explanatory principle. The trouble with Democritus was that he tried to make of mere happenings *reasons*, and so he missed even the necessity in the case, let alone the proper cause:

People who say, like Democritus of Abdera, that 'this is how they are always formed', and regard this as a starting-point (first principle) in these cases, make a mistake, nor do they even succeed in stating the necessity involved in the cause. Their argument is this: what is limitless has no starting-point, and what is *always* is limitless; therefore (says Democritus) to ask for a cause in connection with anything of this kind (sc., anything that always is) is the same as trying to discover a starting-point in something that is limitless. (742 b 18ff.)

This kind of argument would destroy the very foundation of scientific knowledge, even for eternal things:

Yet on this line of argument, on the strength of which they undertake to dispense with trying to discover the cause, there will be no demonstration of any single one of the 'eternal' things. It is obvious, however, that demonstrations of many of these (some of them things which always come to be, some things which always are) do in fact exist. For instance, the angles of a triangle are always equal to two right angles, and the diagonal of a square is always incommensurable with the side; in both of these cases we have something 'eternal', yet there is a cause for them and they are demonstrable. Thus it is right to say that we cannot undertake to discover a starting-point (a first principle) in all things and everything; but it is not right to deny the possibility in the case of all the things that always are and that always come to be; it is impossible only with the first principles of eternal things, for of course the first principle does not admit of demonstration, but is apprehended by another mode of cognition. (742 b 24ff.)

For generated things, similarly, these philosophers of sheer necessity miss the proper ground of explanation:

Now with those things that are immutable, the first principle is the essence;[1] but as soon as we begin to deal with those things that come into being through a process of formation, we find that there are several first principles, principles, however, of a different kind and not all of the same kind. Among them the source whence the movement comes must be reckoned as one, and that is why the heart is the first part which all blooded animals have, as I said at the beginning; in the other animals, it is the counterpart of the heart that is formed first. (742 b 34–743 a 1)

The motive cause, however, though it plays a unique role in ontogenesis, could not be properly investigated except through reference to the final cause; in the concluding chapter of the *Generation of Animals*, Aristotle, referring again to Democritus (this time to his explanation of the loss of milk teeth in some animals), explicitly rejects the Democritean type of 'explana-

[1] The what-it-is: τί ἐστιν.

143

tion' in these terms, relating both motive and material (instrumental) cause to end:

> Democritus, however, omitted to mention the for-the-sake-of-which, and so all the things which nature employs he refers to necessity. It is, of course, true that they are determined by necessity, but at the same time they are for the sake of something, and for the sake of that which is better in each case. And so there is nothing to prevent the teeth being formed and being shed in the way he says; but it is not on that account that it happens, but on account of the end; those other factors are causes *qua* causing movement, *qua* instruments, and *qua* material . . . But to allege that the causes are of the necessary type is on a par with supposing that when water has been drawn off from a dropsical patient the reason for which it has been done is the lancet, and not the patient's health, for the sake of which the lancet made the incision. (789 b 3ff.)

In other words, instruments are never independent agents, but instruments of and to an end. They are what Plato in the *Philebus* calls the servants of the cause for the purpose of generation, but not the cause itself. Although the house could not be built without the bricks, the bricks themselves would not build a house. The plan of the house must exist as well— and, it is true, in the case of artifacts, the builder. In nature, however, it is the plan itself that is the builder. If a doctor doctors himself, Aristotle says in the *Physics*, he is as it were two people, craftsman and patient; nature is both in one. As both in one—or three in one: agent, end and form—the nature of each kind and of each part of each kind determines the framework within which the available material and the antecedent starting-points of motion can be utilized. The definitions of physics, being physical, must indeed refer to the hypothetical necessity, the conditions and instruments of change: snub is a shape of flesh and bone, not disembodied concavity. But such reference is always subordinate to the end which in the pattern of nature it is made to subserve. Noses, of whatever shape, must have a function; the material without which they cannot exist subserves the end for which they do exist.

Hypothetical necessity, then, as against the absolute necessity

144

of eternal things, is a correlate of final cause. Aristotle makes a further distinction, however, between hypothetical and simple necessity within nature itself. Some characteristics of animals are necessary agents or instruments of the final cause: they are hypothetically necessary. Others, not being indispensable to the λόγος of the animal, occur one way or another, as antecedent conditions and available materials determine. These are the products of necessity simply, or of *material* necessity. So, e.g. an animal to whose nature it belongs to see must have eyes; on this hypothesis, the development of a visual organ is necessary to its being. Whether its eyes be blue or of some other colour is indifferent; eye colour is the result of material and motive cause let loose from end, that is, of necessity simply. Book V of the *Generation of Animals*, for instance, is devoted to the study of such products of necessity, although at the outset of the book and in the refutation of Democritus already quoted, Aristotle takes care to tie the overall lines of development firmly to final cause. Simple, or material, necessity operates within a range left free within the development pattern of a given organism; it is in no way sovereign over the λόγος of development itself. To take another example, Aristotle argues that, of the viscera, heart and lungs are essential to life, but the spleen, having no indispensable positive function but simply using up excessive waste, is the product of necessity.

Aristotle's distinction here is reminiscent of Darwin, who recognized that minor variations, if non-functional, are not controlled by his sovereign principle of natural selection. They are exceptions within the rule, not against it. Only, of course, unlike Aristotle, and like Democritus, Darwin conceived of his ruling principle as itself begotten by necessity out of chance. He believed, like Democritus, that he had explained function without recourse to teleology. This Aristotle believed to be impossible. *Within* the bounds of the nature of each kind of thing, there is a certain field of free play for mere 'necessity'; but without those bounds and the ends or forms that eternally delimit them, there would be neither things to know nor minds to know them.

145

Before we proceed to Aristotle's own analysis of chance—
the twin of necessity in ancient as in modern mechanistic
thinking—one more comparison between Aristotelian and
evolutionary explanation may clarify further Aristotle's conception of material necessity. When he deals with the subject
of horns in the *Parts of Animals* (III, 2), Aristotle follows his
usual practice of expounding first the function (the for-the-
sake-of-which) of such appendages, and then the 'necessary
nature' present for other (material) reasons, which 'rational
nature' has made use of to subserve her ends. Although in
some animals, such as deer, Aristotle says, horns are useless,
and nature has provided such animals with some other means
of defence, in general the function of horns is for defence and
attack. Having shown why horns should come in pairs, be
situated on the head, etc., he proceeds;

We must now describe the character of that 'necessary nature',
owing to which certain things are present of necessity, things which
have been used by 'rational nature' (ἡ κατὰ τοῦ λόγου φύσις) for
the sake of something.

To begin with, then: the larger the animal, the greater the quantity
of corporeal or earthy matter there is in it. We know no really small
horned animal—the smallest known one is the gazelle. To study
nature we have to consider the majority of cases, for it is either in
what is always or for the most part that things according to nature
are to be found. Now all the bones in animals' bodies consist of
earthy matter; so if we consider the majority of cases, we can say
that there is most earthy matter in the biggest animals. At any rate,
in the larger animals, there is present a surplus of this corporeal or
earthy matter, produced as a residue, and this nature makes use of
and turns to advantage to provide them with means of defence. That
portion of it which by necessity courses upwards she allots to form
teeth and tusks in some animals, and to form horns in others. And we
can see from this why no horned animal has incisor teeth in both
jaws, but only in the bottom jaw. Nature has taken away from the
teeth to add to the horns; so that the nourishment which would
normally be supplied to the upper teeth is here used to grow the
horns. Why is it, then, that female deer, although they have no horns,
are no better off for teeth than the male deer? The answer is: both of

them are, by nature, horned animals; but the females have lost their horns because they would be not only useless but dangerous. The horns are indeed of no more use to the males, but they are less dangerous because males are stronger.

Thus in some animals this part of the body is secreted for the formation of horns; in others, however, it causes a general increase in the size of the teeth, and in others again it produces tusks, which are like horns springing out of the jaws instead of the head. (663 b 23–664 a 12)

Aristotle has here observed a correlation between body-size and the growth of 'bony' appendages, which suggests comparison with Julian Huxley's principle of *allotropy*. It had been a stumbling block of Darwinism that some animals developed structures (like the appendages of the Irish elk or of the American titanotheres) in apparent excess of their utility, thus outrunning the control of natural selection, which supposedly eliminates the less in favour of the more useful at every stage of evolution. This seems to suggest an inner dynamic of development let loose from selective control, and Darwinism would have none of that. But, Huxley argued, if increased body size is advantageous, and appendages increase with body size but at a more rapid rate, we shall have the larger animal with a *still* larger horn: the unwieldy appendage being a necessary if unhappy concomitant of the advantageous overall body size. Thus we have here a quantitative expression which replaces and, because quantitative and subordinated to natural selection, 'explains' an apparent inner dynamic. It reduces its *explicandum* to a correlation between two variables, the independent variable, body size, being in its turn dependent on the necessitation of selection. For Aristotle, on the other hand, the quantitative correlation between body size and the presence of appendages is on the one hand a static one: it is a simple observation of the kinds there are, not of how they came to be. And within this static situation, the use of horns is the sovereign principle for the most part (some exceptions there are, but nature always has room for exceptions); but subject to the sovereignty of function there is the complementary aspect of necessity: there is in the case of large animals material present which nature might use and has in fact used for the invention of weapons of defence or attack. For the Darwinian, necessity, quantitatively expressed if possible, produces function. For Aristotle, a quantitative observation, expressing material cause, takes note of a 'second nature' subordinate to the control of a more-than-quantitative nature, an operating principle which puts to use the stuff made available by necessity. Were the extra earthy stuff of the larger animal body not available, nature could not have fashioned horns of it; material necessity is the condition for what nature makes of it. But quantity and necessity subserve function, not the other way around. Moreover, even the non-functional appendage where he finds it fails to worry Aristotle: nature works always *or* for the most part. For the modern Darwinian, it is essential to tie all major phenomena directly and logically to utility, which alone selection can control. The useful and only the useful can be generated, by natural selection, of necessity; so that, to be thoroughly necessitarian, it is necessary to be thoroughly utilitarian, thoroughly teleological, in fact. Aristotle, for whom inherent teleology reigns supreme in nature, can allow an area for the non-functional, the merely necessary within his 'rational' nature. He, the prophet of the 'for-the-sake-of-which', is less obsessed with finding 'ends' than are the Darwinian evolutionists, who deny 'teleology' while seeking it everywhere in order to reduce it to necessity.

One final remark: on logical necessity. All three of Aristotle's necessities, absolute (of eternal things), conditional, and material, are real, not logical necessities. With logical necessity as we understand it he is not primarily concerned. True, scientific knowledge, for Aristotle, is 'necessary', and, *a fortiori*, the first principles of a science are *necessary* basic truths. But they, again, are *really* necessary; in fact, they must be necessary, one supposes, in the absolute sense, for the kinds of things there are, and the peculiar form of each kind, are eternal, even though their instances perish, and it is these eternal verities, which cannot be other than they are, that the knower knows.

The principal reference to what we should call logical necessity is in the puzzling chapter on Cause in the *Posterior Analytics* (II, 11). There Aristotle seems to put the fact that the premises necessitate the conclusion in the place of material cause, and one might suppose therefore that logical necessity would be a case of material necessity in Aristotle's sense. But the analogy between matter/form and premises/conclusion is a very weak one. In general it is the reference back to the real, and absolute, necessity, of real definitions on which the methodology of the *Posterior Analytics* rests. Of course, syllogistic arguments are logically necessary, but it was not that sort of necessity that interested Aristotle most.

8. *Luck and chance*

If for Aristotle necessity is bound to form and function, so are contingency and chance. The analysis of propositions about future events in *On Interpretation* may lead one to conclude that Aristotle's world had room for real contingency, for realities uncomprehended in the demands of finality and the being-what-it-is of each kind of thing. But real contingency in this sense could be no wider in extent than material necessity: it is whatever happens for no serious reason, but just happens, and that can be only within the confines of the rational order of things. Aristotle's account of contingency in the *Physics* confirms this view.

In Book II of the *Physics* Aristotle discusses the possibility that contingency should be added as a fifth to his list of 'becauses'. In his analysis he distinguishes between two concepts, 'luck' and 'chance' (which are similarly distinguished in the *Metaphysics* also). Luck operates in the sphere of deliberate action. Thus, e.g. if a man goes to the market place to buy wine and happens to meet his debtor, his collecting the debt was a matter of luck. We are here not only within the bounds set by final cause, but, narrower still, of deliberate actions. Luck is a perfectly recognizable factor in human behaviour, but not a kind of natural cause to be added, as a serious

149

consideration for the physicist, to form and matter, end and moving agency. Chance or randomness, on the other hand, does operate in nature, but again in the interstices of its inherent patterns. The products of 'the automatic' are the stray bits which nature need not keep tidy. Again, they are like the evolutionist's non-functional variations which fail to add up to overall trends. In themselves, they do not constitute a principle of explanation of importance to the student of nature; chance need not be added as another sort of cause to the list of four.

In chapters 8 and 9 Aristotle proceeds to argue for his type of inherent teleology against the physicists who have tried to elevate necessity to the principle of nature and shows how the physicist must use the concept of hypothetical necessity in subordination to the end and nature of each kind of thing. The subordinate place of chance emerges very plainly from the first part of this argument, which is directed in particular against Empedocles.

So here the question arises whether we have any reason to regard nature as making for any goal at all, or as seeking any one thing as preferable to any other. Why not say, it is asked, that nature acts as Zeus drops the rain, not to make the corn grow, but of necessity (for the rising vapour must needs be condensed into water by the cold, and must then descend, and incidentally, when this happens, the corn grows), just as, when a man loses his corn on the threshing-floor, it did not rain on purpose to destroy the crop, but the result was merely incidental to the raining? So why should it not be the same with natural organs like the teeth? Why should it not be a coincidence that the front teeth come up with an edge, suited to dividing the food, and the back ones flat and good for grinding it, without there being any design in the matter? And so with all other parts in which we suppose that something is happening for the sake of something.[1] In cases where a coincidence brought about such a combination as

[1] The Loeb translation of this sentence is: 'And so with all other organs that seem to embody a purpose'. Wicksteed regularly renders the Aristotelian phrase 'for-the-sake-of-something' as 'purpose'. With the Loeb Library's permission, I have avoided this term (which seems to me seriously misleading), and in the next two quotations have substituted 'action for an end' or 'processes for the sake of something'.

might have been arranged for something, the creatures, it is urged, having been suitably formed by the operation of chance, survived; otherwise they perished, and still perish, as Empedocles says of his 'man-faced oxen'. (198 b 17–32)

This is a theory which, like Darwinism so many centuries later, makes coincidence the mother of necessity. But it is impossible, Aristotle contends, that things should really be this way. His argument, or the first part of it, is a revealing instance of Aristotelian induction, or at least of one brand of it:

Such and suchlike are the arguments which may be urged in raising this problem; but it is impossible that this should really be the way of it. For all these phenomena and all natural things are either constant or normal, and this is contrary to the very meaning of luck or chance. No one assigns it to chance or to a remarkable coincidence if there is abundant rain in the winter, though he would if there were in the dog-days; and the other way about, if there were parching heat. Accordingly, if the only choice is to assign these occurrences either to coincidence or to an end, and if in these cases chance coincidence is out of the question, then they must be for an end. But, as our opponents themselves would admit, these occurrences are all natural. There is action for an end, then, in what is, and in what happens, by nature. (198 b 33–199 a 8)

'No one assigns it to chance,' etc.—the plain man's use of plain language is given as support for a philosophical point of considerable importance. Why should not the plain man be wrong? Why should 'ordinary usage' be so plainly relevant to what things are really like? Or why must coincidence and finality be the only conceivable alternatives? Things are constant or usual = natural, or unusual = by chance or coincidence, Aristotle argues. The growth of teeth and the like are usual, therefore not by chance, therefore for the sake of something. This is in itself a circular argument so narrow as to seem no argument at all.

Aristotle then proceeds to back it up, however, by pointing to the directedness of natural phenomena, basing his point on the usual analogy of nature and art; and he argues further that even monstrosities such as Empedocles envisages would

151

have resulted not from *no* principle, but from the occasional failure of a principle, 'as monstrous births are actually produced now by abortive developments of sperm'. (199 b 6–7) But the fundamental objection to Empedocles' view becomes apparent when Aristotle generalizes the Empedoclean picture:

> In plants, too, though they are less elaborately articulated, there are manifest indications of processes for the sake of something. Are we to suppose, then, that as there were 'ox-creatures man-faced' so also there were 'vine-growths olive-bearing'? Incongruous as such a thing seems, it ought to follow if we accept the principle in the case of animals. Moreover, it ought to be a matter of chance what comes up when you sow this seed or that. (199 b 9–13)

It is by no means a matter of chance what comes up when you sow this seed or that, and a theory which would lead us to such a conclusion in fact 'does away with the things that are by nature and with nature itself':

> For natural things are exactly those which do move continuously, in virtue of a principle inherent in themselves, towards a determined goal; and the final development which results from any one such principle is not identical for any two species, nor yet is it any random result; but in each there is always a tendency towards an identical result, if nothing interferes with the process. (199 b 15–18)

This is where, as we have seen before, Aristotle's predecessors had gone astray. *Each* kind of thing has its own intrinsic finality; that is what makes it the kind of thing it is. Only the understanding of this fundamental principle makes scientific knowledge possible. But once it is understood, the nature of our minds and of our discourse enables us to rely even on such seemingly superficial testimony as the plain man's use of the term 'chance' and to infer from it the contrast between the natural and the merely coincidental. For our natures and other natures, each in its constant place in the ordered universe, are naturally atune to one another. There is no need to explain the obvious by the non-obvious, but we may rest assured that the stabilities we observe in things are the stabilities of nature itself, including the powers, sensory and intellectual, by which we observe them. True, there are coincidences, as well as occasional spontaneous happenings:

A desirable result and the means to it may also be produced by luck, as for instance we say it was by luck that the stranger came and ransomed the prisoner before he left, where the ransoming is done as if the man had come for that purpose, though in fact he did not. (199 b 18–22)

But here 'the desirable result is incidental',

for chance is an incidental cause. (199 b 23)

And again, the usual or normal is the contrary of the casual or coincidental:

when the desirable result is effected invariably or normally, it is not an incidental or chance occurrence; and in the course of nature the result always is achieved either invariably or normally, if nothing hinders. (199 b 24–26)

Thus chance events occur only within the limits not of necessity, but of inherent aim: an aim not imposed on nature from without but intrinsic in and peculiar to the specific character of each natural kind of thing: the being-what-it-is of each thing and the definition of each kind of substance. Substance as essential form, substance as end, is the ground within which alone the study of nature has its proper starting-point. In relation to this sovereign principle, with its fourfold expression in the right form for the appropriate material conditions, and the appropriate end directive of each moving agency, both chance and necessity must take their fitting and subordinate place.

Let me emphasize once more, in conclusion, the significance of the statement, in the refutation of Empedocles, of the separateness of each nature from every other:

the final development which results from any one such principle is not identical for any two species, nor yet is it any random result; but in each there is always a tendency towards an identical result, if nothing interferes . . . (199 b 17–18.)

It is the process of development uniquely determined for *each*

153

kind of thing which expresses, in the world of change, the being-what-it-is, the peculiar substance of each kind, its being as such a substance and not another. Nature is first and foremost function, but function as determinate; not as indefinite ongoing, but as the structure and limited life-history of each species.

An example from the *History of Animals* may fittingly show us the kind of thing—or one of the many kinds of things— that Aristotle seems to have had in mind. In describing the habits of fishes, he has this to say:

Of river-fish, the male of the sheat-fish is remarkably attentive to the young. The female after parturition goes away; the male stays and keeps on guard where the spawn is most abundant, contenting himself with keeping off all other little fishes that might steal the spawn or fry, and this he does for forty or fifty days, until the young are sufficiently grown to make away from the other fishes for themselves. The fishermen can tell where he is on guard: for, in warding off the little fishes, he makes a rush in the water and gives utterance to a kind of muttering noise. He is so earnest in the performance of his parental duties that the fishermen at times, if the eggs be attached to the roots of water-plants deep in the water, drag them into as shallow a place as possible; the male fish will still keep by the young, and, if it so happen, will be caught by the hook when snapping at the little fish that come by; if, however, he be sensible by experience of the danger of the hook, he will still keep by his charge, and with his extremely strong teeth will bite the hook in pieces. (621 a 21ff.; Oxf.)

The species so described is known to zoologists as Parasilurus Aristotelis. Aristotle first observed its habits; but it was rediscovered only by the American naturalist Louis Agassiz in the nineteenth century. Here as in other instances Aristotle shows himself pre-eminent in the precise observation of the life-histories of animals. This is if you like mere 'observation', not explanation, teleological or otherwise; indeed on Aristotle's own account the *History of Animals* provides a body of information, reasons for which will be given in the other biological works. Yet it is, it seems to me—and as the great editor of the *History of Animals*, D'Arcy Thompson, himself believed—

precisely this naturalist's attention to minute and differentiating detail which lies at the root of Aristotle's conception of nature itself. Nature as finite process and as the finite structure expressed in finite process: this is the intelligibility in the real, the form in things, which Aristotle is everywhere seeking to articulate and to defend.

9. *Attributes of nature*

In speaking of the causes, necessity, teleology and so on, I have been drawing out some of the implications of Aristotle's definition of nature: that is, I have been elaborating on the *second* constituent, or the starting-point, of Aristotelian physics. The third constituent of a science consists in a set of attributes of which at the outset we know the meaning and for which we demonstrate their inherence in the subject-genus of the science in question. So in Books III and IV Aristotle proceeds to deal with a number of concepts that have been thought to belong to the subject-matter of physics and considers how and to what extent they do in fact characterize natural things and natural events. I am by no means attempting to survey Aristotle's work in general or the treatise *On Nature* in particular, but I want to consider some points about these arguments, in so far as they emphasize more strikingly than ever the way in which the concept of finite or determinate form lies at the root of Aristotelian 'nature'. Aristotle's concept of change I have already mentioned; what concerns me here are some parts of his analysis of the further and subsidiary concepts essential to natural science: the infinite, place (and the void) and time. (III, 4–8; IV, 6–9, 10–14; esp. 14)

The study of the infinite is proper to natural science, Aristotle admits, since all reputable philosophers have treated it and have in fact in some sense accepted it as a constituent of nature. Yet, however essential to the practice of mathematics a certain conception of infinity may be, the *actual* infinite is not physically a viable concept. There is no actually infinite body; Aristotle's meticulous and complex argument to this effect may be followed with the help of Ross's commentary on the *Physics*. It is sufficient here to mention some points about it.

First, the argument is again organized with reference to the *substances* whose natures we are discussing. Infinity is considered as a candidate first for substantial, then for attributive character and rejected in each case. It may be said that such arguments are routine in Aristotle. That is just the point. Whatever there is in nature is either a first substance or something that qualifies such a substance: any candidate for natural reality must stand this test.

Secondly, in the case of his argument against the infinite as substance, Aristotle puts strikingly, in a single remark, the root of the contrast between his cosmology and what one might call the ontology of modern mathematics. The infinite is not a substance, Aristotle argues, because if it were, each part of it would have to be infinite also (as part of air is air), 'but for one thing to be many infinites is impossible'. (204 a 25) Thus Aristotle seems implicitly to recognize the nature of an infinite class: that a part of the whole is equal to the whole (can be put into one to one correspondence with it), and hence rejects as absurd the whole conception of actual infinites. He leaves, he feels, in the concept of infinite divisibility and unlimited counting, sufficient scope for mathematics: but to face, as modern mathematicians must, the paradox of infinite magnitudes, would be to take a course for him unnecessary and incomprehensible.

What there is, for Aristotle, thirdly, is not an actual but a potential infinite: 'the open possibility of taking more, however much you have already taken'. (207 a 7–8) But again, fourthly, such open possibilities are relative to their contrary, 'that of which there is nothing more to take', and this is not unlimited but 'whole or completed':

For we define a whole precisely as that from which nothing is absent, for example, a 'whole man' or a 'whole chest'. (207 a 9–10)

Thus Parmenides, who held the whole to be finite, spoke truer than Melissus, who thought it infinite:

So Parmenides was nearer the mark than Melissus; for Melissus speaks of 'the Whole' as 'unlimited', whereas Parmenides sets boundaries to his 'whole', that is 'equipoised on the centre'. For 'whole' and 'all' and 'unlimited' are terms that cannot run in double harness. What led them to give to the Unlimited the impressive attributes of 'all-embracing' and 'all in itself containing' was the fact that it has a certain resemblance to the whole; *for the 'unlimited' is really the 'material' from which a magnitude is completed, and is the potential, though not the realized whole.* It is 'divisibility without limit' in the direction of reduction or converse expansion, and is not any determined whole in itself, but only in relation to something else [*My italics*],

or, in Wicksteed's paraphrase, 'only as the unlimited and "material" factor of the whole which is constituted as such by the limiting and "formal" factor'. 'As unlimited,' Aristotle continues,

it is embraced and not embracing. Therefore *qua* unlimited it is unknowable, since 'material' as such is formless. So the unlimited were evidently better defined as a part than as a whole, in the sense in which 'part' means the 'material constituent' as bronze is a part or constituent of the bronze statue. For, if in things of sense the undetermined 'great and small' were the continent and not the contained, analogy would demand that in the noetic world also the unintelligible should embrace the objects of thought; but it is contradictory and impossible that the unknowable and undefined should embrace and define anything. (207 a 15-32)

The unlimited, then, is the indeterminate, the material cause, subordinate to and relevant to form. For number, it is in the outward direction that we find it: of units we can always take one more, but the one, the least unity, is atomic:

It is quite as it should be that in number there should be an inferior limit, whereas it is always possible to transcend any given number . . . The reason is that unity, as unity, is atomic, the human unit, for instance, being one man and not more than one; whereas number is of more units than one, and specifically of 'so many', so that you cannot go further back than the indivisible (for 'two' and 'three', that is, two ones and three ones, are both numbers, *qua* more than one,

157

but different numbers, *qua* two or three respectively, and so with the rest). (207 b 1–10)

Of magnitudes, on the other hand, there is an upper but not a lower limit:

> . . . in magnitudes, on the other hand, it should always be possible to make the small smaller, but there can be no magnitude of unlimited greatness. (207 b 3–5) . . . for a continuous magnitude can be divided beyond any given smallness, but cannot be increased above every assignable greatness. For any magnitude that can exist potentially can exist actually; so since, as we have seen, nothing sense-perceived can be unlimited, a magnitude in excess of every definite magnitude is an impossibility; it would have to transcend the universe. (207 b 16–21)

Here once more we come to rest in the perceptible, intelligible, manageable world: *nothing sense-perceived can be unlimited*, and it is the sense-perceived, comprehensible things there are—men and bees and plane trees and Parasiluruses— with which, concretely and really, the student of nature has to deal. We may count them as far as we like, and divide them as minutely as we like; but none of them in itself is infinite. If it were, it would 'transcend the universe'. The tidy cosmos of kinds, each following its own course in distinction from every other, casts forth from itself wholly such grotesque leviathans. We live and move and have our being, as do all things, as finite wholes within one finite whole; breezes of haphazard may ruffle a little the trappings incidental to each entity within this well-run dwelling-place, but against the wild winds of infinity its windows are securely barred.

In the Aristotelian universe, secondly, everything has its proper place, in modern jargon, its ecological niche; and there are no wholly empty spaces. It is the thing, and the place of the thing, the river in its bed, the frog in its pool, the hare in its form, that go to make up this universe. What would a place be that was the place of nothing? Place is an attributive category; it cannot be itself a thing. A place is not a natural subject, able to assume and shed contrary qualities and remain itself, but merely an accident of such things. Again, Aristotle argues in detail against the Democritean void. One point (which I have already mentioned in another connection), seems to me especially revealing here: that is, Aristotle's objection that the void accounts only for local motion, whereas any one can see that a theory of change must take into account qualitative change as well. Things that have natures or are by nature are more than bundles of smaller things moving here and there; they are substances, each expressing its peculiar form, its peculiar pattern of development, which includes seeking its proper place, upward or downward or alongside other things, but includes much more as well: growth, and perception, and memory, the development of habits, in general, the fulfilment of its appropriate ends.

Even time, finally, which is the measure of motion, is tied to substance, since it is substances that move, and time is but the numerable aspect of these movements. Moreover, though time has no end, 'being always a beginning', it is not one infinitely stretched out receptacle of change, but the unit of concrete change:

> Time is a number not as counted but as counting; whence it follows that earlier and later are different because the nows are different; just as the number of a hundred horses is the same as that of a hundred men, but that which is enumerated is different, the horses from the men. (220 b 8–12; MG)

It is the concrete processes, as it is the concrete things, that *are*, and each, as time-spanning, is different from each other, even though the measure used is uniform. Moreover, where events recur, different in number but one in kind, time too is measured by recurrences:

> when one and the same motion takes place over and over, so with time too, like the year or the spring or the autumn. (220 b 12–14; MG.)

This does not, as Wicksteed points out, mean that 'time circulates'; perhaps, as he suggests, Aristotle is here preparing for the selection of the rotation of the celestial spheres as the right measure of time, as distinct from his previous association of time-measurement with rectilinear motion. But he may also be referring to the recurrent processes of the sublunar world, the finite life-histories which the Aristotelian physicist studies and measures by their time of year or time in years and seasons: the circular self-perpetuation of species through which the processes of life imitate the celestial motions, so that becoming will never fail. First and last it is the recurrent finite processes of determinate kinds of things, whether under or in the heavens, of which Aristotelian natural science treats.

V

'On Memory and Recollection'

The treatise *On Nature* outlines the principles for second philosophy as a whole, but Aristotle's method will be applied, appropriately to each division of the subject, to a whole range of natural sciences. The conceptual strength of the method, with its predilection for form, is nowhere more apparent than in the study which concentrates on the forms, in Aristotle's terms, the souls, in modern language, the operating principles of living things as distinct (though never in existence separate from) their matter: that is, the branch of physics which we call psychology. Before turning to First Philosophy, therefore, we may glance at one example of Aristotle's study of mind, the treatise *On Memory and Recollection*. This is one of the brief studies collectively referred to as the *Shorter Treatises on Nature* or *Parva Naturalia*; it deserves more attention than it usually gets from philosophers, for its contrast both to Plato and to the point of view of modern associationist theories of mind like that of Hume. To compare it, for example, on the one hand with the *Meno* or the *Phaedo* and on the other with Hume's argument in the *Treatise* brings into sharp relief the power of Aristotle's method. His confidence that their natures, their several definable forms, are written on the face of things, makes intelligible to him in a straight-forward empirical way processes that for philosophers with other starting-points need elaborate justification, whether transcendental as with Plato or reductive and behaviourist in import as with Hume. Let us look at it here as a study of the form of a natural process, the kind of thing we have been talking about in a more general way in the preceding chapter.

161

There are two chapters in the little treatise, dealing in turn with each of its two subjects. The two must be distinguished, for

Men who have good memories are not the same as those who are good at recollecting, in fact generally speaking the slow-witted have better memories, but the quick-witted and those who learn easily are better at recollecting. (449 b 6–8)

As to memory: first, it concerns not future or present, but past: 'what has become':

For instance one cannot remember a particular white object when one is looking at it, nor can one remember a subject of theoretical speculation while one is actually speculating and thinking about it. One merely claims to perceive the former, and to know the latter. But when one has knowledge or sensation without the actualization of these faculties, then one remembers: in the former case that he learned or thought out the fact, and in the latter that he heard or saw it or perceived it in some other such way; for when a man is exercising his memory he always says in his mind that he has heard, or felt, or thought this before. (449 b 15–23)

Thus, secondly, memory is:

neither sensation nor judgment, but . . . a state or affection of one of these, when time has elapsed. (b 24–25)

This means that:

only those animals which perceive time remember, and the power by which they perceive time is also that by which they remember. (b 28–30)

How simple and economical a statement is this, obvious, yes, yet impossible on Platonic or on pure empiricist principles. What is 'the perception of time' and how do animals, ourselves or others, perceive it? For Plato only the ascent to the Forms makes even perception itself, let alone its return through memory, intelligible. Only those 'really reals' provide a standard of comparison between the experience of 'now' and 'then'. For Hume the difference between an idea (a memory) and an

162

impression (a percept), though all-important to his argument, is inexplicable except in terms of the limping criterion of vividness, a criterion which he himself admits is not wholly satisfactory. But to invoke the 'perception of time' on his principles would be impossible. It is just because there is no perception of time, but only a succession of disconnected atoms of sensation that the problem of the structure of the real, of necessary connection, of induction, becomes so urgent and so insoluble.

Hume, indeed, like Aristotle, makes ample use of the analogy between men and animals. But for him this means that he explains human memory and human inference as arising from sources identical throughout with the operations of animal psychology: the psychology of all animals uniformly, even down to those stupidest creatures, barnyard fowl. Aristotle, starting from the recognition of the different nature of each species, can cut out of the wider range of animals the class of those which uniquely and characteristically perceive time and identify this class with those which remember, just as he can make a further cut within this class to include those, and those alone, which deliberate. Hume must try to build a world, human and animal alike, out of a mere agglomeration of isolated data. He is committed, as the Platonic Protagoras had been, to 'man the measure', to the construction of nature, both physical and mental, out of the bits of each man's experience and nothing more—as if, Aristotle would say, we expected the bricks—and only mental bricks at that—to build the building. Plato himself, opposing the relativism of Protagoras, yet opposed it in its own terms, and so only a conversion, a radical turning from the surface flow of the individual's sensations, could suffice for his reply. Aristotle, safe within the framework of the categories and of his knowledge of the stability of natural kinds, can distinguish among and identify structures accessible neither to the philosopher of pure sensation nor to the metaphysician who tries to meet him on his own ground. Here his direct and discriminating empiricism, his natural historian's confidence that to describe the habits of kinds of things, is to make them directly intelligible, triumphs over a more abstract and analytical attitude.

Aristotle proceeds to consider the relation of memory to the image-forming faculty which he has already analysed in the treatise *On the Soul*. He summarizes his position, denying that there is any thinking without images:

> It is impossible even to think without a mental picture. The same affection is involved in thinking as in drawing a diagram: for in this case although we make no use of the fact that the magnitude of a triangle is a finite quantity, yet we draw it as having a finite magnitude. In the same way the man who is thinking, though he may not be thinking of a finite magnitude, still puts a finite magnitude before his eyes, though he does not think of it as such. And even if the nature of the object is quantitative, but indeterminate, he still puts before him a finite magnitude, although he thinks of it as merely quantitative. (449 b 30–450 a 7)

The visualization of magnitudes is linked to the awareness of time; thus memory, entailing time-sense, also depends on imagination:

> Why it is impossible to think of anything without continuity, or to think of things which are timeless except in terms of time, is another question. Now we must cognize magnitude and motion with the faculty with which we cognize time, and the image is an affection of the common perceptive faculty. Thus it is clear that the cognition of these things belongs to the primary power of perception. (450 a 7–12)

Memory, therefore, entailing imagery, is primarily the work of a power of perception, and only incidentally of thought:

> But memory, even of the objects of thought, implies a mental picture. Hence it would seem to belong incidentally to the thinking faculty, but essentially to the primary power of perception. Hence memory is found not only in man and beings which are capable of opinion and thought, but also in some other animals. If it formed part of the intellectual faculty, it would not belong, as it does, to many other animals; probably not to any mortal being, since even as it is it does not belong to all, because they have not all a perception of time; for, as we said before, whenever a man actively remembers

that he has seen, heard or learned something, he always perceives in addition that he did so before; now, before and after relate to time. Thus memory belongs to that part of the soul to which imagination belongs, all objects which are imaginable are essentially objects of memory; all those that necessarily involve images (i.e. thoughts) are objects of memory incidentally. (450 a 12–25)

The remark about a possible 'intellectual memory', like so many of Aristotle's suggestions about pure thought, is difficult to interpret. Is he suggesting that only a separate (and therefore non-mortal) mind could think without images, and therefore remember intellectually, unaided by pictures? We may leave the question open, as a small part of the age-old controversy on Aristotle's view of immortality and of 'active reason'.

To identify the power that remembers with the power that imagines is a step in the account of memory, but not enough. 'The question might be asked,' Aristotle continues,

how one can remember something which is not present, since it is only the affection that is present, and the fact is not. For it is obvious that one must consider the affection which is produced by sensation in the soul, and that part of the body which contains the soul—the affection, the lasting state of which we call memory—as a kind of picture; for the stimulus produced impresses a sort of likeness of the percept, just as when men seal with signet rings. Hence in some people, through disability of age, memory does not occur even under a strong stimulus, as though the stimulus or seal were applied to running water; while in others owing to detrition like that of old walls in buildings, or to the hardness of the receiving surface, the impression does not penetrate. For this reason the very young and the very old have poor memories; they are in a state of flux, the young because of their growth, the old because of their decay. For a similar reason neither the very quick nor the very slow appear to have good memories; the former are moister than they should be, and the latter harder; with the former the picture does not remain in the soul, with the latter it makes no impression. (450 a 25–b 11)

The reference here to the basic qualities, like most of Aristotle's physiology, seems crude and antiquated; not so the conceptual analysis which follows:

165

Now if memory really occurs in this way, is what one remembers the present affection, or the original from which it arose? If the former, then we could not remember anything in its absence; if the latter, how can we, by perceiving the affection, remember the absent fact which we do not perceive? If there is in us something like an impression or picture, why should the perception of just this be memory of something else and not of itself? For when one exercises his memory this affection is what he considers and perceives. How, then, does he remember what is not present? This would imply that one can also see and hear what is not present. But surely in a sense this can and does occur. Just as the picture painted on the panel is at once a picture and a likeness, and though both are one and the same, their being is not the same, and we can look at the painting both as a picture and as a likeness, so too we must take the image within ourselves both as an object of contemplation in itself and as an image of something else. In so far as we consider it in itself, it is an object of contemplation or an image, but in so far as we consider it in relation to something else, e.g. as a likeness, it is also an aid to memory. Hence when the stimulus of it is operative, if the soul perceives the impression as independent, it appears to occur as a thought or image; but if it is considered in relation to something else, it is as though one contemplated a figure in a picture as a portrait, e.g. of Coriscus, although he has not just seen Coriscus. As in this case the affection caused by the contemplation differs from that which is caused when one contemplates the object merely as a painted picture, so in the soul the one object appears as a mere thought, but the other, being (as in the former case) a likeness, is an aid to memory. And for this reason sometimes we do not know, when such stimuli occur in our soul from an earlier perception, whether the phenomenon is due to perception, and we are in doubt whether it is memory or not. But sometimes it happens that we reflect and remember that we have heard or seen something before. Now this occurs whenever we first think of it as itself, and then change and think of it as referring to something else. The opposite also occurs, as happened to Antipheron of Oreus, and other lunatics; for they spoke of their mental pictures as if they had actually taken place, and as if they actually remembered them. This happens when one regards as a likeness what is not a likeness. Memorizing preserves the memory of something by constant reminding. This is nothing but the repeated contemplation of an object as a likeness, and not independently. (450 b 11–451 a 14)

How direct and lucid a statement this is of much that modern psychologists and philosophers, freed of the trammels of substance-accident metaphysics—of the knowledge of each kind of thing's being-what-it-is and of the inherent finality of each natural process—have had to labour and experiment and argue to discover and to state! If the schoolmen, by their use of 'insignificant speech', made obscure much that only modern science could make plain, Aristotelian thought, conversely, can also grasp simply and lucidly much that modern thinking can approach only by more devious and difficult paths.

Chapter 2 is concerned with recollection. Here even more than in the account of memory Aristotle's model of a determinate natural process, with its proper *terminus a quo* and its proper *terminus ad quem*, clearly facilitates and governs his analysis. No need, as with Plato, to invoke the separate Forms and immortality, let alone, as with Hume, to beat about the neighbouring fields in search of non-existent *a priori* or external compulsions, before we settle with comfortable resignation into the habitual acceptance of the habitual.

First, Aristotle tells us, we must accept the truths already stated, and proceed to distinguish recollection from our previous subject:

For recollection is neither the recovery nor the acquisition of memory; for when one first learns or receives a sense perception, one does not recover any memory (for none has gone before), nor does one acquire it for the first time; it is only at the moment when the state or affection has been induced that there is memory; so that memory is not induced at the same time as the original affection. Moreover, as soon as the affection is completely induced in the individual and ultimate sense organ, the affection—or knowledge, if one can call the state or affection knowledge (and there is nothing to prevent our remembering incidentally some objects of our knowledge)—is already present in the affected subject; but memory proper is not established until time has elapsed; for one remembers in the present what one saw or suffered in the past; one does not remember in the present what one experiences in the present. Moreover, it is evident that it is possible to remember things which are not recalled at the moment, but which one has perceived or suffered

167

all along. But when one recovers some previous knowledge or sensation or experience, the continuing state of which we described before as memory, then this process is recollection of one of the aforesaid objects. Yet the process of recollection implies memory, and is followed by memory. Nor is it true to say without qualification that recollection is the re-introduction of something which existed in us before; in one sense this is true, in another not; for it is possible for the same man to learn or discover the same thing twice. Hence recollection must differ from these acts; it must imply some originative principle beyond that from which we learn in the first instance. (451 a 20–b 10)

This is Aristotle's refutation of Plato's identification of learning with recollection, but also his inductive restriction of the field he is describing here as against neighbouring areas. Recollection is to be distinguished both from memory and from learning. But how is the distinction to be made? What singles out the field of recollection is the fact that it occurs only when there are movements (in the soul) *in series*:

Acts of recollection occur when one impulse naturally succeeds another: now if the sequence is necessary, it is plain that whoever experiences one impulse will also experience the next; but if the sequence is not necessary, but customary, the second experience will normally follow. But it happens that some impulses become habitual to us more readily from a single experience than others do from many; and so we remember some things that we have seen once better than others that we have seen many times. When we recollect, then, we re-experience one of our former impulses, until at last we experience that which customarily precedes the one which we require. This is why we follow the trail in order, starting in thought from the present, or some other concept, and from something similar or contrary to, or closely connected with, what we seek. This is how recollection takes place; for the impulses from these experiences are sometimes identical and sometimes simultaneous with those of what we seek, and sometimes form a part of them; so that the remaining portion which we experienced after that is relatively small. (451 b 11–22)

Both for natural and merely habitual sequences and for effortless as well as sought-for recollection this general method is the same:

This is the way in which men try to recollect, and the way in which they recollect, even if they do not try to: viz. when one impulse follows upon another. Generally speaking, it is when other impulses, such as we have mentioned, have first been aroused that the particular impulse follows. We need not inquire how we remember when the extremes of the series are far apart, but only when they are near together; for it is clear that the method is the same in both cases, I mean by following a chain of succession, without previous search or recollection. For custom makes the impulses follow one another in a certain order. Thus when a man wishes to recall anything, this will be his method; he will try to find a starting-point for an impulse which will lead to the one he seeks. This is why acts of recollection are achieved soonest and most successfully when they start from the beginning of a series; for just as the objects are related to each other in an order of succession, so are the impulses. Those subjects which possess an orderly arrangement, like mathematical problems, are the easiest to recollect; ill-arranged subjects are recovered with difficulty. (451 b 22–452 a 4)

We can see now how recollection and learning differ:

It is in this that the difference between recollecting and learning afresh lies, that in the former one will be able in some way to move on by his own effort to the term next after his starting-point. When he cannot do this himself, but only through another agency, he no longer remembers. (452 a 4–7)

Recollection, moreover, is not always spontaneous, but can be accomplished by an effort:

It often happens that one cannot recollect at the moment, but can do so by searching, and finds what he wants. This occurs by his initiating many impulses, until at last he initiates one such that it will lead to the object of his search. For remembering consists in the potential existence in the mind of the effective stimulus; and this, as has been said, in such a way that the subject is stimulated from himself, and from the stimuli which he contains within him. But one must secure a starting-point. This is why some people seem, in recollecting, to proceed from *loci*. The reason for this is that they pass rapidly from one step to the next; for instance from milk to white, from white to air, from air to damp; from which one remembers autumn, if this is the season that he is trying to recall. Generally speaking the middle point seems to be a good point to start from; for one will recollect when one comes to this point, if not before, or else one will not recollect from any other. For instance, suppose one were thinking of a series, which may be represented by the letters ABCDEFGH; if one does not recall what is wanted at A, yet one does at E; for from that point it is possible to travel in either direction, that is either toward D or toward F. If one does not want one of these, he will remember by passing on to F, if he wants G or H. If not, he passes on to D. Success is always achieved in this way. The reason why we sometimes recollect and sometimes do not, is that it is possible to travel from the same starting-point to more than one destination; for instance from C we may go direct to F or only to D. (452 a 7–26)

The place of custom relative to nature in this proceeding is again reminiscent of Hume:

If one is not moving along an old path, one's movement tends towards the more customary; for custom now takes the place of nature. Hence we remember quickly things which are often in our thoughts; for as in nature one thing follows another, so also in the actualization of these stimuli; and the frequency has the effect of nature. But since in purely natural phenomena some things occur contrary to nature, and owing to chance, so still more in matters of habit, nature is not similarly established; so that the mind is sometimes impelled not only in the required direction but also otherwise, especially when something diverts it from that direction, and turns it toward itself. This is why when we want to remember a name, we remember one rather like it, but fail to enunciate the one we want. (452 a 26–b 7)

'The frequency has the effect of nature': literally, the frequency produces or makes nature. Custom is second nature; but for Hume equally nature is only second custom: there is nothing but the conjunction of independently imaginable bits with the 'gentle force' mysteriously accruing to them. For Aristotle the existence of real natures, of processes with their internal rhythms, anchors the drift of custom, in itself less reliable than nature because not in the same full sense 'natural'.

Aristotle now returns to the awareness of time and considers its role in recollection, comparing the awareness of spaces with that of temporal distances:

But the most important point is to cognize the time, either exactly or indeterminately. Let it be granted that one possesses a faculty by which to distinguish greater and lesser time; it is natural to suppose that we can distinguish these as we distinguish magnitudes. For the mind does not think of large things at a distance by stretching out to them, as some think the vision operates (for the mind will think of them equally if they are not there), but one thinks of them by a proportionate mental impulse; for there are similar figures and movements in the mind. How then, when the mind thinks of bigger things, will its thinking of them differ from its thinking of smaller things? For all internal things are smaller, and as it were proportionate to those outside. Perhaps, just as we may suppose that there is something in man proportionate to the Forms (sc. of external objects), we may assume that there is something similarly proportionate to their distances. (452 b 7–17).

This temporal element is essential; but it is right co-operation of the movement relating to the fact and that relating to the time which in fact produces recollection:

Thus it is when the impulse relating to the fact and that relating to its time occur together that one actually remembers. If one thinks he experiences these impulses without doing so, he thinks that he remembers; for there is nothing to prevent a man from being deceived about it, and from supposing that he remembers when he does not. But when a man actually remembers he cannot suppose that he does not, and remember without being aware of it; for remembering, as we have seen, essentially involves awareness. But if the impulse relating to the fact takes place apart from that relating to the time, or vice versa, one does not remember. (452 b 23–29)

The temporal component may be precise or general:

The impulse relating to the time is of two kinds. Sometimes one remembers a fact without an exact estimate of time, such as that one did so and so the day before yesterday, and sometimes with an exact estimate; but it is still an act of memory, even if there is no exact estimate of time. Men are accustomed to say that they remember an

171

occurrence, but that they do not know when it occurred, when they do not know the length of the period exactly. (452 b 29–453 a 4)

Aristotle had started by distinguishing between those who retain images easily, often the slower-witted, and those who are quicker in recollection; he now returns to the distinction between memory and recollection and considers the relative range of their occurrence among animals as a whole. All animals with a time sense remember, but only men can *recall* their memories:

Recollecting differs from remembering not merely in the matter of time, that is, between the quick and the slow witted,

but also because, while many other animals share in memory, one may say that none of the known animals can recollect except man. This is because recollecting is, as it were, a kind of inference; for when a man is recollecting he infers that he has seen or heard or experienced something of the sort before, and the process is a kind of search. This power can only belong by nature to such animals as have the faculty of deliberation; for deliberation too is a kind of inference. (453 a 4–14)

Once more, as against the Platonic theory, recollection, though uniquely human, is discovered to be so by making the right cut among all animals to include all, and only, inference-making animals, that is, 'among the animals we know of', man. All living things grow and are nourished; of these some, namely, animals, perceive; of these again, some, namely time-perceiving animals, remember; of these once more, some, inference-making animals, recall. The series of inductions can be marked out clearly and unambiguously *within* nature, without recourse to unnecessary and unintelligible Forms. Within the orderly array of kinds of substances, each showing to the knower its being-what-it-is, the animal that recollects can be identified as the animal that deliberates: deliberation being one kind of inference, and for the purposes of this inductive argument, presumably the most conspicuous by which to identify the species we are seeking. For 'man', as Aristotle says in the *Ethics*, is 'a source of actions, and deliberation is

172

concerned with one's own actions, aimed at ends beyond the actions themselves'. (1112 b 31–33)

The nature of natures, as the *Physics* has defined this concept, holds this whole series of inductions firmly in its grasp. Hume's associationist psychology, on the other hand, like Aristotle's, is wholly 'natural'; but this very distinction between memory and recollection Hume's atomic, merely associative 'nature=custom' will not allow him to make. Recollection, Aristotle and common experience affirm, may be spontaneous, but it may also result from effort. It is, like deliberation, a kind of *seeking*, not just a routine habit, but something that may issue from an effort of will. And that for Hume is inconceivable. Aristotle's 'nature', however, assimilates with ease the facts both of learning and recall: the mind seeking to make actual a movement which it potentially contains is mirroring other natures in their orderly progression from what may be to what is. The acceptance of intrinsic finality elsewhere in the world makes it easy to accept its like in the sphere of mental processes. As for the developing embryo, so for the groping mind, the process, the becoming, is for the sake of its end point: the growth toward and for the adult organism, the effort toward and for the memory it is seeking to recall.

But minds for Aristotle are the operational principles of bodies, and he concludes with a reference to the somatic basis of recollection. This is in part tied to his inadequate 'hot-moist' physiology, but still vivid and precise in its account of the psychological factors:

That the experience is in some sense corporeal, and that recollection is the search for a mental image, is proved by the annoyance which some men show when in spite of great concentration they cannot remember, and which persists even when they have abandoned the attempt to recollect, especially in the case of the melancholic; for these are especially affected by mental pictures. The reason why the recollecting does not lie in their power is that, just as when men throw stones it no longer lies in their power to stop them, so the man who is employed in recollecting and search sets in motion a bodily part in which the affection resides. And most disturbed are

173

those who have moisture about the sensitive region; for the moisture, once set in motion, does not readily stop until the object sought comes round again, and the impulse follows a straight course. For this reason too outbursts of temper or fear, when they have once produced an impulse, do not cease even when the subjects of them set up counter movements, but continue their original activity in spite of these. This affection is like that which occurs in the case of names, tunes and sayings, when any of them has been very much on our lips; for even though we give up the habit and do not mean to yield to it, we find ourselves continually singing or saying the familiar sounds. (453 a 14–31)

Distinctions in memory also have their physical root:

Dwarfish people and those who have large upper extremities have poorer memories than their opposites, because they carry a great weight on their organ of perception, and their impulses cannot, from the first, keep their direction, but are scattered, and do not easily travel in a straight course in their recollecting. The very young and the very old have inferior memories because of the forces at work in them; for the latter are in a state of rapid decay, and the former in a state of rapid growth; small children, moreover, are dwarfish, until they are advanced in age. (453 a 31–b 7)

The reference to the heart as the organ of perception, and the extreme crudity of this as of many of Aristotle's physiological theories, remind us how mistaken were his beliefs about the actual working of our bodies. But at the same time his erroneous physiology sets off the more sharply the accuracy and precision of his psychological account: an account governed and held to its due course by the plainly determinate shape of this as of every natural process. Where such processes are exhibited, as wholes, as rhythms, on the face of our experience—whether in ontogeny, in ethological life-histories, or in the processes of perception and thought—Aristotle was justly esteemed 'master of those who know'.

VI

First Philosophy

1. *Being*

'Being' is the hardest word in philosophy. In fact, the easiest way to practise philosophy is to do without it. For often in the speculations of philosophers—for example, of those who have walked in the shadow of Hegel and the German idealists—outsiders may follow a reasonable argument, an argument concerned with meaty and meaningful problems about knowledge or conduct or nature, until suddenly there looms up what appears to be a gap, a nothing. 'Being', we are told, is what it was all about; but what this 'Being' is, no one seems able to say. Where there was pertinent reflection on our common problems, on the nature of moral standards, for example, or the meaning of 'explanation', or the relation of mind to body, suddenly there is vacuity. 'Being', but what is that? Better, many philosophers have thought, to abandon all this windy nonsense, to leave 'deeper meanings' to the poets and the mystics, and let the philosopher stick with common sense: with the language and concepts of ordinary, unmisguided men. The man on the bus chats of this and that, of test matches, space travel, holiday weather, the latest plane crash or bank robbery, but never of Being as such. Why should we, who can only reflect on other men's experience, claim to have access to some special realm of our own, with Being for its magic name? If there were such a place every one would know it; on the contrary, nobody knows it, not even the philosophers who talk as if they did.

One might think, in particular, that such a vague and

generalized term as 'Being' would have no place in the concrete, compartmentalizing thought of Aristotle. Every kind of thing, from bees and catfish through kings and magnanimous men to the celestial spheres and the intelligences that move them, all these and more interest him as subjects of investigation, each in the right way and the right place. But if, as we have said over and over and must say yet again, Aristotelian knowledge must always be directed to one subject-genus *inside* a wider genus, if each discipline must aim at just the right accuracy and start from just the right premises for its *particular* subject, why should we have to concern ourselves, in studying Aristotle, with such a tenuous, overall, unrestrained subject as Being itself? Even if Aristotle as a pious ex-Platonist still made a bow to metaphysics, could he, as Aristotle, have devoted himself seriously to a subject without limits, which seems to descend on us from nowhere and leave us wholly uninstructed?

With the first of these two protests I confess to feeling a certain sympathy. The path of Hegel or Schelling or the later Heidegger leads, I cannot help believing, but to the grave of meaningful argument. Nevertheless, there are problems traditionally belonging to metaphysics which even empirically minded philosophers find it hard to escape. Consider as one example a problem of peculiar importance for Aristotelian metaphysics: the problem of first principles. Every particular science rests on appropriate starting-points; but it must belong to some discipline or other to consider the source and nature of *all* these starting-points. Lacking Aristotle's unique self-evident principles, we may want to deny the need for such a discipline. On the contrary, however, the want of Aristotelian first principles makes reflection on the character of the presuppositions of the sciences even more urgent a problem. What justifies the presuppositions of physics or chemistry or biochemistry or genetics? How are they interrelated? Or is science just a patchwork of isolated bits of 'know-how'? How are the principles of one generation related to those of another which appear to supersede them? 'The unity of science,' 'the advance of science': these slogans demand explication and elucidation in critical reflection that is meta-scientific, or, in traditional language, metaphysical. Of the great body of traditional speculation this interdisciplinary problem, at least, survives.

Besides, there is a fringe to even the most anti-speculative philosophizing which, if it is not metaphysical, at least reflects a metaphysic. Everyone has *some* convictions about what is really real, some vision, broad or narrow, that confines and directs his reflections about more empirical matters. That every philosopher fails to sympathize with *some* ontologies, shows not that speculation is mere verbiage, but that minds and the world are full enough realities so that minds can comprehend the world and the world be understood in a variety of ways. *I* can interpret what there is only out of my own vision, not someone else's, and I may be missing what another sees; but some fundamental bent in the reading of experience each of us has, or learns, or develops. And this 'emphasis of attention' is in fact our concept of 'being'. It is not, and cannot be, a wholly (or almost wholly) explicit concept, like the concept of 'vertebrate' or 'natural number'. Hence, for example, the myths and other indirections in Plato's handling of it. Hence also, in modern philosophy, Kierkegaard's 'indirect communication'. But concepts that cannot be fully and easily articulated are not therefore nonsense.

As for Aristotle, it was being he had been schooled to seek under Plato's tutelage, first, in a common-sense enumeration of 'things', τὰ ὄντα, the things there are, the 'beings' that pre-Socratic philosophers had begun reflecting on, and then in the discipline of Platonic dialectic, in considering the purely intelligible 'beings', like 'one' and 'justice', that for Plato give such ephemeral existence as they have to the images flitting before us in this changing scene. Further, it was being that Aristotle himself had found in his own way. For his own method of separating and articulating each distinctive discipline depends wholly on the presence, the empirical self-evidence of being, the being that speaks to us in and from the things surrounding us. It depends, first, on the distinction between

177

being-a-substance, an entity (οὐσία) or concrete being, and being an accident of such a concrete being; and secondly, on the meticulous differentiation between separate classes of substantial beings or between separate aspects of one class of such beings. And this double procedure in turn rests, as Aristotle himself has told us, on the discovery of the being-what-it-is of each thing and the definition of substance which that discovery makes possible. Aristotle's conception of being, therefore, underlies the whole range of his empirical investigations.

More than that, too. There are, we have already noticed, three branches of Aristotelian philosophy, and of these the one that treats of being *qua* being is the one that Aristotle designates as *first* philosophy. This is *par excellence* the science of the causes, the science of form, the science most to be desired, the science the possession of which is wisdom. Whatever the delights of biologizing, of watching chicks develop or catfish guard their young, it is the contemplation of *being as such* that is the first and highest study, the worthiest end of human life. As between Plato and Aristotle, here is another paradox. Plato's philosopher, who climbs painfully aloft to gaze on the Sun and the Good, must return to the cave to rule among the shadows. Aristotle's wise man, though discovering being *in* the inspection of the sensible world itself, revels in contemplation of being-itself for its own sake alone. Seeing that there are higher things in the universe than man, he looks down, in his detachment, on all practical, human concerns as second best. But does this not present us with a paradox also in Aristotle himself? For if there are higher things in the world than man, surely the humble animals that so captivate the interest of the biologist are lower still. There may be gods in the kitchen; but there are temples elsewhere. Whatever our interest in those humbler entities and their life-stories, we must not give them more than their due place. In the order of things, as in the order of science, the first of things, the being that is most excellently being, and the first of studies, the wise man's contemplation of being, must hold secure first place. Many passages in the *Metaphysics*, indeed the whole tenor of

178

the argument, confirm this; we may take as one example the passage in Epsilon where Aristotle distinguishes between the three branches of theoretical science:

. . . physics deals with things which exist separately but are not immovable, and some parts of mathematics deal with things which are immovable but presumably do not exist separately, but as embodied in matter; while the first science deals with things which both exist separately and are immovable. Now all causes must be eternal but especially these; for they are the causes that operate on so much of the divine as appears to us. There must, then, be three theoretical philosophies, mathematics, physics, and what we may call theology, since it is obvious that if the divine is present anywhere, it is present in things of this sort. And the highest science must deal with the highest genus. Thus, while the theoretical sciences are more to be desired than the other sciences, this is more to be desired than the other theoretical sciences. For one might raise the question whether first philosophy is universal, or deals with one genus, i.e. some one kind of being . . . We answer that if there is no substance other than those which are formed by nature, natural science will be the first science; but if there is an immovable substance, the science of this must be prior and must be first philosophy, and universal in this way, because it is first. And it will belong to this to consider being *qua* being—both what it is and the attributes which belong to it *qua* being. (1026 a 13–32; Oxf.)[1]

Can this be the Aristotle of the *Introduction to Biology?* Is this not rather a more than Platonic Platonist, an over-zealous academician, not yet experienced in biological research? Are there after all two Aristotles, facing Janus-like in opposite directions: one a Platonist, a gazer upon being; the other a scientist, intent upon the first pulsing of the embryonic heart or the flight of bees to the hive?

To those who segregate 'metaphysics' and 'Platonism' from 'science' and 'empiricism', this would be comforting; but it would be false to Aristotle, to the Aristotle who speaks to us from the texts themselves, whether in the *Parts of Animals,*

[1] All quotations from the *Metaphysics* are from the Oxford translation. See Bibliographical Note, p. 253.

179

the *Organon*, the treatise *On Nature*, or the *Metaphysics* itself.
There is but one Aristotle, he who discovered the 'being-what-
it-is and the peculiar substance of each kind of thing', and this
discovery is as fundamental to first as it is to second philosophy
or to the methodology of all or any single discipline. Even
enmattered forms can be studied, can be known, in physics,
only *as* forms. It is the universal latent *in* the individual that
makes this frog this *frog*, this developing egg this *bird*, this
child in due course this *man*. Everywhere, form is superior to,
prior to, gives intelligibility to matter. But this is a world, a
uniquely ordered, delimited, intelligible world, in which each
form, each kind, has its place. If therefore there is a being
beyond other visible, tangible beings, if there is a pure form
existing in separateness from all matter, it will be the best of
beings and to study it will be the highest study. Yet both in
his method of approach to such a being and in his conception
of its nature and function in the universe Aristotle remains
constant to his consuming interest in the kinds of things there
are and the kinds of processes that make them just those kinds.
And this is still, as in the physical treatises, a biologizing
interest of the type I have been trying to sketch so far. The
logic is founded on the distinction between substance and
accident, the physical treatises deal with the kinds of change
that happen to substances, and the *Metaphysics* will come to
grips with the character of substance itself, as that which
primarily and *par excellence is*. The over-arching interest in the
character of concrete individual entities as members of natural
classes, persists throughout.

For the *Metaphysics* as for the *Physics* and the *Organon*
I can do no more than barely to indicate this persistent theme.
What I want to do is to underscore the connection with
Aristotle's biological interests that seems to me to emerge
once more from the reading of the *Metaphysics* itself as it has
from the other treatises. I shall try to do this by touching on
three facets of the work: first, the path from beings to the
primary instance of being; secondly, the study of sensible
substance, especially in Book Zeta; and thirdly, the dis-

tinction between the potential and the actual elaborated in Book Theta.[1]

2. The path to the primary instance of being

Logic treats of terms, propositions, arguments; yet the *Categories* opened with a classification of *things*, a classification which necessarily preceded the analysis of terms, their use and their conjunction in scientific discourse. This was the distinction between things as univocally, equivocally and derivatively named, a classification of things according to the different ways in which they are open to our discourse. Some things can be named in such a way that whenever they are spoken of the definition remains constant. Other things can be named with the same name, but a different definition, like the man and his picture. 'There's Dick,' we say, when we hear a knock at the door; or, 'There's Dick,' searching him out in the school photograph. Still other things, whether univocal or equivocal, are named derivatively, as, in Aristotle's example, grammarian from grammar. Science depends, we have seen further, on the possibility of *universal univocal predication*. The definition of a blooded animal, for example, must apply literally and constantly to all such animals and to such animals only, if we are to have knowledge, rather than merely opinion, about them. Definitions, the starting-points of science, must be literal and fixed for each distinctive subject-matter. Both Aristotle's method as set forth in the *Posterior Analytics* and its application

[1] It may be objected that I am selecting from a work of unique intricacy and massive scope just those parts which bear out my thesis. But a more substantial confirmation of it may be found, I believe, in Father Joseph Owens' brilliant and definitive exegesis of the *Metaphysics* (72). Owens refers only in an aside to the possible biological foundation of Aristotelian metaphysics; but his analysis of Aristotle's doctrine of being is entirely consonant with such a possibility. In fact my present essay seems to me to be in a sense an extension of his view of Aristotle to some other works. To this acknowledgment I should add another. I have found the argument of Zeta very much clarified by the reading of an essay on 'Substantial Form in Aristotle's Metaphysics Z' by Dr. Ellen Stone Haring (43). If I have misinterpreted either of these authors, however, the fault, needless to say, is mine.

in the physical treatises depend on the existence of univocal things, that is, things susceptible to knowledge through the correct use of univocal language. It is the things that are accessible to such treatment that can be known. And these are the things, as we have also noticed in considering the logic, which can be marked out as one class within a wider class.

Can we do this with being? Clearly not, for 'being' is not a genus. The highest science, Aristotle says in Chapter I of Book Epsilon, deals with the highest genus, but this is true only in a very special sense. Being is not a genus like birds or blooded animals; and there is no *summum genus*, since a *summum genus* could not be carved out from any genus wider than itself. If there is a 'genus', that is, a proper subject-matter studied by first philosophy, it must be a subject-matter isolated by some technique other than the univocal predication characteristic of other sciences. On the other hand, if there were no such subject-matter, second philosophy would be first, there would be no 'wisdom', no science of pure form, of the principles of all the other sciences. That there *is* such a science, however, Aristotle seems entirely confident.

What then, is the technique that replaces univocal predication when we come to study being itself? Since we cannot pin being down to one genus within a wider area, and so cannot define it literally, it will have to be a technique suitable to equivocal things: it is in fact the technique described by Aristotle as *equivocation by reference*. The 'things' in question are referentially equivocal, that is, they are different things named in reference to some one thing which uniquely bears the character named by the name, and our speech about them if true exhibits the same equivocal nature.

Book Kappa, which repeats the aporetic arguments of Beta, sometimes in simpler form, presents a lucid discussion of this method. In enumerating, in chapter 1, the difficulties that face the student of first philosophy, Aristotle has asked:

Does Wisdom investigate all substances or not? If not all, it is hard to say which; but if, being one, it investigates them all, it is

182

doubtful how the same science can embrace several subject-matters. (1059 a 26–29)

This difficulty is dealt with in chapter 3. It is the method of *equivocation by reference* that provides the way out. True, it would seem at first sight that the use of equivocation only intensifies the difficulty, since terms that were wholly equivocal could not form the basis for a common science; but referential equivocity is less drastic. So Aristotle argues:

> Since the science of the philosopher treats of being universally and not in respect of a part of it, and 'being' has many senses and is not used in one only, it follows that if the word is used equivocally and in virtue of nothing common to its various uses, being does not fall under one science (for the meanings of an equivocal term do not form one genus); *but if the word is used in virtue of something common, being will fall under one science.* (1060 b 31–36) [*My italics.*]

And it is this use *in virtue of something common* which in fact applies here. Aristotle explains what he means by the use of an analogy (the same analogy used also in the same connection in Book Gamma):

> The term seems to be used in the way we have mentioned (i.e. in virtue of something common), like 'medical' and 'healthy', or each of these also we use in many senses. Terms are used in this way by virtue of some kind of reference, in the one case to medical science, in the other to health, in others to something else, but in each case to one identical concept. For a discussion and a knife are called medical because the former proceeds from medical science and the latter is useful to it. And a thing is called healthy in the same way; one thing because it is indicative of health, another because it is productive of it. And the same is true in the other cases. (1060 b 36–1061 a 7)

Aristotle now shows how this applies in the case of being:

> Everything that is, then, is said to 'be' in this same way; each thing that is is said to 'be' because it is a modification of being *qua* being or a permanent or transient state or a movement of it, or something else of the sort. (1061 a 7–10)

'Being' is here used in the widest possible extension: to include all the 'things' there are, accidents as well as substances. Each

183

of them in some way, though not the same way, is said to be. Yet the different meanings are not wholly diverse, since they are all meanings of 'being' with respect to 'something single and common' that corresponds, for being, to medical science for things medical, or health for things healthy.

What is this something common, the single referent, *par excellence*, of being in all its meanings? What is the primary instance of being, by analogy with which all other 'beings' are so called, as healthy things are called so in reference to health? That is the inquiry to which the whole text of the *Metaphysics* is directed. It is an inquiry of great difficulty. Aristotle uses (if we follow Owens' interpretation) a series of texts, or school λόγοι, to guide his students through it step by step, often covering the same ground from a somewhat different perspective, but still advancing toward the single goal: the knowledge of being in its primary instance, and the relation of this primary instance to all the beings so called in reference to it.

This general conception of the text seems to me almost certainly the correct one, and I must stress it here once more before proceeding with the argument of Kappa 3. Books of philosophy sometimes look on the surface like formal arguments, pieces of logic which we could put into the form of axiom systems if we liked. But not all philosophical texts are meant to be read in this, or in any one spirit. Plato's dialogues are at most hints, not statements of doctrine. So, we are told, are the *Philosophical Investigations* of Wittgenstein. Descartes's *Meditations* are what their title indicates: not a formal axiom system, but a series of mental exercises which the student is meant to follow, i.e. himself to live through, to practise, in the same sequence, in order to arrive at the right starting-point of universal knowledge. Aristotle's treatises, we know, were in some sense instruments of *teaching*. They represent the courses given in the Lyceum on a series of subjects. And the method, in adherence to Aristotle's conception of scientific procedure, is tailor-made in each case to suit the subject. It is reality—each distinctive kind, or aspect of reality

—that dictates how we shall know it. Most branches of know-ledge, whether theoretical or practical, demand but a brief historical introduction, and a brief initial induction from the experience of 'all, the many, or the wisest'. We can then state our principles and begin demonstration—pausing always, as with the argument on the infinite or the void in the *Physics*, for example, to treat dialectically whatever opinions of other authorities need correction or refutation. But when it comes to wisdom, both the highest and the hardest discipline, the lesson to learn, and therefore the way of teaching it, will be more devious and more elaborate. Aristotle is always fond of 'making a fresh start' and taking up a problem from a slightly different angle. (Not for nothing was he so shrewd an observer of the ways of memory and recall!) But in the course on First Philosophy the fresh starts are multiplied exceedingly—whether because the lecturer had a series of useful essays at his, and his students' disposal, or because he conceived this as the best way of dealing with so abstruse a subject, I think it unlikely that any one can definitely say. Nor does it matter much. Whatever their origin, the λόγοι of the *Metaphysics* form a series of texts to be studied by Aristotle's hearers in the course of their training as philosophers: the crown of their training, for this is Wisdom, the crown of philosophy.

Nor are the λόγοι strung together like separate beads on a string. They overlap both with one another and each in its own sub-divisions, so that the organization proceeds on many levels at once. Take for example the central chapters of Zeta, with which we shall be concerned in the next section. Zeta and Eta deal with the first major meaning of being, being as sub-stance. The central chapters of Zeta (3–15) consider four candi-dates for the status of substance: substrate, being-what-it-is, universal and genus; the argument of these chapters is osten-sibly divided according to this outline. The chapter on sub-strate, however, concludes with the statement that we must now consider substrate as form. Yet it is the treatment of the second candidate, being-what-it-is, that follows; substrate seems to have been dropped. But in fact being-what-it-is *is* form as

185

expressed in definition; so Aristotle is really proceeding with substrate as form, as well as beginning to examine the next of the four candidates. Again, the universal is dealt with in 13–15; but 12, which concludes the treatment of definition and being-what-it-is, already deals with the universal as the object of definition. And 12 itself constitutes a relatively slight introduction of a theme to be studied in the discussion of Eta on the actuality of form, and again in the analysis of unity in Iota. The passage in Eta, moreover, will itself serve as prelude to the next meaning of being, potency and act, to be studied in Theta. The doubling of themes throughout is much too careful not to be intentional. It is reminiscent of the piling of subject on subject, the searching through the universe, of the Platonic dialogues, yet even the overlapping, even the overtones, have an Aristotelian precision. In short, this is Aristotelian dialectic. The groping Socratic seeker after wisdom, whose knowledge of his own ignorance is the highest knowledge, has become, at two removes, the master who executes with light precision an intricate pattern of formally designated steps toward a finale familiar to him and possible of attainment, once they have become experts in this initiatory dance, to his pupils too.

I have already sketched in my first chapter (when setting Owens' view of the text against Jaeger's), a general outline of the *Metaphysics* as a whole. For the better orientation of the reader, let me list again briefly the main blocks in the series of λόγοι. First there is Alpha, the introduction of the problem with reference to the attempts of Aristotle's predecessors. In other disciplines, this dialectical introduction suffices, but in the case of Wisdom a further dialectic is necessary to prepare the students for the major task. In fact, this further dialectic constitutes, as I have said, the balance of our text. Beta, the 'book of knots', enumerates a formidable list of obstacles which the student of first philosophy must overcome. Some, like the problem of the One or the Ideas, form part of the common heritage of Greek philosophy. Some, like the one considered in Kappa 3 (the unity of a science which seems to lack a unified subject-matter) are difficulties that will impede the progress of Aristotle's own students, trained in his scientific methodology, and in the scientific disciplines as he has taught them. The next book (Gamma) attacks one of these problems: the question of principles in the science of sciences, the science which examines the principles of other sciences, and so offends, apparently, against a major canon of Aristotelian methodology, that is, the segregation of starting-points, subject-matter by subject-matter. Next in this sequence Epsilon 1 both concludes the argument of Gamma and forms a transition to the central argument of Epsilon 2 to Iota. The latter refer back, however, not to Beta to Epsilon 1, but to Delta, the philosophical dictionary, which lists for reference by the student variant meanings of important philosophical terms, thus providing a useful base for the development of the technique of referential equivocation which is to be explicitly put into practice throughout the subsequent course. The basic concept, of course, is being, and of this there are four meanings: being as accidental, being as in the categories, being as actual and potential, being as the true. The first of these, e.g. as when a pale man is musical and we say 'the musical is pale', is no object of knowledge, and Aristotle dismisses it. These chance togethernesses need not concern the philosopher. Being as truth is secondary (since truth belongs properly to propositions, not to things), and it will be dealt with briefly at the end of the central analysis. The two major meanings for the purpose of the student are the second and third: being as in the categories, and being as act and potency. To treat of being as in the categories, however, is principally to treat of substance, and of first substance, the concrete entities that make up the world around us. For we are proceeding *to* first principles, and our proceeding as always must be empirical and inductive. Everything in the world around us, Aristotle's students know, is either a substance or some modification of a substance; but if a modification of a substance *is*, it is because the substance is, not the other way around. A science merely of attributes would not be a science at all because its object would *be* only in dependence on the entity in which it is or of which it is predicated. So it is substance we must study, beginning with the list of things that are usually called substances and trying to refine and correct the catalogue, always with an eye to the question, what is the primary instance of being—and that will be the primary instance of *substance*—of which we are in search. This is what Aristotle does, or what he guides his hearers to do, in Zeta and Eta. Parallel to the substance/accident distinction, however, and just as fundamental, is the difference between potential and actual. This meaning of being Aristotle treats in Theta, and finally being as truth is briefly examined at the close of this book. Book Iota treats unity, which (as we shall see presently in connection with Kappa 3) is in a sense conterminous with being. In this survey of being in its four fundamental senses Aristotle has laid the groundwork for the study of its primary instance: the unique instance of being in which substantial, independent existence and pure form, free of all matter, or pure actuality, free of all potency, are to be found. To the study of such being, the unmoved movers, he proceeds in Nu/Lambda. Mu considers and refutes once more other conceptions of separate, unmoving form, the Pythagorean and Platonic. (Both α, i.e. small alpha, and Kappa in different ways are parallel to this main structure.)

After this introduction, let us return to the text of Kappa 3. Despite the many meanings of its central term, we shall find the one subject-matter for the science of being, Aristotle has suggested, in a reference to something 'single and common', taking for all beings the role that health has for all things healthy or medical science for all things medical. If there is one science of being, moreover, whatever is contrary to, or contrary in, being will be studied by the same science, for a single science always studies contraries:

And since everything that is may be referred to something single and common, each of the contrarieties also may be referred to the first differences and contrarieties of being, whether the first differences of being are plurality and unity, or likeness and unlikeness, or some other differences. (1061 a 10–15)

We are reminded again of *Physics* I and the *underlying nature*. A concrete entity, a first substance, is peculiar in having no contrary, but assuming contrary qualities, positions, places, etc. while remaining the same concrete entity. If therefore each science studies one given class of substances, or a certain aspect of some such class, it will necessarily study not only the characteristic attributes of such substances (or some of these characteristic attributes), but the contraries (privations) of those attributes as well. True, Aristotle proceeds to explain, we must not, in moving to the contrary, deny the whole definition, but only part of it. For example,

if the just man is 'by virtue of some permanent disposition obedient to the laws', the unjust man will not in every case have the whole definition denied of him, but may be merely 'in some respect deficient in obedience to the laws', and in this respect the privation will attach to him; and similarly in all other cases. (1061 a 24–28)

We must still keep to the same basic subject-genus, or the precision, the scientific character, of our method will have slipped from us. So in the case of being, we may study likeness and unlikeness, plurality and singularity or the like, but non-being *as such* is not a subject of study at all.

The same reference to substance as subject, that is, as the subject of scientific predicates, accounts for Aristotle's next comment also, on the relation between being and unity. 'It makes no difference,' he continues,

whether that which is be referred to being or to unity. For even if they are not the same but different, at least they are convertible; for that which is one is also somehow being, and that which is being is one. (1061 a 15–18)

This remark is necessary, perhaps, because the concept of unity had appeared conspicuously in the speculation of Plato as well as of the generation of Parmenides. For Aristotle, however, the correlation of being and unity is a commonplace, not a problem. 'X is' and 'X is one' are somehow equivalent. If we ask: what does it mean for something to be? or: what does

189

it mean for something to be one? the answer will be the same both in content and extension. For whatever is is in some sense a unity, and every sense of being corresponds to a sense of unity. Every concrete thing is a this-such, a unit in a class of things like itself, a unit as distinct from members of other classes. 'Man, one man, existent man, all are one and the same.' (1003 b 26.) The naturalist's experience here sweeps aside the problem of traditional ontology. There need not be one Parmenidean being, nor even such a being divided into Platonic Forms, but there are beings, each of which is one because it is a unit, one member of a natural class, a whole of its kind.

That is not to say that the path of the Aristotelian first philosopher is easy. Quite the contrary. The object of his science does not lie ready to hand, like the subject-matter of embryology or ethics. He must seek it by an abstraction which Aristotle compares with the abstraction of the geometer:

As the mathematician investigates abstractions (for before beginning his investigation he strips off all the sensible qualities, e.g. weight and lightness, hardness and its contrary, and also heat and cold and the other sensible contrarieties, and leaves only the quantitative and continuous, sometimes in one, sometimes in two, sometimes in three dimensions, and the attributes of these *qua* quantitative and continuous, and does not consider them in any other respect, and examines the relative positions of some and the attributes of these, and the commensurabilities and incommensurabilities of others, and the ratios of others; but yet we posit one and the same science of all these things—geometry)—the same is true with regard to being. (1061 a 28–b 4)

This characteristic abstraction marks off the philosopher (i.e. the first philosopher, the man in pursuit of wisdom) not only from the mathematician (who abstracts from other characteristics of substance to concentrate on quantity, not on being), but from the physicist, dialectician and sophist as well:

For the attributes of this in so far as it is being, and the contrarieties in it *qua* being, it is the business of no other science than philosophy to investigate; for to physics one would assign the study of things

190

not *qua* being, but rather *qua* sharing in movement; while dialectic and sophistic deal with the attributes of things that are, not of things *qua* being, and not with being itself in so far as it is being; therefore it remains that it is the philosopher who studies the things we have named, in so far as they are being. (1061 b 4–11)

Thus physics deals with things *qua* moving, not *qua* being pure and simple. And note, again, that dialectic fails to achieve the status of scientific knowledge because it deals with attributes only, let loose from the beings to which they are attributed, that is, from substance. The demonstrative arguments of the scientific knower are tied to certain kinds: they predicate essential attributes of a carefully restricted subject-genus. The dialectician, however, deals in predications irrespective of this restrictive range; according to the classification of the *Topics*, he deals in ascriptions of definition, genus, property or accident, which he handles in question and answer *whatever the context of his argument.* He does not direct his inquiry to the substance of each kind of thing, the being-what-it-is which his 'predicables' characterize. Therefore his arguments, though formally valid, are rootless and unscientific. The Sophist in turn is a mere imitator of the dialectician; his arguments are tricks. This conception of being *qua* being, then, grounded in the technique of referential equivocation, marks off successfully the subject-matter of philosophy, the first of the sciences, from all others:

Since all that is said to 'be' in virtue of something single and common, though the term has many meanings, and contraries are in the same case (for they are referred to the first contrarieties and differences of being), and things of this sort can fall under one science, the difficulty we stated at the beginning appears to be solved—I mean the question how there can be a single science of things which are many and different in genus. (1061 b 11–17)

There is, then, one science of being *qua* being, even though being is not a genus; and the road to the knowledge of it must be the road to the 'something single and common' in view of which whatever is is said to be. A man, as a substance, is simply

191

a man; that is literally, as substance, what he is. But he *is*, he is a *being*, in view of a reference to something other than himself, in view of a reference to the primary instance of being, which is to him and to all other entities as medical science to all things medical: the source in reference to which they have their nature and their name.

We may take this little chapter as illustrative of the way in which Aristotle unties the 'knots' that impede his hearers' progress and in particular of his success in segregating the subject-matter of Wisdom and so indicating that there is a philosophy anterior to physics, which studies the being itself, or beings themselves, from which other disciplines set out. The careful technique of separating subject-matters which characterized Aristotle's biological method and the scientific method applied elsewhere in the light of his biological insight, has proved successful here too in this most abstruse of subject-matters.

There is a problem here, however, for which, it seems to me, our texts provide no definitive solution. If Wisdom is a science, its method must be not merely dialectical but demonstrative. Yet the whole of the *Metaphysics* as we have it consists of the dialectical and inductive part of first philosophy: the path to its first principle, that is, to the primary instance. For even though Aristotle arrives in Lambda at a treatment of pure separate form, that is, of the unmoved movers, he does not go further to treat the unmoved source of motion in relation to other beings, and show how it is and functions as the primary instance of being. He does not move from dialectic to demonstration and give us first philosophy itself, but only, through the devious route of a series of school exercises, the introduction to it, the road *to* first principles, which is not itself the science we seek. νοῦς, insight into the principles, we may or may not have at the end of the road; but the full structure of a demonstrative science of Wisdom we certainly have not.[1]

---

[1] It may indeed be objected that the other sciences are not demonstrative either: certainly they are not written, on the face of it, in syllogistic form. But at least we do, for instance, in the *Physics* or the *De Anima*, have the dialectical

Why has Aristotle not written down his science of first philosophy? The chapter in Kappa that we have been considering, and other passages as well, strongly suggest that he thought this science not merely dialectical, as our text is, but demonstrative. Where are those demonstrations? They may be, as Owens seems to think, arguments which it simply happened that Aristotle did not write down, or, one might surmise, which we do not happen to possess. But is it not also possible that they do not exist because they could not? Because the science of being *qua* being is non-existent and unattainable? Aristotelian science is always realist, always empirical, in the sense that the things themselves speak to the knower of the inherent forms, the ordering principles, the rhythms of life that make them the things they are. That natural things should strike him as having the sort of structure he found in them seems, in the light of the natural historian's or the embryologist's approach to living organisms, plausible enough. But could the principles of first philosophy, the relation between the unmoved movers and the moving movents moved by them, could the relation between the primary instance of being and the beings characterized in reference to it, be explicitly articulated in the fashion in which, to satisfy Aristotle's own canons, they would have to be? The question is at best an open one.

3. Sensible substance

The question that has been asked of old and now and always, and is always puzzling: what is being, is the same as the question, what is substance. (1028 b 2–4)

To students who have mastered the doctrine of the categories, this initial step along the road to the primary instance is easy, since they know that 'without first substances none of the other things could be'. If 'being' has many senses, however, so does

treatment of Book I followed by definitions, the starting-points of the science in question, then a treatment of the attributes to be predicated of the subject-matter. The *Metaphysics* does not have this kind of structure.

'first'. Books Zeta to Iota, and especially Zeta to Eta, the central argument of the central group of books of the *Metaphysics* examine the concrete entities described in the *Categories* as first substance with a view to seeking out a substance that is first in another sense: in the sense that it is the fitting subject-matter for first philosophy:

For it is for the sake of this that we are trying to determine the nature of perceptible substances as well, (1037 a 13–14)

although in a sense, Aristotle continues, it is physics that studies these, since even physics, or second philosophy, must deal, not only with the matter, but primarily with the form of sensible things. Thus the substances studied in the physical treatises, by the method laid down in the *Categories* and *Analytics*, are now to be subjected to fresh study for the sake of discovering that primary instance in virtue of which all beings are said to be. Aristotle is examining, as Owens points out, his own principles of procedure and his own doctrines in other disciplines, with a view to the treatment of the most fundamental question: what is being? He is asking his students to revise the ground already covered in order to advance to higher ground, to the highest of all, to the science which reflects on and criticizes the principles of the other sciences. And in this revision, which is at the same time an advance, it is Aristotle's great discovery, the being-what-it-is and the definition of substance that is being scrutinized: for the argument of Zeta moves between these two as between two poles. It examines sensible substances, showing that in them form is prior and superior to matter; this even the *Physics* had already demonstrated. But here form is in turn linked with the being-what-it-is, and this is what, indirectly, definition is said to exhibit. So the enmattered forms of the *Physics*—the natures of perceptible processes and structures in the living world—are expressly linked with the targets of definition as expounded in the *Analytics*: the being-what-it-is of each kind of thing. Zeta is thus an expansion and a deepening in an ontological direction of the remarks about biological method in the *Parts of Animals.* Through the reference to form, it binds together substance, definition, and being-what-it-is, in careful discrimination from the search for an underlying matter on the one hand or transcendent Forms on the other.

THE CHAPTERS OF BOOK ZETA

1. Introduction: substance versus other categories
2. Things thought to be substances
3. Substance as substrate
4–6. Substance as being-what-it-is: definition
7–9. Substance as being-what-it-is: generation
10–12. Substance as being-what-it-is: definition
13–15. Universal as substance?
16. Return to list of Chapter 2
17. 'New beginning' linking substance with cause

The opening chapter introduces substance, in distinction from the other categories, as our theme. (See outline.)

Chapter 2 gives us a list of things commonly or sometimes thought to be substances:

Substance is thought to belong most obviously to bodies; and so we say that not only animals and plants and their parts are substances, but also natural bodies such as fire and water and earth and everything of the sort, and all things that are either parts of these or composed of these (either of parts or of the whole bodies), e.g. the physical universe and its parts, stars and moon and sun. But whether these alone are substances, or there are also others, or only some of these, or others as well, or none of these but only some other things, are substances, must be considered. Some think the limits of body, i.e. surface, line, point, and unit, are substances, and more so than body or the solid.

Further, some do not think there is anything substantial besides sensible things, but others think there are eternal substances which are more in number and more real; e.g. Plato posited two kinds of substance—the Forms and the objects of mathematics—as well as a third kind, viz. the substance of sensible bodies. And Speusippus made still more kinds of substance, beginning with the One, and

195

assuming principles for each kind of substance, one for numbers, another for spatial magnitudes, and then another for the soul; and by going on in this way he multiplies the kinds of substance. And some say Forms and numbers have the same nature, and the other things come after them—lines and planes—until we come to the substance of the heavens and to sensible bodies. (1028 b 8–27)

The analysis of the succeeding chapters will enable Aristotle to return in chapter 16 to decide which of these things are in fact substances. Chapters 3 to 15 give us the means for making this decision. They are twofold. On the one hand, Aristotle asserts at the start of 3 that substance is ascribed, if not else-where also, at least to four kinds of things: 'the being-what-it-is, the universal, the genus and the substrate'. (1028 b 34–36.) On the other hand, a further pair of criteria are shortly to be applied to the last of these four candidates, substrate, which is considered first. These are the criteria of 'separability' and 'thisness', which all four candidates must be shown to possess. The central series of arguments in Zeta will then consider the four, being-what-it-is, universal, genus and substrate, as candidates for the status of substance, in the light of the two criteria, separability and thisness, and the checking of the original list in 16 will depend upon the results of this inquiry.

Let us see first how the characters of *separability* and *thisness* are introduced. 'Substrate', Aristotle argues in chapter 3, seems to mean 'underlying matter', but this interpretation will not do. Matter is the indeterminate, the not-yet-definite which is to become definite, or the no-longer-definite which has lost its determinacy: the seed or the cadaver, not the man. And as indeterminate it cannot exist without determinacy, without form. Matter is in itself nothing in particular, nothing existing 'separately' from the form *for* which it is material, the function of which it is the instrument. Therefore matter in itself, matter in abstraction, prime matter, is not substance, since what chiefly distinguishes substance is *separability* and *thisness*. Substance is, as the *Categories* have taught us, what is neither predicated of nor present in another: not predicated, therefore not general, but *this*; not present in, therefore not

196

dependent on, but independent, existing in itself, *separate*. To be separate and a this: these are the characters which all four candidates for substantial status must exhibit if they are to pass the test. (It is typical of Aristotelian dialectic that these two canons of substantiality are discovered in the course of the argument itself which will apply them. Inside the framework of the list of chapter 2 we have the four kinds of things to which, ultimately, we shall refer the items on the list; and when examining the first of the four, we establish, in turn, the criterion by which all four, and so in the last analysis, the listed items themselves are to be tested. The spiral of the student's progress is carefully maintained.)

Before we consider further how our four candidates fare, we may look once more at the four themselves. Why these four? Why not, for example, matter, form, compound and universals, or some such list? 'Substrate' must be considered, Owens points out, because it is the term for logical *subject* in the *Categories*. It is the subject of predicates that is a substance, and Aristotle must show that even as subject substance is form (or at any rate compound of form and matter) before it is matter. For the inquiry into being proceeds at every stage through analysing out the *form* in the thing, the order of letters in the syllable, the functioning of the bodily organs in the whole animal (that is, its 'soul'), as the principle that makes each substance substantial. It must be made plain that the 'subject' is not a material 'element', as many philosophers had believed, but a concrete entity, capable of bearing predicates or being modified by accidents in one sense, admittedly, because of its matter, or not without its matter, but more precisely and more profoundly because of its form. This is doubtless correct; but I believe there may also be a reference here to the *underlying nature* of *Physics* I, the nature which underlies the flow of contrary into contrary and holds it within intelligible bounds. Nature, Aristotle has shown in *Physics* II, belongs only to substances and pertains to their form primarily rather than (though always in reference to) their matter. But the 'underlying nature' of *Physics* I has been primarily associated with matter, or at

197

best with the compound matter-and-form. This seems to leave a disparity which the metaphysician reflecting on sensible substances must surely reckon with. Both logical subject and physical substances-as-substrate, therefore, are germane to this argument.

Substrate, then, must be included in the four. Secondly, if substances are subjects of predicates and the underlying ground of natural change, it is from the definition of their essences, from the insight into the being-what-it-is of each kind of thing, that our scientific demonstrations about them must take their start. And again, form will be the mediating concept to guide us from the substrate, which, as intelligible, as subject-matter of science, is primarily form, to the being-what-it-is, which *is* the form that our definitions formulate. Thus after the study of substrate in chapter 3 we have a preliminary statement about being-what-it-is from the point of view of logic (4–6), then, in 7–9, an analysis of generation with particular emphasis on the role of form, and this will enable us to return, in 10–12, to a more detailed account of the formulaic expression of essence in relation to substances and their parts. So we are confronting directly the two ontological pillars of our methodology: concrete entity and its being-what-it-is, substance and the definable essence of substance; considering at the same time how, in virtue of their forms, the changing things which we have principally studied in second philosophy are themselves, as beings, though necessarily in union with an appropriate matter, the expressions of essence. Thus Zeta treats first (in 3) substance as substrate, then, in 4 to 12, substance as being-what-it-is, in the former reflecting both on logic and on physics; in the treatment of essence dealing explicitly with the *Posterior Analytics* and definition, but embracing the subject-matter of the physical treatises on the way.

Both these two candidates for substantiality are individual. Substrate, especially as form or compound of form and material, is plainly individual; but so is being-what-it-is, for it is present as a this-such, both this and intelligible, in each individual thing. The essence of an animal, its soul, is what it is to be

198

that animal, not accidentally and idiosyncratically, as differentiated from others of its kind, but as an individual-member-of-its-species, as this *octopus*, this *man*. 'Universal' and 'genus', on the other hand, are non-individuals, and Aristotle's discussion of them amounts to a consideration of the question whether anything general can be a substance. This is, or seems to be, a single question, and on the face of it these two candidates are not treated separately in the later argument (13–15). At any rate, if there is a separation it is certainly a very obscure one. Yet the two are emphatically distinguished in the initial list. This is puzzling. Besides, why have we 'universal' and 'genus' instead of species and genus? In terms of the *Categories* we should expect first substance or the concrete entity (here represented by 'subject' or 'substrate'), then species, then genus to be considered, in that order, under the heading of the category substance with which, Aristotle has told us, we are here concerned. Perhaps the answer to this second question, at any rate, is not far to seek. The term for species is εἶδος, i.e. 'form', which here plays a different role, since it stands for the correlate of matter in a sensible (primarily a natural) thing. For it is the '*form*' of the primary instance of being that is the object of our inquiry. Thus 'genus' would be used here to designate 'second substance' in general, and 'universal' would mean predicates of all kinds, whether substantial or not, including the Platonic Forms like 'equal' and 'just' which Aristotle is especially concerned to attack. At the same time it seems that for the purpose of the present argument the two terms, universal and genus, can be treated together, since the argument amounts to a refutation of a theory of the substantial status of generals of any kind, whether narrower and specific or wider and generic in their range. The fact remains, however, that the two are formally separated in the initial listing, but that they are treated at least with less formal separation later on. For our very schematic exposition here, in any case, we may take them together as 'the universal', the non-individual, of whatever scope.

We have, then, in effect, three candidates for substantiality, substrate, being-what-it-is, universal, all well known from other disciplines to Aristotle's hearers. Let us see how the argument of Zeta deals with them. 'Substrate', as we have seen, means either matter, form or the compound of the two. Matter, however, taken on its own, i.e. prime matter, which is mere possibility, mere openness to form, fails to pass the test of 'thisness' and separate existence. It has, as Dr. Haring terms it, only 'receptive' but not 'factual' reality. The compound of form and matter, this man, this horse, is clearly a substance; but it is, as compound, posterior to its components, and it is therefore, Aristotle suggests, substrate as *form* which, though more difficult, must be treated first. Form is also, one would suppose, more important than the compound from his point of view as pedagogue, since it is the orientation of the whole investigation toward form—yet without leaving the full, factual reality of the natural world—that is to guide the student from enmattered things to the simply separate formal substance (if there be such) which, if anything, will *be par excellence*.

We are to deal, therefore, Aristotle concludes in chapter 3, with the subject as form; but we turn instead, in 4, to being-what-it-is. Yet that is to continue the same theme, since the essence of a thing is clearly its formal aspect, its form as embodied in its matter. Aristotle goes a long way round to prove this, however, building the formmatter distinction of the *Physics* into the subject–being-what-it-is foundation of the *Organon* and so achieving the solid metaphysical edifice of which in fact these two pairs of concepts are distinctive and essential parts. It is as if instead of the techniques of the syllogism in the *Prior Analytics* we now had the real ongoings of the natural world connecting the substances of the *Categories* with their definable essences in the second book of the *Posterior Analytics*. This is what 3 to 12 accomplish.

Chapters 4 and 5, as Dr. Haring points out, identify substance and essence (being-what-it-is) by a process of elimination: for definitions are of essences, and only, or primarily, substances are definable. Chapter 6 goes on to show that if there are self-subsistent things, such as Platonic Forms were supposed to be, they must be identical with their essences. This identity appears to hold good in some sense even for substances not dissociated from a material base, for instance, Socrates:

Clearly, then, each primary and self-subsistent thing is one and the same as its being-what-it-is. The sophistical objections to this position, and the question whether Socrates and to be Socrates are the same thing, are obviously answered by the same solution; for there is no difference either in the standpoint from which the question would be asked, or in that from which one could answer it successfully. (1032 a 4–10)

Self-subsistent things, in other words, are the same as their essences; in enmattered things this simple identity does not hold, and yet for these things too the question of the unity of essence and being will be answered by the same approach. The thing considered with respect to form will be brought into proximity and even identity with its being-what-it-is despite its incarnation.

This hint is elaborated in the analysis of generation in chapters 7 to 9, where generation, like the substrate of 3, is oriented to form in preparation for the more elaborate identification of form and being-what-it-is in the subsequent analysis of definition (10–12). As Dr. Haring states the purport of these chapters:

Despite the fact that form and matter both constitute an individual, and despite the fact that each gives something to the other—matter gives scope to form and form gives character to matter—Aristotle does not treat them as though they were on a par. Matter falls below the level of factuality and substantial form stands above it. If, as is probably the case, only living beings among perishables are genuine ousiai, this regard for substantial form is plausible. Matter provides only a base for the order and dynamism of nature. Living individuals are the natural world, in a way, but only if they are seen non-atomistically, as parts of a genetic continuity. The substantial forms corresponding to living species provide not only the determinacy of each individual but the continuity of the races; they are in this way supra-individual binders which go a long way toward accounting for the ongoing harmonious totality which is the natural world. The series —matter, individual, form—is a sequence in the direction of superior whatness; it is also a sequence in the direction of greater binding force. Matter is a diffusion determined within the individual; the living individual is a brief existent connected with others through form. (**43**, 24)

Form is therefore prior both to individuals and to matter:

A substantial form is a *per se* what. An individual has whatness from form. Prime matter stands at even a further remove from form. It is potential individuals. It can be compared to form in point of determinacy and intelligibility only because it can be raised, by form, above the threshold of intelligibility. Form stands opposed to matter not as one to many but—more extremely—as one to the potential of many. (**43**, 25)

But this prior form *is* the being-what-it-is:

Therefore it follows that in a sense health comes from health and house from house, that with matter from that without matter; for the medical art and the building art are the form of health and of the house, *and when I speak of substance without matter I mean the being-what-it-is.* (1032 b 11–14 [*My itals.*]; cf. 1033 b 5–10, 1034 a 30–32)

Having established the primacy of form even in generated things and suggested its identity with the being-what-it-is, Aristotle returns in 10–12 to the discussion of definition. This raises thorny questions, since on the one hand form as substance must be individual, but definition is of the universal; and the being-what-it-is which definitions formulate must be simple, while definitions are compound. Further, definitions of sensible substances must contain a reference to matter, though, being definitions of the form of the substance, they contain no matter. By the close of 11, Aristotle's analysis has guided the student through some at least of these perplexities, so that he has sorted out (1) the concrete substance with its matter, (2) the formula of the substance 'with reference to its primary substance', that is, to its form or its being-what-it-is, and (3) the kind of substance (if such there be) which contains no matter and so is identical with its own essence. And of course he has eliminated (4) the quasi-unity formed by the togetherness of accidents, which does not constitute a substance at all. Aristotle

can now summarize the discussion of being-what-it-is, referring back to 4 and 5 as well as 10 and 11:

What the being-what-it-is is and in what sense it is independent,
has been stated universally in a way which is true of every case. . . .
And we have stated that in the formula of the substance the material
parts will not be present (for they are not even parts of the substance
in that sense, but of the concrete substance; but of *this* there is in a
sense a formula, and in a sense there is not; for there is no formula
of it with its matter, for this is indefinite but there is a formula of
it with reference to its primary substance—e.g. in the case of man
the formula of the soul—for the substance is the indwelling form,
from which and the matter the so-called concrete substance is derived; e.g. concavity is a form of this sort, for from this and the nose
arise 'snub nose' and 'snubness'); but in the concrete substance, e.g.
a snub nose or Callias, the matter also will be present. And we have
stated that the being-what-it-is and the thing itself are in some cases
the same; i.e. in the case of primary substances, e.g. curvature and
the being of curvature, if this is primary. (By a 'primary' substance I
mean one which does not imply the presence of something in something else, i.e. in something that underlies it which acts as matter.)
But things which are of the nature of matter, or of wholes that include
matter, are not the same as their being-what-it-is, nor are accidental
unities like that of 'Socrates' and 'musical'; for these are the same
only by accident. (1037 a 21–b 7)[1]

What we have established so far, therefore, is that substrate
is correctly thought to be substance, but primarily with
reference to its form, and being-what-it-is is also substance,
because, again, the form of the thing—the *such* that this thing
is—is the being-what-it-is, and therefore the substance, which
our definitions aim to formulate. Definition, Aristotle will
remind us later (Eta 6), is not just a string of names, externally

[1] Notice that 'first substance' has a somewhat different definition here from its
definition in the *Categories*. The two do not contradict one another, however, but
reflect the different context of the inquiry. For both substance and primary
things are equivocal in fact and therefore in our way of speaking of them. 'First'
here is first in being, i.e. form over against compound: 'first' in the *Categories* is
first in the series of questions 'What is it?', that is, the individual, which is in fact
form-in-matter, and not ontologically as 'first' as the form *of* this matter.

joined together, like the *Iliad*; it is a formula directed to an *object*: and that object is substance as form, the being-what-it-is of the thing defined.

A special problem remains about definition, however, i.e. the question of the *unity* of the definiendum. For the definiens, of course, is verbally double: consisting of genus (as *animal*) plus differentia (as *two-legged walking*). Man is a two-legged-walking animal. Yet substance, form, being-what-it-is, must be one and apprehended as one. In Zeta 12 Aristotle makes a first approach to this question, 'considering especially the definitions which are made by division'. In such divisions, he points out, it is the last differentia that pins down the *one* form, the one species, we are defining:

the last differentia will be the substance of the thing and its definition. (1038 a 19–20)

This discussion reminds us that definition is of *species*, and that in talking of the essence it is the being-what-it-is of each *kind* that we have been referring to. Trained in Aristotelian method and in Aristotelian biology, the philosophers' hearers scarcely needed this reminder; but it raises the problem that troubles critics like Robin and that Aristotle himself well knew he must face. It is first substances, this man, this horse, concrete entities that exist independently (as *separate*) and as *individuals* (as a *this*) on which the reality of all else in the perceptible world depends. Yet knowledge, hanging as it does on the grasp of the right definitions as starting-points of demonstration, is of universals—of the reasons why this species—man, frog, horse—is as it is, not why Socrates, Jumbo, Dobbin is this singular unique individual rather than another of the same kind. The candidacy of the universal to be counted substance must now be pondered, not only in respectful opposition to the Platonic theory, but in the light, too, of the Aristotelian study of nature, which hinges on the careful recognition and discrimination of natural kinds. For we study, not singulars, but specimens, and it is their species that, in and through them, we come to know. How, as we asked at the very start of our inquiry, can knowledge be both real and universal, if only individuals, not generals, are fully real?

In Zeta 13–15 Aristotle sketches the outline of his solution to this problem by means of a critique of the Platonic Forms, and he develops his own position further in Eta. The negative side of the answer is emphatic and simple. Universals fail both the tests for substantiality. Generality and thisness are flatly contradictory; generality and separateness, as Aristotle argues, are equally incompatible. No one has ever met a universal existing as a separate, independent thing. In the order of being, universals simply are not substances at all. This puts us into a very perplexing situation indeed. Definition is of the universal. But the object of definition is the real substance, the being-what-it-is of the thing. This is substance and *not* universal. What is this real substance, which is expressed, universally, in definition, yet is, individually, as a this; which is *in* the thing, not apart like a Form, yet somehow fulfils the criterion of separability as well? It is the form in the thing, which is separate in formula (λόγῳ), though (for sensible substances) not separate simply. It is *specific* form, the form of man or frog or horse, but *in* the specimen, the individual man or frog or horse. The compound of form and matter, on the other hand, Socrates, Jumbo, Dobbin, is separate simply, not only in formula; and is of course an individual, a this. But the compound, being enmattered, is not wholly intelligible. The universal is superior to the individual in intelligibility; it is the direct object of definition, which the mind confronts. In being, however, it is inferior to the individual, and above all to the *form-in-the-individual*, because it is common to many individuals, and is only potentially, not actually, itself a concrete entity. Whatever *fully* is, is substance; whatever is substance is both individual and independent, a this and a separate: in short a τόδε τι, a this-such. A *this* which was not a *such* could not be separate; and a such which is not a this is not fully but only potentially real. As far as the perceived world goes, the naturalist's specimen, the individual of a type, the member of a class, is the prototype of the real.

205

The relation of the individual to the universal, as Aristotle understands it (with special reference to sense-perception), is well expressed in an article by Professor R. P. McKeon:

> . . . the individual things which exist are not strictly the objects of scientific knowledge, and the universals which are known do not exist apart. What is better known to us is perceived by sense, and the objects of sense are not in themselves particular or universal, but may be said in one context to be particulars, in another context to be universals, and in a third context to be universals in particulars. If it is a question of the stimulation or actualization of sense, actual sensation apprehends individuals, while knowledge apprehends universals which are in a manner of speaking in the soul . . . If it is a question of the form of what is perceived by sense, the object of sense is a kind of confused whole or 'universal', and analysis yields from it elements and principles as 'particulars' which constitute its parts, in much the same fashion as the meanings of words are established, by differentiating in definition properties involved in the meanings of unanalysed words. . . . If it is a question of content, the content of sense perception is universal, although the act of perception is of a particular, for what is perceived is man, not the man Callias, and induction yields from such rudimentary universals an explicit knowledge of true universals. (56, 30)

All non-individuals, species and genus alike, therefore, fall short of full substantial status. But we must make a distinction here. As we move from individual to general, *infima species*, the narrowest universal in the series, does have a unique place. It is the 'ultimate indivisible unit' expressed in definition. The situation is clarified in Book Iota in the discussion of unity and contrariety, and it may help us to cite it here. A thing's differentia consists in a contrariety within a genus: as e.g. horse and man are *different* kinds of *animal*. But a definition is a formula itself containing no contrariety. It states the 'what' of the most restricted universal, the species, which is just the kind it is and can be subdivided no further. Where there are further contrarieties, they are incidental only, making no difference in species, because they correspond to no contrariety in definition. For example, Aristotle points out, the contraries 'with feet' and 'with wings' make a difference in species, but 'paleness' and 'darkness' do not. (1058 a 35–36) Why is this?

Perhaps it is because the former are modifications peculiar to the genus, and the latter are less so. And since one element is definition, in other words one element in the thing is stateable essence, namely the form,

and the other is matter, contrarieties which are in the definition make a difference in species, but those which are in the thing taken as including its matter do not make one. And so paleness in a man, or darkness, does not make one, nor is there a difference in species between the pale man and the dark man, not even if each of them be denoted by one word. For man is here being considered on his material side, and matter does not create a difference; for it does not make individual men species of man, though the flesh and the bones of which this man and that man consist are other. The concrete thing is other, but not other in species, because in the definition there is no contrariety. This is the ultimate indivisible kind. (1058 a 36–b 10)

Thus we may alter a little our form-and-matter account of individual entities, and say that

Callias is definition plus matter; the pale man, then, is so also, because it is the individual Callias that is pale; man, then, is pale only incidentally. Neither do a brazen and a wooden circle, then, differ in species; and if a brazen triangle and a wooden circle differ in species, it is not because of the matter, but because there is a contrariety in the definition. (1058 b 10–15)

The distinction between first substances and their accidents is still fundamental; but the concrete thing *fits* its definition in a way different from the way it carries its accidents. It *is* its definition plus matter. The matter is the potential *for* the substance; the definition, the form, enmattered, *is* the substance. Yet in the definitions of physics matter is included; is not matter then itself essential to the differentiation of species?

But does the matter not make things other in species, when it is

207

other in a certain way, or is there a sense in which it does? For why is this horse other than this man in species, although their matter is included with their definitions? Doubtless because there is a contrariety in the *definition*. For while there is a contrariety also between pale man and dark horse, and it is a contrariety in species, it does not depend on the paleness of the one and the darkness of the other, since even if both had been pale, yet they would have been other in species. (1058 b 15–21)

In other words, it is the unity of the definition of this species, itself, as formula, containing no contrarieties, which marks the intelligible real. When, as Dr. Haring points out, we advance from this *infima species* to wider genera, we only go from the more precise to the vaguer generality; we advance neither in being nor in intelligibility. On the other hand, when we step from the species understood as such, as universal and common, to the individual bearer of specific form, we lose in direct intelligibility, to be sure, but we gain in direct confrontation with the fully real. To grasp, in the natural world, *both* reality and its intelligible character, we must apprehend the universal *in* the individual, the class in a member of it, the intelligible form *in* the sensible thing. If, on the other hand, there are fully real entities—individuals—existing without matter, they will be still better objects of knowledge, for the element of mere potency, of opacity to intellect, will be wanting. They will be pure, simply separate, individual forms, more wholly real than any sensible substance would ever be. If there are such substances, they are not Platonic Forms, which try to be self-existent and yet partaken of by countless individuals, and end by being mere verbiage; but they are the supreme objects of knowledge, toward the apprehension of which this whole argument is meant to move.

In Zeta 16, Aristotle returns to the list of chapter 2, and checks it off in the light of the analysis of the four (or three) candidates, substrate, being-what-it-is, and genus-universal. The 'elements' (fire, air, earth, water) and the parts of animals, not being full individuals, rank as only quasi-substances:

Evidently even of the things that are thought to be substances, most are only potencies—both the parts of animals (for none of them exists separately; and when they *are* separated, then too they exist, all of them, merely as matter) and earth and fire and air; for none of them is a unity, but as it were a mere heap, till they are worked up and some unity is made out of them. One might most readily suppose the parts of living things and the parts of the soul nearly related to them to turn out to be both, i.e., existent in complete reality as well as potency, because they have sources of movement in something in their joints; for which reason some animals live when divided. Yet all the parts must exist only potentially, when they are one and continuous by nature—not by force or by growing into one, for such a phenomenon is an abnormality. (1040 b 5–16)

Universals, of course, let alone general concepts like being and unity, are wholly excluded:

Since in general nothing that is common is substance; for substance does not belong to anything but to itself and to that which has it, of which it is the substance. Further, that which is one cannot be in many places at the same time, but that which is common is present in many places at the same time; so that clearly no universal exists apart from its individuals. (1040 b 23–27) . . . Clearly, then, no universal term is the name of a substance, and no substance is composed of substances. (1041 a 3–5)

The concluding chapter of Zeta, finally, makes a 'fresh start', considering substance as 'a principle and a cause', again with the aim of getting 'a clear view also of that substance which exists apart from sensible substances'. (1041 a 7–9) In this context once more and even more emphatically, it is *form* that is substance as 'principle and cause'. For every being is a unity, and every unity is made a unity, rather than a mere aggregate, by something other than its constituents, i.e. by its form:

Since that which is compounded out of something so that the whole is one, not like a heap but like a syllable. (1041 b 11–12)

But plainly . . . the syllable is not its elements, *ba* is not the same as *b* and *a*, nor is flesh fire and earth (for when these are separated the wholes, i.e. the flesh and the syllable, no longer exist, but the elements of the syllable exist, and so do fire and earth); the syllable,

209

then is something—not only its elements (the vowel and the consonant) but also something else, and the flesh is not only fire and earth or the hot and cold, but also something else. (1041 b 12–19)

And with this 'something else', the infinite regress argument shows us we must stop: for if in terms of analysis into components, we ask what the something is, we shall have to say:

if . . . that something must itself be either an element or composed of elements, (1) if it is an element the same argument will again apply; for flesh will consist of this and fire and earth and something still further, so that the process will go on to infinity. But (2) if it is a compound, clearly it will be a compound not of one but of more than one (or else that one will be the thing itself), so that again in this case we can use the same argument as in the case of flesh or of the syllable. (1041 b 19–25)

This 'other', then, this 'something else', is something, but not an element or compound of elements; in fact,

. . . it is the *cause* which makes *this* thing flesh and *that* a syllable. And similarly in all other cases. And this is the *substance* of each thing (for this is the primary cause of its being); and since, while some things are not substances, as many as are substances are formed in accordance with a nature of their own and by a process of nature, their substance would seem to be this kind of 'nature', which is not an element, but a principle. An *element*, on the other hand, is that into which a thing is divided and which is present in it as matter; e.g. *a* and *b* are the elements of the syllable. (1041 b 26–33)

Substances are natural entities, and the substance of them, the primary cause of their being, is their form.

At the start of our exposition of Zeta we noted that the inquiry into being is identified with the investigation of substance. The central strand of the argument of Zeta has been the analysis of substance as form. Finally we come now to the identification of form with cause. Is not this a very sweeping series of identities? Being = substance = form = cause. How can all these be alike? To say 'x is' is one thing; to say 'y is the cause of x' is surely another. But consider Aristotle's favourite example of substance: this horse or this man. What does it mean to say 'Callias *is*'? It means primarily: Callias is a substance, an individual—but an individual *man*. His material differences from Socrates—having a straighter nose and less disposition for philosophy, for instance—are accidental. What makes him what he is is first and foremost his specific form, the being-what-it-is peculiar to a *man* and to every man as man. This is his formal cause, the most essential why of his being; it is also, remember, the final cause, for the goal of his generation, that for the sake of which he was born, was again: this *man*, that which it is to be man. Even the efficient cause, the male parent, is, once more, identifiable with the form—another man, indeed, but still *man*, numerically distinct but in species one. Only the less intelligible, less significant material cause resists this overall identity. It is the *form in* the individual that is *causal, substantial* and *real*.

One final remark. Historians of pre-Socratic philosophy have lately fathered on Parmenides a confusion between an 'existential' and a 'predicative' 'is', which, they say, still troubled Plato, and which only Aristotle, with his invention of 'pure' logic, disentangled. But although Aristotle did indeed make such a distinction analytically, with his two questions 'whether it is' and 'what it is', he nevertheless held the two together firmly, both metaphysically and methodologically, in the conception of each thing's being-what-it-is, which is the ground at one and the same time of substance, of definition (i.e. of essential predication), and of form.[1]

4. *Potency and actuality*

When, in the first book of the *Physics*, he had singled out matter, form and privation as the principles of nature, Aristotle remarked:

This, then, is one way of formulating the solution of the problem. But there is also an alternative formula based on the distinction between existing as a potentiality and existing as an actuality. But this is developed more fully elsewhere. (191 b 27–9)

[1] See also Chapter VII, p. 249-51.

That fuller development occurs in *Metaphysics* Theta, and the distinction there expounded holds, for Aristotle, equal rank with the division of things into substances and their accidents, or of sensible substances into matter and form. For as substance is prior to its modifications, or the instance of specific form to the incidental modifications its matter may assume, so is what Aristotle calls 'actuality'—something like 'fulfilment'—to the potentiality for that fulfilment. And as the other 'things'—quantity, quality, place and so on—could not be except in reference to the being of substances, so the potential, the seed, the embryo, that which can be other, could not *be* except in reference to the full issue of its development: the flowering plant, the man, the fully and necessarily real. If, moreover, it is the connoisseur of species, the morphologist, who finds in substance as form the approach to the primary instance of being, so is it the connoisseur of organic development, the embryologist, who finds in the relation of the seed to the adult the clue to causality in the world as a whole. For as the issue of development, its τέλος, governs the course of ontogenesis, so in general, Aristotle believes, the real precedes and dominates the possible. 'Nature as generation is the path to nature as goal.' The goal *is*; the path, too, is, but secondarily, as the way to its goal. The end-point, the developed individual, is the *being* to which and from which the runner nature moves. And by analogy, even in eternal things, the fulfilled, ἐντελέχεια, being that is completed or self-contained, precedes and presides over the lesser being, the merely potential, which has its fulfilment not in itself but in another.

Both the foundation of this principle in the natural world and its extension to first philosophy are presented in the argument of Theta, and we are thus given another and more direct stepping-stone to separate substance: to the pure form which is purely actual, containing no matter and no potency, and which will be, when he confronts it, the subject-matter of the wise man's science of being *qua* being, because it is the being *par excellence*, act without passivity, God. The path from Plato's cave to the sun is troublesome. From the unfolding egg to the Unmoved Mover the way is gentler. No wrench, no conversion is needed, but only a careful extension to other areas of a principle self-evident in its own sphere.

Aristotle begins by referring once more to the meanings of being:

> We have treated of that which *is* primarily and to which all the other categories of being are referred—i.e. of substance. For it is in virtue of the concept of substance that the others also are said to be— quantity and quality and the like; for all will be found to involve the concept of substance, as we said in the first part of our work. And since 'being' is in one way divided into individual thing, quality, and quantity, and is in another way distinguished in respect of potency and complete reality, and of function, let us now add a discussion of potency and complete reality. (1045 b 27–35)

There were four principal meanings of 'being' listed in the 'philosophical dictionary'. Accidental being (as 'the pale is musical') has been dismissed as of no consequence for science. Being as truth and falsity, though not of primary interest, will be dealt with briefly in Theta 10. Substance, especially our natural starting-point in sensible substance, has been analysed in Zeta–Eta. Being as actual/potential remains for discussion here. The first five chapters deal with the potential, first, as Aristotle says, 'in the strictest sense, which is, however, not the most useful for our present subject'. (1045 b 35–1046 a 1). For, he continues,

> potency and actuality extend beyond the cases that involve a reference to motion. (1046 a 1–2)

This indicates, as does the discussion of potency in the next chapters, that the 'strictest sense' of potency and actuality refers to the things that *move*, i.e., in Aristotle's usage, things that change, whether in quality, quantity or place, or even (to judge from the context) generation, the becoming of the things themselves. In fact, in chapter 3, Aristotle says explicitly that

> the word 'actuality', which we connect with 'complete reality', has,

213

in the main, been extended from movements to other things; for actuality in the strict sense is thought to be identical with movement. (1047 a 30–32)

Thus it is first and foremost in the things that move that we distinguish possible from actual: the sleeping child awakes, the acorn grows to an oak, the stone is picked up and thrown; the water that is (because it *can* be) heated, steams, and so on.

But why is this strict sense 'not the most useful for our present purpose'? Because what we want to understand in first philosophy is the distinction between the pure actuality of necessary and eternal things and the balance of actuality and potentiality in all others. We want to extend our distinction first to substance and its matter in general rather than to motion alone; and then to eternal things in relation to other beings. This, Aristotle says,

is the reason of the inquiry in the course of which we have discussed these previous senses also. (1048 a 30)

For this purpose, again, we start with our common experience of sensible things, including our experience of ourselves. Thus among potencies, e.g., are the senses, or the ability to play the flute, or artistic power (1047 b 31f.), or the statue as contained in the wood (1048 a 32–33), or the power of animals, ourselves and others, to get what they want. (1048 a 12f.) From an account of these potencies we move to actuality, still in things subject to motion, and distinguish actuality as their contrary:

Actuality, then, is the existence of a thing not in the way which we express by 'potentially'; we say that potentially, for instance, a statue of Hermes is in the block of wood and the half-line is in the whole, because it might be separated out, and we call even the man who is not studying a man of science, if he is capable of studying; the thing that stands in contrast to each of these exists actually. Our meaning can be seen in the particular cases by induction, and we must not seek a definition of everything but be content to grasp the analogy, that it is as that which is building to that which is capable of building, and the waking to the sleeping, and that which is seeing to that which has its eyes shut but has sight, and that which has been shaped out of the matter to the matter, and that which has been wrought to the unwrought. Let actuality be defined by one member of this antithesis, and the potential by the other. (1048 a 30–b 6)

Gilson has commented on the resignation with which Aristotle declines to attempt a further explication of the nature of actuality: 'We must not seek a definition of everything'. Just this very key point in the ascent to the primary instance is left to be known by induction and analogy: *as* that which is building to that which is capable of building, and so on. We can say no more than this about it. Yet what could be more evident to the student of living things than the relation of the organ with its function to its exercise, the possession of limbs to walking, the possession of molars to grinding or incisors to tearing food, the development of a placenta to viviparity, and so on? In introducing his present subject Aristotle has said, 'We may consider being also according to potency and complete reality, and to function (ἔργον)', and it is the functional study of living things that will have formed, for his students, the broad inductive basis from which to proceed in their training as philosophers. They are already biologists; by applying biological distinctions, with a difference, to being as such, they may become Wise.

The difference is significant, for 'all things are not said in the *same sense* to exist actually, but only by analogy—as A is in B or to B, C is in D or to D'. (1048 b 6–8) In the list of instances quoted above, the relation of 'that which has been shaped out of the matter to the matter' is a crucial one: for some things 'are *as movement to potency, and the others as substance to some sort of matter*'. (1048 b 7–8) After clearing out of the way still a third kind of potency, the infinite, void, etc., which have no corresponding actuality, Aristotle proceeds to elaborate this distinction in terms of a differentiation between two kinds of *action*. First:

Since of the actions which have a limit none is an end but all are relative to the end, e.g. the removing of fat, or fat-removal, and the

215

bodily parts themselves when one is making them thin, are in movement in this way (i.e. without being already that at which the movement aims), this is not an action or at least not a complete one (for it is not an end). (1048 b 18–22)

These are what Aristotle will from now on call *movements*, whereas he will reserve *'actuality'* for complete actions, in which the end is present:

but that movement in which the end is present is an action. E.g. at the same time we are seeing and have seen, are understanding and have understood, are thinking and have thought (while it is not true that at the same time we are learning and have learnt, or are being cured and have been cured). At the same time we are living well and have lived well, and are happy and have been happy. If not, the process would have had sometime to cease, as the process of making thin ceases; we are living and have lived. Of these processes, then, we must call the one set movements, and the other actualities. For every movement is incomplete—making thin, learning, walking, building; these are movements, and incomplete at that. For it is not true that at the same time a thing is walking and has walked, or is building and has built, or is coming to be and has come to be, or is being moved and has been moved, but what is being moved is different from what has moved. But it is the same thing that at the same time has seen and is seeing, or is thinking and has thought. The latter sort of process, then, I call an actuality, and the former a movement. (1048 b 22–36)

We have now separated out the *whole* of movement (originally conceived as the locus of potency *and* actuality) from actuality itself, a title now reserved for situations in which the end itself is present: for, literally, 'entelechy', things or actions or events that have their goal within themselves—for achievements, we might say. Thus to slim is not an achievement, but only to *have* slimmed, whereas to see is already to have achieved seeing, to know to have achieved knowing, and so on. In this manner actuality is brought close to end, that for the sake of which: and that means, in their functional aspect, to substance and form. And substance and form, as we shall see presently,

216

are thus brought close to actuality, to the kind of ongoing that is its own fulfilment.

An Aristotelian substance is a common-sense *thing*, this man, this horse, but a thing ongoing, most truly itself in its achievements, of well-being, of sensation, of thought. All substances, being natural, move, and have their source of movement in themselves; but they are pre-eminently themselves in those processes which are their own justification, which contain in themselves their own ends. To move is characteristic of the living; in common Greek usage as Plato had adopted it, this was ground for the definition of soul, the principle of life, as 'that which moves itself'. But all movement is toward a goal, and the goal must be intrinsically worth attaining. This in turn, self-enjoyment, well-being, the intrinsic self-satisfaction of living, sensing, and, in man, of knowing, is the primary characteristic against which we must see movement itself if we are to understand it. John Dewey explains that a man builds a house for the pleasure of the activity of building, not to live in it—for he might die before the roof is on. In Aristotle's terms (and in fact, it seems to me), this is nonsense. All skilful employments do indeed, in so far as they are skills, carry an aspect of intrinsic value, of self-enjoyment; they are all achievements. But first and foremost they are instrumental; and instruments are just those things and actions which are *not* self-justifying. We do build houses *to live in*; if we are happy settled into a comfortable shelter that is our very own, then *that* is self-justifying. We both are happy and have been happy; we both live and have lived; this, not the means to it, is the sheer activity.

I have laboured this distinction partly because, in the form in which Aristotle makes it, it seems a point alien to our way of thinking; partly also because, to me at least, the most difficult step in Aristotle's argument for God as an unmoved mover is the equation of pure form, of God, with sheer *activity*. And this is the passage in which Aristotle most clearly tries to take his hearers' minds along the road to this equation. Even in sensible things, in enmattered substances, we distinguish between movement, which is instrumental, and another kind of ongoing which is self-sufficient, an end in itself, yet an active end, not death, which is less than potency, but sheer living, which is much more. And the highest, and therefore most *actual* form of living, is thinking; and the highest form of thinking is thought *without* matter, thought self-contained, directed only to itself. Whether we can follow this last step, remains to be seen, but Aristotle has laid the foundation for us—or for his students, who had other qualifications which we lack, and lacked disabilities which we have—in Theta 6.

This chapter, moreover, laying the ground for the equation of actuality and activity, has also introduced the link between actuality and substance as form. For matter is potency, the indeterminate ground of what can be—and actuality is the determinate, the achieved, the form that is the end of development, and this, even in enmattered things, is their substance, *what* as beings they primarily are. The link between actuality and substance is forged firmer in the next chapter (7), in which Aristotle once more considers potency, the contrary of actuality, and identifies it in effect with proximate matter, the contrary, for an individual sensible thing, of its form. Thus for man, the potency is not earth (too far removed from his actuality) but the seed: that is, earth already transformed in the semen and planted in the womb where it can grow. Or of the casket, the potency again is not earth, but wood: earth so informed as to be directly, 'proximately' matter for caskets or tables or statues or what the carpenter wills. Thus potency is identified with matter, and conversely, we should suppose, form, or substance as form, with actuality.

That this is so is hammered home in chapter 8, the most important text for our purpose: for here Aristotle argues (dialectically, of course) for his fundamental thesis—fundamental in all his thinking—that actuality is prior to potency, that every potency presupposes a full reality *from* which it takes its origin. The character of Aristotle's finite universe, the absolute primacy for him of finite structure, of eternal pattern, in things, is nowhere more apparent than in his use of, and here, his argument for, this principle. As he applies it elsewhere it often seems—especially to those who live a century after 1859—arbitrary and absurd; but here, in Theta 8, Aristotle shows us why for him, and as he hoped for his hearers, it was reasonable, borne out by experience in every field whether of theoretical inquiry or of practical concern.

The thesis to be confirmed is laid down at the opening of the chapter:

From the discussion of the various senses of 'prior', it is clear that actuality is prior to potency. And I mean by potency not only that definite kind which is said to be a principle of change in another thing or in the thing itself regarded as other, but in general every principle of movement or of rest. For nature also is in the same genus as potency; for it is a principle of movement—not, however, in something else but in the thing itself *qua* itself. To all such potency, then, actuality is prior both in formula and in substantiality; and in time it is prior in one sense, and in another not. (1049 b 4–12)

First, it is prior in formula (λόγῳ), that is, in the expositions of science, as elaborated in the *Organon*, where, in the finished statement, first things stand first. From this point of view it is clear that the scientific knowledge of the actuality must precede that of its corresponding potency. Only an experienced musician, e.g., knows a likely pupil when he meets him; it takes experienced doctors to make an effective selection of medical students, and so on. Aristotle puts this point as follows:

(1) Clearly it is prior in formula; for that which is in the primary sense potential is potential because it is possible for it to become active; e.g. I mean by 'capable of building' that which can build, and by 'capable of seeing' that which can see, and by 'visible' that which can be seen. And the same account applies to all other cases, so that the formula and the knowledge of the one must precede the knowledge of the other. (1049 b 12–17)

Secondly, the actual is also, in one sense, prior in time:

(2) In time it is prior in this sense: the actual which is identical in

species though not in number with a potentially existing thing is prior to it. I mean that to this particular man who now exists actually and to the corn and to the seeing subject, the matter and the seed and that which is capable of seeing, which are potentially a man and corn and seeing, but not yet actually so, are prior in time; but prior in time to these are other actually existing things, from which they were produced. For from the potentially existing the actually existing is always produced by an actually existing thing, e.g. man from man; musician by musician; there is always a first mover, and the mover already exists actually. We have said in our account of substance that everything that is produced is produced from something and by something, and that the same in species as it. (1049 b 17–29)

Here we have once more the unending cycle of generation. *Omne vivum ex ovo*: all things living spring from an egg—and every egg (for Aristotle, every seed) comes from an adult of the same species as the offspring into which in due course it will mature. Though not the same actual individual, yet an actual individual of the same εἶδος, species = form, must precede development, even in time.

The same temporal priority holds for learning also; for as Aristotle has said elsewhere, all knowledge springs from some pre-existent, though partial knowledge:

This is why it is thought impossible to be a builder if one has built nothing or a harper if one has never played the harp; for he who learns to play the harp learns to play it by playing it, and all other learners do similarly. And thence arose the sophistical quibble, that one who does not possess a science will be doing that which is the object of the science; for he who is learning it does not possess it. But since, of that which is coming to be, some part must have come to be, and, of that which, in general, is changing, some part must have changed (this is shown in the treatise on movement), he who is learning must, it would seem, possess some part of the science. But *here* too, then, it is clear that actuality is in this sense also, viz. in order of generation and of time, prior to potency. (1049 b 29–1050 a 2)

These reflections once more draw together the knowledge of nature, the skills of the craftsman, the disciplined method of the demonstrative scientist, into the purview of first philosophy. With this broad foundation in mind, the student is ready to focus his attention on the third and most basic point. Actuality is prior, also, in substantiality, in οὐσία, and this for two reasons, reasons which bring us ever closer to the insight into the primary instance that is the goal of our quest. First:

(3) It is also prior in substantiality; firstly, (a) because the things that are posterior in becoming are prior in form and in substantiality (e.g. man is prior to boy and human being to seed; for the one already has its form, and the other has not), and because everything that comes to be moves towards a principle, i.e. an end (for that for the sake of which a thing is, is its principle, and the becoming is for the sake of the end), and the actuality is the end, and it is for the sake of this that the potency is acquired. For animals do not see in order that they may have sight, but they have sight that they may see. And similarly men have the art of building that they may build, and theoretical science that they may theorize; but they do not theorize that they may have theoretical science, except those who are learning by practice; . . . Further, matter exists in a potential state, just because it may come to its form; and when it exists *actually*, then it is in its form. And the same holds good in all cases, even those in which the end is a movement. And so, as teachers think they have achieved their end when they have exhibited the pupil at work, nature does likewise. For if this is not the case, we shall have Pauson's Hermes over again, since it will be hard to say about the knowledge, as about the figure in the picture, whether it is within or without. For the action is the end, and the actuality is the action. And so even the *word* 'actuality' is derived from 'action', and points to the complete reality. (1050 a 4–23.)

Here again we have, drawn from our experience of animals and men, the primacy of the form over the matter, the end of the process over the process itself. Matter is posterior in being to form, potency to the actuality that eventuates from it, whether that actuality be, as in useful arts, an object beyond the practice of the art, or as in some skills the exercise of the art itself. Of course, these two cases, as I have already pointed out, must be duly distinguished; but in the present context it becomes evident that even the instrumental activity is superior to the mere possibility of its exercise. The builder builds a house so that a man may live in it; but he has acquired the art of building so that he may build:

And while in some cases the exercise is the ultimate thing (e.g. in sight the ultimate thing is seeing, and no other product besides this results from sight), but from some things a product follows (e.g. from the art of building there results a house as well as the act of building), yet none the less the act is in the former case the end and in the latter more of an end than the potency is. For the act of building is realized in the thing that is being built, and comes to be, and is, at the same time as the house.

Where, then, the result is something apart from the exercise, the actuality is in the thing that is being made, e.g. the act of building is in the thing that is being built and that of weaving in the thing that is being woven, and similarly in all other cases, and in general the movement is in the thing that is being moved; but where there is no product apart from the actuality, the actuality is present in the agents, e.g. the act of seeing is in the seeing subject and that of theorizing in the theorizing subject and the life is in the soul (and therefore well-being also; for it is a certain kind of life). (1050 a 23–b 2)

Here again also we have the argument moving toward the affirmation of a certain form of awareness, a certain form of life, as the paradigm of actuality, and therefore of being itself. For the issue of the whole chapter so far is the equation of substance = form with actuality:

Obviously, therefore, the substance or form is actuality. According to this argument, then, it is obvious that actuality is prior in substantial being to potency; and as we have said, one actuality always precedes another in time right back to the actuality of the eternal prime mover. (1050 b 3–6)

The reference to the first mover leads us on to the second and stricter sense in which actuality is prior to potency; we are coming, indeed, within sight of our goal:

. . . (b) actuality is prior in a stricter sense also; for eternal things are prior in substance to perishable things, and no eternal thing exists potentially. The reason is this. Every potency is at one and the same time a potency of the opposite; for, while that which is not capable of being present in a subject cannot be present, everything that is capable of being may possibly not be actual. That, then, which is capable of being may either be or not be; the same thing, then, is capable both of being and of not being. And that which is capable of not being may possibly not be; and that which may possibly not be is perishable, either in the full sense, or in the precise sense in which it is said that it possibly may not be, i.e. in respect either of place or of quantity or quality; 'in the full sense' means 'in respect of substance'. Nothing then, which is in the full sense imperishable is in the full sense potentially existent (though there is nothing to prevent its being so in some respect, e.g. potentially of a certain quality or in a certain place); all imperishable things, then, exist actually. (1050 b 6–18)

The imperishable, then, is purely actual; so is the necessary:

Nor can anything which is of *necessity* exist potentially; yet these things are primary; for if these did not exist, nothing would exist. (1050 b 18–19)

This is the simply necessary in the prior sense—not the materially necessary of biology, which is necessary only in a third degree: since, depending merely on material conditions, it must be inferior in being even to the hypothetically necessary which, though occurring only in changing, and therefore partly potential things, is nevertheless anchored to that-for-the-sake-of-which, and so to form and substance. But the purest and simplest necessities, that is, again, the eternal things, are simply actual. Moreover, the necessary things, in this sense, are 'first': 'if these did not exist,' Aristotle says, 'nothing would exist.' For the non-necessary may be or not be; and what may or may not be depends always, as we have already seen, on what *is*: the process on its principle, the accident on its subject, the possible or probable on the fully real. So for the world as a whole too: necessity must precede possibility. And thus if necessary things, which are prior, are actual, we must acknowledge once more the priority of act to potency.

Moreover, the same relation of priority holds between eternal motion and the change of perishable things:

> Nor does eternal movement, if there be such, exist potentially; and, if there is an eternal *mobile*, it is not in motion in virtue of a potentiality, except in respect of 'whence' and 'whither' (there is nothing to prevent its having matter which makes it capable of movement in various directions). And so the sun and the stars and the whole heaven are ever active, and there is no fear that they may sometime stand still, as the natural philosophers fear they may. Nor do they tire in this activity; for movement is not for them, as it is for perishable things, connected with the potentiality for opposites, so that the continuity of the movement should be laborious; for it is that kind of substance which is matter and potency, not actuality, that causes this. (1050 b 20–28)

This descending scale, once begun, continues to the corruptible world; even here, the actual takes ontological precedence. So, as Aristotle also stressed in the treatise *On Generation and Corruption*:

> Imperishable things are imitated by those that are involved in change, e.g. earth and fire. (1050 b 28–9)

The imitation, here, however, consists not (as there) in the circularity of their mutual transformation, but in their constant activity:

> For these also are ever active; for they have their movement of themselves, and in themselves. (1050 b 29–30)

Thus the elements, which are only quasi-substances in one sense, are substantial in so far as they are always *actually* what they are, and produce the changes they produce. Other powers, already discussed both in 8 and in the earlier chapters of Theta, are less constant in their effects, and so come, in this perspective, lower down the scale. Arts, e.g. medicine, may produce their right effect or its contrary, health or disease; so with all change governed by a rational formula. Non-rational powers too move to contraries simply by their presence or absence: as, for instance, hunger causes the animal to seek food: satiety makes it stop. As Aristotle puts it:

> But the other potencies, according to our previous discussion, are all potencies for opposites; for that which can move another in this way can also move it not in this way, i.e. if it acts according to a rational formula; and the same *non-rational* potencies will produce opposite results by their presence or absence. (1050 b 30–36)

This is the bottom of the scale; throughout, it is now plain, 'actuality is prior both to potency and to every principle of change'. (1051 a 2–3)

The difficult chapter which follows, and which concludes the discussion of being as actual and potential, seems to add two points. First, where potency may be for good or ill, 'actuality is better and more to be honoured than the good potency' (1051 a 4–5) and correspondingly in bad things the actuality is worse. In eternal things, however, where there is no potency, and so no possible defect,

> there is nothing bad, nothing defective, nothing perverted (for perversion is something bad). (1051 a 20–21)

Secondly, even in the 'eternal things' of mathematics, though but abstractions, the potency, the possibility, of proof depends on the activity of construction and hence on an actuality. Here as elsewhere actuality shows its primacy.

This completes Aristotle's analysis of being as act and potency. Chapter 10 disposes of the fourth meaning, being as truth. In Iota he is still concerned with material substances, with reference to the concepts of unity and contrariety. Not till Lambda does he move to demonstrate directly the existence of separate substance, the unmoved movers of all things, celestial and sublunar. I shall not attempt to deal here with Aristotle's proofs, in Lambda, of the existence of his primary instance; once the dependence of all changing things on a prior actuality has been established, the course of the argument is plain. There is, of course, the question, which I referred to in my first chapter, whether the unmoved mover is one or many. This, I believe, Owens has solved very plausibly, by showing that there may be many but in series: one, and others ordered in relation to the first.[1] There is also the question, which I have already mentioned, why Aristotle never makes explicit *how* pure actuality or separate substance serves as primary instance of being. Even Lambda is still dialectical: the last stage on the road to the first principles of Wisdom, not the science itself. Yet, in the series of λόγοι which constitute the text of the *Metaphysics*, the ground for the student's approach to Wisdom has been firmly laid.

[1] See also Professor H. A. Wolfson's article in the Jaeger *Festschrift* (116).

VII

The Relevance of Aristotle

1. *The biological theme*

My portrait is finished—a few rough strokes by an amateur where professional Aristotelians, and philosophical geniuses among them, have spent lifetimes. Reflecting on this partial and hasty sketch, I wonder, finally, what lessons its subject, seen in this one rather special perspective, has for a twentieth-century student of philosophy. Every great thinker speaks with a different voice to every age. Even the thirteenth century, applying its industry and energy to the interpretation of the Latin Aristotle, had to refashion the philosopher for itself. As Owens says, 'Aristotle, like every catechumen, had to be instructed.' I shall not attempt so formidable a task. But I may suggest, in conclusion, a few places where we find the Aristotelian cosmology and method alien to us, some where we cannot help rejecting Aristotle's view, others where the difference may teach us to clarify and enrich our own vision. Most of these points I have already touched on in one context or another, but it may help to bring our picture better into focus if we enumerate them more explicitly now.

Let me begin with the model of science, and with an aspect of it which lies close to what has been in effect our central theme: the relevance of biological thinking for philosophy. True, Aristotelian biology itself is founded on the conception of the being-what-it-is of fixed kinds of things in an eternally existing universe, a conception which our acceptance of evolutionary principles compels us to reject. Yet the very fact that *living* nature is made the focal point of philosophical reflection may be instructive. The authoritative position of 'science' in our culture stems largely from the successes of the exact sciences. Others, be they biologists, sociologists, psychologists, hope to copy the rigour, the power of prediction of the sciences of inanimate nature, and so become more 'scientific' in their turn. Descartes began it, with his beast-machines, his belief that nothing existed but thinking mind and inert, extended matter, that the whole range of living creatures to whom we are so evidently akin were but automata, simulating the feelings, drives, perceptions which we alone possessed. What a deadly vision of the world, and how dearly we have paid for its influence on our minds! A world of men (=minds) and machines—and then, if you like, animals reinstated in a sentimental niche to be our toys. Even evolutionary biology, founded on the kinship of men and animals, has gloried in reducing all alike to the single status of machinery-for-staying-alive, or strictly speaking, machinery-for-not-being-annihilated. The mysterious multifariousness of living nature, formerly a massive obstacle to mechanistic thinking, was transformed by Darwin's genius into an indefinite aggregate of random changes mechanically maintained. Life itself became machinery, made by no one for no purpose except barely to survive.

Yet if this is a dreary image, perhaps it is the truth. Life, we surmise, at least life as we know it on this earth, is but a tiny accident of chemistry on a tiny speck in a world among countless worlds. Why magnify it? The answer is: because we *are* it, and the only place to begin thinking is where we are. And we are, not only in death, but in the midst of life. Not only evolution, but embryology, comparative anatomy, common experience itself if unperverted by Cartesian prejudice, show us our kinship with all living things. This is a common ground, broad enough for generalization, narrow enough for some degree of empathy, from which to consider who and what we are, what and how we can know of the realities about us. To focus our attention on constants of acceleration and the like, we must wholly forget ourselves, or else transform ourselves into pure mathematicians, into calculators. In our existence as animals among animals we may have a richer starting-point for reflection even on the nature of our knowledge of inanimate things.

A simple lesson. And we might have learned it, the reader may object, from Bergson or Whitehead. Why take, to so little purpose, all this trouble with the arid texts of Aristotle? Because the Aristotelian universe is, in itself, in its strange austere fashion, a thing of beauty? Because of the overwhelming historical importance, once upon a time, of Aristotelian thought? These are good reasons, but there is another, too, related to our general biologizing theme. Biology can teach us better and more directly than the exact sciences, the all-important role of *pattern* in the world and of *comprehension* in our knowledge of it. If we reflect on both these points as our picture of Aristotelian science exhibits them we shall have learned something important both to the founder of the Lyceum and to ourselves who stand in so many other ways so far from where he stood.

2. *Pattern*

Pattern in things—and that means also, though modern thinkers find it hard to credit, directedness in process. The whole before the part, the goal before the way to it:

In my end is my beginning.

Act before potency then? In its full Aristotelian range this is surely not a formula we can accept, and we must take issue with it before acknowledging the core of truth we find that it contains.

Considered as an ultimate metaphysical principle, the be-all and end-all of a finite world, the priority of act to potency is difficult for us to understand, let alone to believe. What it means, in the last analysis, is that cosmologically the necessary precedes and determines the contingent, and the eternal the things that change. In Aristotle's cosmology, as we have seen, the contingent is strictly limited in scope. It is in fact two things, both slight in their metaphysical implications. Either, in the restricted field of purposive behaviour, it is what happens at cross-purposes, or incidentally to purpose: as when going to the market to buy corn I happen to meet my debtor—who happens to be in funds—and so collect the debt. Or in natural happenings in general, the contingent is simply the exceptional: what does not happen 'always or for the most part', like dog days in winter. What happens in general, however, is, in the last analysis, controlled by necessity, not a blind necessity like the Democritean, or like Plato's receptacle, but a rational necessity, the necessity of 'eternal things'. This is the ultimate metaphysical significance of the priority of the actual over the potential, the fully over the partly real. Even in things that change it is the ἐντελέχεια, the immanent goal of change, that *is* their being. Although the individual perishes, this being, as specific form, is constant in the never-ceasing succession of beings of each kind. And more than this, even such being seems to depend—so Aristotle has argued in Theta—on being that is wholly necessary: containing no source of movement or alteration, but being itself wholly within itself, the being which all other beings imitate and to which they are drawn. Everywhere: the actual *before* the possible, the fully developed before the embryonic and immature, the end of the road, as present goal, before the road that leads to it.

For us the very opposite is and must be the case. In some sense the potential takes precedence over the actual, the road ahead over its end (if indeed it has an end) in every evolutionary universe. And we are faced with the incontrovertible fact that the organic world we live in has evolved. The record of the rocks, unknown to Aristotle, presents to the modern knower a vast body of evidence that directly contradicts and reverses his fundamental principle. True, metaphysics is not for the most part based on facts. A man's metaphysics reflects his basic attitude to reality, not any special body of empirical knowledge that he may possess, like his French or his chemistry or his accounting. A man *can* be more or less of a Platonist, or Hobbesian, or Humean at any time. Yet some pieces of factual knowledge do bear significantly and even fatally on some metaphysical beliefs, and such is the case, in its cosmic application, for Aristotle's principle of the priority of actuality. For him, the chicken *must* precede the egg, eternally. He was wrong. There was a time on this globe when there were neither eggs nor chickens, there was a time when the first eggs that could reasonably have been called hen's eggs produced the first day-old chicks. They were not, or had not been hen's eggs, however, but the eggs of hen-ancestors. Since that day there have been hen eggs and chicks hatching from them; and this may go on as now for a long time yet. But it has not been so always, nor will it always be. Becoming does become; it begins and some day it will fail. In short, organic forms are achievements, not only, as Aristotle believes, because the seed succeeds in becoming a full-blooming plant, the fertilized egg a mouse or a man, but because each type of ontogenesis itself has been achieved in this world of process out of a different, preceding, and as a general rule a simpler form. Forms themselves are potencies for other forms. Nothing, it seems to me, separates us more fundamentally from Aristotle than does this principle, based on the massive fact of organic evolution.

Biologically oriented thinkers will indeed find Aristotle's comparative way of seeing man as one animal among others congenial to their views. Even the phrase 'rational animal' does not seem to be Aristotle's own; man is the two-legged animal, or two-legged-walking animal—a naturalist's definition delightfully free of dogmatic insistence on the sanctity of mind or the pre-eminence of man over all things. 'There are better things in the world than man.' This is the very spirit of T. H. Huxley: the naturalist's humility before the astounding range and variety of life. But if for Aristotle as for the modern evolutionist man is but one animal among others, for Aristotle man and every other animal has its place, and that a fixed one—and it is on the fixity, as part of a uniquely and wholly articulated universe, that Aristotelian science entirely depends. If each kind or species of thing had not, once and for all, its being-what-it-is, if we could not define once and for all the peculiar substance of each kind of thing, we should have no stability, no knowledge, and be back, in Aristotle's view, with the Cratylean flux and the Platonic or Parmenidean or who knows what fanciful way out of it. For us, on the other hand, a 'species' is but a slow and relatively stable pattern in the constantly changing rhythms that are life. Every successful pattern of plant or animal life is a triumph over chaos, which may, given other circumstances, sink back into chaos again. It was an overworked thesis of late nineteenth-century evolutionary theory that 'ontogeny recapitulates phylogeny'. But that, conversely, phylogenies are long-term ontogenies no modern student of nature can deny. And like ontogenies, they may succeed or fail. The hazards of mutation, of environmental change, of inter- and intra-specific competition, all these and more furnish a background of contingency against which the great proliferation of new patterns of living has taken place and will take place, on this planet and perhaps elsewhere, so long as life lasts. Therefore there is no being-what-it-is of each kind of thing, no ultimate and final definition of each natural class of substances, from which, with the necessary definiteness and precision, an Aristotelian science could take its start. We live for better or worse in an evolutionary universe, and, in the last analysis, evolution and Aristotelian science will not mix.

This is a drastic contrast. Yet we can go too far in our emphasis on process, our insistence that the possibility precedes, in all senses, its actualization. Applied to the *history* of life, the principle of the primacy of act to potency must appear mistaken: but applied to the *analysis* of living things—and by a legitimate extrapolation, to all analysis—it carries an important truth. For taken in a less sweeping but still Aristotelian sense it amounts to the principle that wholes precede parts, and ordering principles the data that they order. Mechanistically inclined philosophers have long tried to banish from our minds and from reality *any* kind of wholeness either in space or time. The founders of the Royal Society were confident that the behaviour of matter could be explained by the 'shape, size and texture' of its minute parts. Looking with delight through their brand-new microscopes, they may have felt that living nature too would yield to such analysis: and so indeed many, perhaps even most, biologists and biochemists, working with immensely greater knowledge and precision, feel today. But living things resist their efforts. The particulate genetics of orthodox Mendelism, for example, has had to be modified to take account, not only of isolated genes, or even the gene pool, but the gene *complex*, representing, as an eminent elder statesman of genetics puts it, 'the unity and integration of the organism'. And in embryology the 'developmental mechanics' of Roux has had to be modified to include such teleological concepts as 'the morphogenetic field'. Things do not speak to us of permanent, natural kinds, but they do show us, both in space and time, *some* pattern emergent out of flux.

Aristotle anticipates here, if you like, the lesson of *Gestalt* psychology. So have other philosophers; so, as Wertheimer once pointed out, did Spinoza, who found the part intelligible only as part of, as deducible from, the whole of wholes. But this would be, for Aristotle, and for us too, I believe, too sweeping an application of the whole-part principle. We must ask of *each* concrete entity what *its* structure is; of each natural process, what *its* function is. The form, the function of *this* organ in *this* organism, *this* ontogenetic sequence in *this* life-history, the right universal in this individual-of-this-kind: that is the limited whole which must forever guide us in all analysis, however refined, however extensive, of its parts. We cannot, with Aristotle, define it once for all; but we must aim at it, we must take it into account as our frame of reference. For parts in complete isolation from some such concrete, binding context are not even parts. If we think they are, it is because we have seized upon some shadowy abstraction—like the void in which Democritean atoms move—as a pseudo-whole. Some prior whole, some embracing entity we must have envisaged before we can find aspects, parts, factors, parameters to abstract from it by the use of our intellectual tools. True, Aristotle's structures, Aristotle's means-end processes, are eternal,

233

THE RELEVANCE OF ARISTOTLE

secure against chance or failure. Ours are essentially imperilled; they might not have been, some day they will not be. But if process were not slow enough, rhythmical enough to throw up *some* forms, it would not be process, it would not *be* at all. As it is the order that makes the syllable a syllable, so it is the organizing principle, the specific form, that makes this piece of copper a piece of copper, this paramecium a paramecium, this man a man.

Admittedly, when we have said this much, we have not yet given the *reason* for anything, we have not explained the kind of thing or phenomenon before us, but only specified it, pinned it down on the dissecting board so that we can begin to study it. Aristotelian explanation for us is not yet explanation, but a device for isolating the phenomenon to be explained. We cannot isolate it as substance, in Aristotle's sense of an individual exemplifying the specific nature of an everlasting kind, nor, *a fortiori*, as an accident or set of accidents of such a substance; but we can strive to isolate it as the concretion of an entity out of, and in, flux, as an achievement of being out of, and in, becoming.

3. *Comprehension*

As the world is, finally, so is the intellect that knows it. If there are wholes to be analysed, it is with the awareness of them as wholes, with *comprehension*, that analysis begins— and ends, unless we are to lose our way to knowledge in a meaningless maze of contextless parts. Remember what Aristotle said in the *Physics*: the mind moves, in seeking knowledge, from a crude whole to a more explicit and articulate whole. And what it is moving toward is the being-what-it-is of the phenomenon before it, the comprehensive entity or network of events that it is trying to understand. Provided we remember always the background of contingency, of hazard, we can agree with Aristotle that there is no analysis without comprehension, and no comprehension without an object, without some form susceptible of being understood.

234

Granted, again, that comprehension as we may hope to achieve it differs in a number of essential ways from Aristotelian νοῦς, the end-point of Aristotelian induction and starting-point of demonstration. First, there is nothing unique for us about the *premises* of knowledge: even in axiom systems, axioms and theorems are interchangeable. With the loss of finite kinds, we lose the anchoring of proof to just these definitions of just these subject-genera. Speech circulates freely, pinned down somewhere to experience, but just where, our more hazardous comprehension must tell us, not in the context of a given subject, fixed forever, but of a given problem that puzzles us here and now. Comprehension is the resolution of puzzlement. For Aristotle it results from the elucidation through induction of the universals implicit in perception. But if things are not fixed in kind, as he believed, if perception may lead us anywhere, our choice of roads from puzzlement to understanding will be much freer, much more perilous also, than he thought. And the right starting-point for the resolution of *this* problem will not be the right starting-point for the resolution of another, even about what looks like the same subject. With the advance, or the change, in knowledge, even the priority of some statements to others, the relation of premises to conclusions, will change too.

If starting-points are not unique, however, language in general, secondly, must lose its Aristotelian univocality. I must underscore this point, for it is one that too few modern thinkers recognize. Those especially whose reflections are guided by their admiration for the 'objectivity' of science attempt to follow here an Aristotelian ideal, although they have abandoned the Aristotelian justification—the only justification—for following it. For the emphasis on precision, on the exact and literal use of language, represents an Aristotelian ideal; but, bereft of its root in the fixed and substance-bound subject-genus, it becomes a self-contradictory ideal, impossible of execution.

That 'objectivist' thinkers follow Aristotle is not hard to see. Like him they insist on a sharp division between literal and poetic language, and seek to banish all metaphor and analogy from scientific discourse. I might cite as an illustration of this theme the anti-rhetorical invectives of Bishop Sprat in his *History of the Royal Society*; similar attacks have been conspicuous in every century since. The division of language into 'emotive' and 'cognitive' uses, for example, fashionable in the 1930's, or the story of the 'two cultures', much talked of recently: these and other aspects of modern objectivism, if they are not Aristotelian, at least echo an Aristotelian theme. For they reflect the confidence in a wholly objective, wholly impersonal use of language by the scientist in contrast to the imprecise, and more personal, speech of the artist or the practical man. They reflect an Aristotelian faith in 'universal, univocal predication', in the power of the mind to formulate literal, impersonal, self-sustaining truths.

Is the mind, is language really like that? Can we, in particular, introduce such Aristotelian predication into a contingent, developing, never completed, un-Aristotelian world? My own answer to both these questions must be in the negative, and the second negation, I believe, points to a contradiction implicit in the philosophy—or better, a philosophy—associated with the rise of the exact sciences ever since the intellectual revolution of the seventeenth century.

As to the first question, I may recall here the contrast between Plato and Aristotle on this theme. According to Aristotle there are *real* definitions which are the proper starting-points of scientific disciplines. According to Plato, we never know for sure, as far as verbalization can take us, that a defining formula is the correct form of speech in which to express the essence of the thing we aspire to know. Only a vision *beyond* language can give us the knowledge of the thing. Plato's successors in the Middle Academy, however, admitted their inability to take the last and mystical step to the knowledge of the really real; they had to be content with conjectures tied to the abstractions of language and the changing images of experience. Much the same, I submit, holds for us now. We live in a world in process, like the Cratylean-

Sophistic world on which Plato tried to impose, from beyond, the order of the Forms. We too try to understand, to find an order in that world, and do so by reaching beyond the sheer particularity, the sheer givenness of sense to definitions, inferences, intelligible patterns *through* which we order and explain the inexhaustible range of our experience. But our efforts, though guided always by *some* vision of reality, can never come to rest in a single, ultimate vision. Great discoverers in science are so because of some novel vision of their own, at first personal and odd, but which comes to be shared, to be validated by the community of acknowledged authorities in the discipline concerned. Once so accepted, you will say, it *is* literal and precise and true. Yes, in a way. Yet however widely and deeply such a vision may come to be believed, it is still one among many possibles, to be revised and in part even rejected in the light of some new insight of some new Darwin or Mendel, Newton or Einstein. When we reflect on the character of our scientific disciplines, therefore, we must embrace Plato's more pessimistic, not Aristotle's confident view; and what lies beyond language we must acknowledge also to be as tentative, as groping, as speech itself. Of course within an area included in the scope of common sense—talk about trains or tables—or in a very well-established and routine branch of science—talk of elementary chemical formulae or elementary anatomy, for instance—our language, like our knowledge, will be literal and for practical purposes complete. But reach beyond the limits of routine either to the presuppositions of our everyday knowledge or to the frontiers of discovery, and we find the Academics' relativism amply justified. Acknowledging Plato's wisdom about the limits of language, but lacking his 'flash of fire', we are probabilists through and through.

This is, so far, orthodox 'philosophy of science'. But are not our formulations, though tentative, precise and literal? Can we not—and this was my second question—have Aristotelian predication in a flowing world? Of course not. Aristotle himself would have hastened to admit as much. And that, I believe, is where the modern search for objectivism, from its commencement in Descartes's clear and distinct ideas, has constantly gone astray. Universal univocal predication depends on the limitation of the reality that is there to be known. That is all very well, as I have just said, for 'ordinary usage' or for scientific routine, but not for metaphysical reflection on the nature of things or metalinguistic reflection on the nature of language itself. Aristotelian discourse can be literal because it rests on *real* definitions. And there can be real definitions, in Aristotle's sense, once more, because in them the mind is understanding face to face the being-what-it-is of definite, limited unique, eternal kinds of things. This, as I have argued, was Aristotle's 'discovery', but it is not so for us—it has not been so since Descartes separated out the mind as knower from the flat indefinite spread of extended things it is condemned to try to know. When that happened, the Kantian restriction of knowledge to appearance was already destined to follow. It is, as Kant discovered, our minds that impose the categories through which we know, and we can never reach behind that imposition to the things themselves. Things *are* somehow, but *we* categorize. For Kant and for the Enlightenment, indeed, this categorization was common to all men in all ages; that uniformity once lost, the probabilism of modern epistemology was bound to follow in its turn. Why? Because the attempt to retain self-evident truths in separation from the being-what-it-is, the substance of each kind of thing, was self-defeating from the start. Language can be literal, science certain, in an Aristotelian world, but in no other. For in no other world do things speak to us, of themselves, each in its own kind, without our first invoking and evoking them. We, as Kant showed us, must by our categorizing contribute to the making of the world we know. We must construct our world, a hazardous, never-completed venture.

This means that for us science is in part *poetic*. It depends on imagination as well as accuracy, persuasive analogy as well as explicit proof. Aristotle, secure in the knowledge of each kind of thing's being-what-it-is, could make an absolute

THE RELEVANCE OF ARISTOTLE

division between scientific discourse, founded on real definitions, and poems (like the *Iliad*), which are but words strung
together. For us, since we lack the Aristotelian 'objects' of
definition, the dichotomy must be less rigid. Although the
proofs of our scientific theories, like the proofs of mathematical
theorems, may be elegant and accurate and powerful to con-
vince, their beauty, their power of conviction, though different
indeed from the beauty and truth of the *Iliad*, is not as wholly
different as Aristotle thought. Every scientific theory, however
accurate, however thoroughly supported by experiment, rests
ultimately on analogy and metaphor: on what we feel makes
it explain, because it is familiar or because it is beautiful or
because it is deeply akin to some ultimate hope of ours about
what the world may be. Every scientific theory, in other words,
rests in the last analysis as much on poetic vision as on hard
fact. The dream of literal truth, of total, impersonal objectivity,
itself was one such vision; but in the twentieth century physics,
mathematics, metaphysics, all have converged on its destruc-
tion. If man as agent is condemned to be free, so is man as
knower: he must fashion his knowledge, with the marvellously
powerful yet forever abstract and partial tools of language, in
the light of his faith, hoping for its truth, but acknowledging
its partiality, the possibility of its error. Scientists are poets in
spite of themselves; theirs too the risks, as well as the rewards,
of creation through speech.

The comprehension of the Aristotelian scientist, then, differs in the uniqueness of its premises and the literalness of its
language from that of the modern knower. It follows also,
thirdly, that although the understanding of pattern, of wholes,
when we achieve it, guides us toward new knowledge, toward
possibilities of analysis and explanation, it may *mis*guide us
too. We can never be sure; knowledge for us is a gamble, a
risk for which the individual knower in his knowing assumes
responsibility. The certainty of an Aristotelian intellect it
would be hybristic for us even to hope to acquire. Like Lessing,
we cannot even want that kind of certainty; it would be
mauvaise foi, illusion, death. Aristotelian intuition, the grasp

of the being-what-it-is of each kind of thing, is impersonal: like Cartesian reason, the same for all men everywhere. But for us, comprehension is *en situation*, aiming at universal validity, but never definitively in possession of it. It expresses, not disembodied thought, but the endeavour of the living person to make his world a world.

Yet for all that, Aristotle's great discovery, the discovery of each kind of thing's being-what-it-is, has still its validity for us. In its time it turned the knower's attention from the search for transcendent Platonic Forms or for underlying Democritean parts, to the investigation of the intelligible forms *in* things. We cannot define, literally, once for all, as Aristotle did, the 'substance of each kind of thing'. But we should recognize that for the scientist, groping his way as he must out of any given perplexity, it is the comprehensive awareness of a pattern, and only this, that can lead to a solution. He may be seeking to understand, say, the role of the cytoplasm in inheritance, or the behaviour of electrons at low temperatures, or the origin of the universe: whatever his problem, it is some gestalt, the form of some matter, or the issue of some trend in nature, that he is seeking. He cannot fix such a pattern eternally, nor specify it wholly. Yet it is the universals in the individuals, the general, intelligible content in and through the perceived particulars on which, in all his guesswork, his groping experimentation whether with concepts or with wires and test-tubes, his mind is bent. The cosmos that Aristotle built around his discovery depends on the fixity of kinds and the finitude of being as a whole; so does the formal structure of science as he conceived it. But the need to apprehend as such the existence of comprehensive entities or comprehensive contexts before we can analyse them, in relation to our analysis of them, and as the goal of our analysis of them: the priority of wholes to parts, of principles to conditions, both in reality and in our understanding of reality, both in the known and in the knower: this lesson, translated into our own conceptual framework, where being is stripped of its necessity and knowledge of its completeness, Aristotle, the only great philosopher who philosophized out of a passion for understanding living nature, may still help us to learn.

4. νοῦς

I must close, however, with two further points of contrast, closely connected also with the model of science for Aristotle, that is, on the one hand, the nature of mind and on the other of the object of knowledge, in particular, the finitude of Aristotelian being, of the Aristotelian universe.

As to mind, scientific knowledge, Aristotle believes, must proceed from premises better known than the conclusions to conclusions still possessing certainty. This certainty depends, he admits, on our possession of a power of direct confrontation with the being-what-they-are of things, the power he designates as νοῦς. This, I submit, is the element in the cognitive structure of Aristotelian science which most strikingly cuts it off from contemporary models of mind and of knowledge. νοῦς is foreign to us, it seems to me, in a number of dimensions: in its role in knowledge, in its character of separate mind and, in the unmoved mover, in its divinity.

(a) First, as to νοῦς in science. If we deny it credence we should first of all, however, be sure we know what we are denying. Indubitable first principles: these we do deny; non-Euclidean geometry alone would compel us to deny them. But against Aristotle we must not simply cry, 'No self-evident truths!' We have not to do here with *a priori*'s, with innate ideas, or the Cartesian light of nature. It is not the mind turned inward on itself that discovers the first principles of Aristotelian disciplines, but the mind methodically and appropriately facing a suitable reality, a suitable specimen of the kind that is to be known. *Things* speak to the mind of their being-what-they-are and the mind, finding the universal *in* the perceived individual, putting its insight into words in the correct definition, thus comprehends the substance of the thing, and, as formal grasp of formal, actual understanding of the actual, is identified with it. Knower and known are united because,

241

being in nature suited to each other, they have never been wholly apart. The ultimate question about νοῦς, therefore, is not the Lockean question: does the mind, independently of experience, possess innate ideas? but the Aristotelian question: do things show us their being-what-they-are? Is the peculiar substance of each kind of thing there for us to grasp, vaguely in perception, step by step through induction, directly and luminously through rational, necessary intuition?

For myself, I can only answer, No. It is hard, Aristotle says, to know that we know; but he did know, or believed he did— and he could do so because his world was ultimately determinate, because in it contingency was the servant of rational necessity, matter of form, potency of act. The *what* of each kind of thing held the conjectures of the Aristotelian scientist firmly in check. For us, the strand of contingency is ultimate; we may transcend it, we must transcend it, but in peril. Both the source of nature's reality and nature itself have lost their radical determinacy, and so lost also the radical intelligibility of Aristotelian substances. And so when we understand one aspect or another of the world around us, that understanding becomes our venture, not the world's. If we succeed, that is our achievement; if we fail, our 'understanding' turns out to have been our dream. Aristotelian knowledge could be impersonal because things, including minds, were thoroughly determinate. The determination *we* impose on things is in part at least of our own making, and in what part we can never precisely say. *We* put the questions we put to nature; the answers are nature's, but also partly ours. Is it nature, the essences of things, or our own dreams we are elaborating? Was Kepler's vision of celestial harmonies true or false? Or Newton's world spinning in absolute space through absolute time? Each generation of knowers accredits the reality and rejects the illusions of its predecessors—and the same destiny awaits its own vision. We cannot know that we know; we can only hope we do. And the self-assured comprehension of literal, unique, eternal first principles even for our most developed fields of knowledge we cannot even hope to attain.

'All that we know for certain,' as Tillich says, 'is that we know nothing for certain.'

(b) Aristotelian νοῦς, secondly, is not only the mind's link with the premises of scientific knowledge, with the being-what-it-is of each kind of thing. It is also the highest 'part' of mind itself and the only part of which Aristotle seems to believe there is an existence separate from the body. I have not tried to deal with this crux of Aristotelian scholarship, nor shall I attempt to do so now. I can only record the fact that, cryptic though they are, the texts do agree; they all tell us that Aristotle did believe that rational mind, in its intuitive aspect, was different, in its independence of body, from any other aspect of 'soul'. And I can only record, further, my own bafflement by this view. Platonic separate soul, Platonic immortality one must take seriously as Plato's deepest faith. Soul for Plato is the moving force in the world as in the individual; if one cannot accept literally his arguments and the kind of after-life he deduces from them, one can at least imagine what it was like to see the world in this way. For it is *one* way, unified, from the *Phaedo* to the *Laws*, in the passion that directs it and the concepts around which it is developed. We find no such consistency in Aristotle, not only because his view of the mind-body relation developed, but because even in the works considered by geneticist scholars to be his latest, his general theory and his theory of 'Active Reason' appear so oddly opposed. No one could reject more emphatically than Aristotle a mind- (or soul-) body dualism in general. As we have noticed earlier, he considers the question whether the soul is separate from the body as foolish as the question whether the impression is separate from the wax. Soul is the way the body works: that is all. When it comes to νοῦς, however, the case is different. To begin with, there is the perennially puzzling chapter 5 of Book III of the *De Anima*, where Aristotle seems to say that active reason is immortal and imperishable, but that this reason is prior only in the universe, not in the individual. This in itself suggests that only a single 'world mind' is impassible; but elsewhere in the same work and in the other biological works also, Aristotle speaks, always very briefly, of νοῦς as, unlike other parts of soul, coming *to* the body from outside—and so he appears to think that in the individual as well there is a separate and immortal mind which is not simply the way the human organism functions but something very much more. This seems to me a strange deviation from the principal tenor of his own psychology. Everywhere else we have soul-body unity, but in this one respect a sharp duality.

What accounts for this diversity? Perhaps it springs from the biologist's sense that his own knowledge, his own elaboration of sets of propositions and arguments *about* other living things, is a very strange addition to life itself, so strange that it must have a foreign source, an origin all its own. One is reminded again of the parallel with Darwin, whose belief in evolution made him wonder how man's own evaluations could be trusted: 'Can the mind of man, which has, as I fully believe, developed from a mind as low as that possessed by the lowest animal, be trusted when it draws such grand conclusions?' This doubt a modern biologist has, plausibly, extended to Darwin's own theory itself, for Darwin's and every scientist's theories too are 'grand conclusions'. Perhaps then, Aristotle's νοῦς is the converse of this: a concept necessary to guard the knowledge of life against the collapse into *mere* life.

There is indeed a genuine problem here. Thinking is a form of living. But living as such is successful or unsuccessful, not true or false. This is one aspect, in fact, of Plato's argument in the *Theaetetus*: what he is arguing is that on this basis knowledge is not possible at all. But Plato carries his attack all the way to perception: even our sensory awareness of *things*, he argues, entails conception, the conception at least of unity or of existence, which we know, not by sense but by the mind alone. Thus even in perception something apart from body is at work. But with Aristotle it is the soul-in-the-body, soul as form *of* body, that is concerned in all cognitive activities except for the purely rational and immediate activity of νοῦς: in all activities—and he knew they were many—that we share with other animals. Then suddenly with our power to know the being-what-it-is, to grasp first principles and so elaborate sciences, comes another element in our natures, foreign to body altogether. It is true that a *merely* biological interpretation of knowledge threatens the validity of knowledge, including the knowledge of biology. It is true that to be knowers in a way consistent with the truth of our knowledge, we must distinguish somehow between success on the one hand and validity or truth on the other. Only by some such distinction can we justify our affirmation of our knowledge as knowledge, not merely a set of conditioned reflexes that happen to work. Yet I cannot help feeling it strange that we should do this so suddenly and briefly at the very top of our biological ladder. It seems to me much more plausible to suppose that far down in the history of life itself something like knowing began: that our reaching out to reality is but a fuller development, marvellously magnified by the invention of symbolic systems, of a curiosity common to many kinds of animals, supported by different sensory capacities, different kinds of awareness, different passions, but fundamentally akin. Our instincts, our affections, our deepest values, are developments of similar drives in other animals; so, too, our ways of knowing. This is indeed a precarious view. If knowledge, if morality, are evolutionary elaborations of animal behaviour, we may easily see them, in some moods, as nothing more than what their beginnings were. Or we may become so concerned to analyse the *conditions* of their origin that we forget the *reasons* for their success. But life, even of the philosopher, is more hazardous than Aristotle thought it. There is no royal road to Wisdom, no knowing with certainty one has arrived there, no finality in one's being there. We cannot save ourselves from these hazards by cutting off the impetus of evolutionary thinking, or, in pre-evolutionary terms, of thinking about 'the scale of nature', and assuming a separate rational mind utterly different from the minds of other living things.

(c) Once more, however, the Aristotelian cosmos is and must be free of such hazards. νοῦς as impassible must save the certainty of first principles; and finally, God as the thought of thought must act as the cosmic safeguard, for Aristotle, of both knower and known, the crowning point of pure actuality which keeps steady the priority of act to potency, the unending cycle of generation, throughout the universe. What is this God of Aristotle's, a finite being who is pure act, unmoving, and yet alive; pure thought, but no planner, related causally but not as creator to other things and thoughts? Aristotle describes his unmoved mover as 'pure thought', as 'living', as supreme actuality in the sense—which, as we have seen, he has developed in Theta—of pure *activity*. And it is clear from other contexts also that he considered intellectual activity the highest, purest, most self-sufficient form of life. But what is pure, eternal, unchanging *thought*? What is a *life* not of an animal, a perceptible entity that is born and dies, the life of a determinate, finite entity which is not a developing entity somewhere in place and filling some strand of time? Aristotle himself has argued in Zeta that physical definitions cannot dispense with matter 'since animals are perceptible' and therefore involve matter, potency and change. The unmoved mover is not an animal, not a perceptible being, 'an eternal living thing' like the cosmos of the *Timaeus*. How then can he be alive? The argument of Theta 6, indeed, ties together activity, performance of function, and actuality, or substance and form, in a manner which, as a generalization from the practice of biology and from common-sense experience, is elegant and persuasive. Yet for all that, the transference of this identity to the realm of eternal things this reader at least finds it impossible to follow. To ascribe 'life' to an infinite God is like ascribing to Him 'love' or 'omnipotence' or any other honorific title: it is pure metaphor, for no finite adjective can literally apply to such a deity. But Aristotle's God is finite through and through, wholly determinate Being, pure thought and the purest object of thought, delimited sharply from all other beings, the point of reference for our knowledge of them as beings but not, most emphatically not, the source of their existence as Father or Creator. Aristotle's God cannot love the world; he can be no more than the self-sufficient object of its love, the self-contained being which other beings imitate. How can such a being be said to live? I do not know. And since Aristotle did not write his science of metaphysics, or since at any rate we do not possess it, perhaps no one will ever know. I for one can only confess that the massive and beautifully articulated argument of Zeta-Iota leads, for me, to an empty focus. The many fresh starts, the precise and delicate equivocations, the meticulously wrought transitions, converge upon a climax, a highest object of reverence, that is not there.

5. Finitude

The strangeness of Aristotelian mind, finally, is but an aspect of the strangeness of Aristotelian being. What does it mean to be? To be one, limited, determinate, a member of a fixed, determinate kind. Let us compare, in conclusion, the finitude of Aristotelian being, whether structure (specific form) or function (the directedness of process to specific form as end), with the concept of finitude in contemporary thought. Finitude is a favourite topic for modern, especially for existentialist philosophy. What a different finitude it is! The founder of existentialist philosophy was Søren Kierkegaard. Kierkegaard: the subjective Christian thinker turning inward to the agony of his own defectiveness, to the abyss dividing him from the infinite greatness and goodness of his God. For every Christian thinker finitude is in some sense suspended from infinity; for Kierkegaard this disparity is exacerbated until it fills the whole religious consciousness. 'Over 70,000 fathoms to rejoice' is Kierkegaard's motto. In Aristotle's world, in contrast, there are no such perilous depths. Infinite being, the source of all finitude, would be for him a topsy-turvy fancy; for the infinite, he has argued, must be the contained, not the containing. Formlessness, i.e. infinity, cannot hold, determine, create form. But for the Christian thinker that is just what infinity does. True, God is said to be a positive infinite, not the hazy ἄπειρον, the indeterminate merely; but so much the greater is the gulf that separates us from him. For every positive reality we meet with in our lives is finite; and if the infinite is positive, it must contain a kind of reality, a degree of reality, which exceeds every power of our intelligence, a reality that we can only worship, never understand.

The non-Christian existentialist, moreover, is still scarred by the Kierkegaardian wound. For him finitude hangs, not from infinity, but simply in a void. Thus for Heidegger the quintessence of our being is indeed finitude, but finitude is simply life-facing-death, my life span not as coming to a τέλος in maturity, but literally to an end in the cessation of my life. And the mood that truly reveals my own finite being to myself is not faith, in my confrontation with my infinite Maker, but dread, in my confrontation with Nothingness.

But this is a far cry, the reader may object, from traditional philosophy, whether scholastic and theologically oriented or modern and naturalist in its bent. Yet the existentialist motif is but the intensification, the fulfilment, of a theme common to all Christian or post-Christian thinking, in sharp contrast to Aristotelian thought: that is, the division between the essence of things and their existence. True, 'existentialism' deals with personal, subjective existence, not existence in general, the sort of concepts more common-sense philosophers trade in; but the contrast is the same. Whether it be in the hope of grace or in the courage of dread, every modern, like every medieval, thinker must face the paradox of existence, of sheer being-there, cut loose from essence, from the *kind* of its being. For medieval thinking, the very fact of creation makes this plain. To be a man is what it is to be a man; but when God made Adam, the first man came into existence. Clay became life: this, the first event in history, happened by fiat, not by any logic. Between the species as a *what* and its series of representatives in time, creation makes a cut. In Aristotelian terms, in terms of a non-created universe, to say that a man 'is' offers no information of scientific import beyond the statement what it is to be a man. If there is creation, to say that a man *exists* informs us of something over and above his 'what'. This is true of all Hebrew-Christian cosmologies in contrast

THE RELEVANCE OF ARISTOTLE

to Aristotle. Kierkegaard's more subjective theism only intensifies this theme, and the atheism of Sartre or Heidegger, depriving the mere existent of his creaturely status, intensifies it further still: for the finite person, cast into a meaningless world, must be his own creator, reaching out of the absurdity of existence for an essence, a principle, a meaning, that may, for all he knows, be sheer illusion. Moreover, every naturalism, however self-confident its rejection of all speculation, all romanticizing nonsense, carries at its heart this paradox. Newtonian nature, dead, spread out through infinite space and time, was a nature that 'gave no reasons'. And under the influence of that conception we ourselves, as natures shorn of self-evident truths, have become the blind succession of sensations and habits that Hume made of us. So at the end of the story we have, over against 'brute fact', subjective 'attitudes', emotional posturings called 'ethics', or pure formalisms, systems of mathematical symbols competent to carry our knowledge of nature precisely because we know they say nothing at all. Existence if we could grasp it directly would be, externally, pure unintelligible ongoing, or, internally, sheer thereness, pure feeling tone; essence, over against it, is pure, empty form. The existentialist cultivates the internal wretchedness of this dilemma, while the less introspective philosopher cheerfully applies his analytical techniques to the minute problems left within his range. But they are both working in the same divided universe, where *what* and *that* stand sharply cut off from one another, two pinpoints to hold not only Rabelaisian angels, but all there is, all that becomes, all that might be.

Such has been, for modern minds, the perilous issue of the acceptance of infinity, whether of God or nature. The bonds of finitude were broken and essence and existence fell apart. In Aristotelian metaphysics, as both Gilson and Owens have emphasized, there was no such separation, no such problem. Every *one*, every intelligible whole, is a being, exists; and everything that is a being, that exists, is a one. We start from the things there are, which are units, members of classes,

249

THE RELEVANCE OF ARISTOTLE

containing implicitly the universals, the essences, that make them what they are. We want, in first philosophy, to analyse out the aspect of pure being *in* them, i.e. to demonstrate the form in the individual, and from there to proceed to pure, separate form itself if there be any entity or entities of such a character. But the sheer contingent fact of existence, over against the pure intelligible being, or 'subsistence', of essences is not an Aristotelian dichotomy. This is not to say that Aristotle ignores one of the traditional pair in favour of the other, but that the separation does not arise for him in this form. It arose in one sense for Plato out of the conflict between Heraclitean flux and sophistic relativism on the one hand, and, on the other, the Parmenidean or Pythagorean faith in a noumenal reality and the Socratic faith in moral standards. In its later connotation, however, only the successive infinities first of the Hebrew-Christian God and then of modern nature made it the fundamental dilemma it has become. To be one, to be, to exist: in a finite, uncreated world of natural kinds all these coalesce. To exist is neither to be made by an infinite power out of nothing, nor to 'fall' out of nothing into a meaningless stretch of mere existence. It is to exhibit in a proper place and at a proper time the characters of some one natural class: to be a unit in a class. Aristotle distinguishes, of course, between the questions 'if it is' and 'what it is'; but these are analytical distinctions, free of any suspicion of metaphysical nausea or of theological humility. To know existence is already to know essence, that is, to know the form of the existent, to know it *as this such-and-such.* As Aristotle remarks in Book Zeta:

. . . 'why a thing is itself' is doubtless a meaningless inquiry; for the fact or the existence of the thing must already be evident (e.g. that the moon is eclipsed), but the fact that a thing is itself is the single reason and the single answer to all such questions as 'why the man is man, or the musical musical', unless one were to answer 'because each thing is inseparable from itself; and its being one meant just this.' This, however, is common to all things and is a 'short and easy way' with the question. (1041 a 14–19)

But what is more important than the easy equation of being

and unity, is the differentiation of the principle that makes each thing a thing *of such a kind* and not another:

Since we must know the existence of the thing and it must be given, clearly the question is *why* the matter is some individual thing, e.g. why are these materials a house? Because that which was the being-what-it-is of a house is present. And why is this individual thing, or this body in this state, a man? Therefore what we seek is the cause, i.e. the form, by reason of which the matter is some definite thing; and this is the substance of the thing. (1041 b 4–9)

No gulf here divides the infinite source of order and unity from the sheer existence of the creature; nor conversely does an indefinite ongoing of nature have to look beyond itself for the resolution of its own absurdity. Neither faith nor despair is needed in this universe.

Yet it is not our universe. We may admire its beauty and order, yearn for its security; it is not ours. If we are religious, it is not a finite God we worship; if we are scientists (not that these are contradictories), we have no hope, no desire, for completed systems, whose unique premises could be stated once for all with certainty. Both the infinite and the indeterminate are before us and around us; we live by our very natures on the edge of the abyss. The finite perfection of the Aristotelian world we cannot hope to restore.

Bibliographical Note

The accompanying bibliography is partial and selective. I have included all works quoted in the course of my own essay, and numerous other titles of books and articles which I consulted because they seemed germane to the theme I was hoping to develop. But there are doubtless a great many more that I have overlooked. The vast bibliography on the *Ethics*, *Politics*, *Poetics* and *Rhetoric*, moreover, I have almost wholly ignored. An extensive bibliography centring in the *Metaphysics* will be found in Owens (72), and a still fuller list of publications for the years since 1950 in the *Repertoire Bibliographique de la Philosophie* (*Louvain*), *Section Socrate*, *Platon*, *Aristote*.

A word should be added here about the literature on two particular subjects: on Aristotle's development, and on the relation of Aristotle's biology to his philosophy. On the first of these, Owens' discussion, in combination with the English edition of Jaeger's basic work, forms an excellent introduction to the subject. In addition to Owens, the articles of Düring (30), Moraux (67), and De Vogel (111) are especially relevant. Düring suggests, as I mentioned in Chapter I, not only that Aristotle may have developed his own independent position earlier than Jaeger believed, but that some of the later Platonic dialogues may even have been in part directed against Aristotle's criticisms. As Düring himself remarks, whether or not this was actually the case, the fact that one can argue plausibly for it shows at least how loose is the rein of speculation in this field. Better therefore, if we can, to look at the Corpus in itself, systematically. And that we can do so, it seems to me, is proved for the *Metaphysics* at least by Owens' exegesis, or, at a more introductory level, for the Corpus as a whole by D. J. Allan's excellent *Philosophy of Aristotle* in the Home University Library

(1). Another approach to the same conclusion is provided, for example, by R. P. McKeon's article on 'Aristotle's concept of the development and the nature of scientific method' (56), which I have quoted in connection with the discussion of universals in *Metaphysics* Zeta.

Secondly, the attempt to see Aristotle's philosophy as an harmonious whole, inspired in particular by his activities as a biologist, is also amply supported in the literature. To begin with, there is the famous remark of D'Arcy Thompson (105), and his essay in the collection *Science and the Classics* (106). In the latter, however, Thompson separated Aristotle the biologist from Aristotle the physicist, rather than deriving Aristotelian physics itself from biology. Ritter's article (80), though in part philosophically unsound, is very illuminating in this connection. E. S. Russell's remarks in *Form and Function* (91) are also suggestive though not very detailed; the same is true of Le Blond's introduction to his edition of the *Parts of Animals*, Book I (52). Meyer's *Der Entwicklungsgedanke bei Aristoteles* (66) comments on the organic basis for the distinction between act and potency, and hence for Aristotle's metaphysics generally. The question of Aristotle's attitude to evolutionary conceptions of nature is exhaustively and definitively treated in Torrey and Felin's analysis of the relevant texts (107). His own developed position in biology is carefully worked out in Düring's commentary on the *Parts of Animals* (29), and the articles of East (32) and Moreau (69) are also helpful in this connection.

All the above authors, however, give us hints which point, indeed, in a single direction, but which have not been carried through so far in a detailed and systematic exposition of Aristotelian texts, philosophical as well as strictly biological. There are two books which one might have expected to carry out such a detailed analysis, but they are both disappointing in execution. H. D. Hantz's Columbia dissertation on *The Biological Motivation in Aristotle* (42) should have developed the theme I have tried to argue in this book, but it is for the most part not much more than a résumé of the biological works, with a suggestion that the *Metaphysics, Ethics* and *Politics* are all concerned with 'life'. One interesting point Hantz makes: he alleges that the four causes are taken for granted, not argued for, in the biological writings; and therefore, he infers, these concepts are derived directly from Aristotle's biological experience. Now I certainly agree that Aristotle's experience in biological research was probably definitive for his theory of cause and of nature in general; yet I cannot find much basis for Hantz's argument. The introduction of the four causes at the opening of the *Generation of Animals*, for example, seems to me, on the contrary, to suggest that these are concepts which Aristotle had developed and justified elsewhere (e.g. in *Physics* II) and was now applying in the detailed biological works. Their introduction here is not direct and empirical, but conceptual and systematic, in the nature of revision of 'what we already know'. More recently, J. H. Randall Jr. (78) has followed up Hantz's work with a lively and readable study of a 'functionalist' Aristotle, but in this case (as Dr. Haring's review (44) points out), we have an Aristotle so instrumentalist, so Deweyan, as to have little connection with the founder of the Lyceum. In particular, the careful compartmentalizing, the univocality of Aristotelian thought, in short, the basic structure of Aristotelian science, seems to me to be almost wholly ignored.

For the rest, I have referred in the course of my own argument to most of the secondary sources that I have found especially useful. Miss Anscombe's essay (4) was published when my manuscript was on the point of completion; it seems to me, in connection with the fundamental concepts of substance and being-what-it-is, to lend further support to my central thesis.

Two further points should perhaps be made here about Chapter II. First: in discussing Plato, I have retained the traditional view of his development, following an interpretation roughly in agreement with F. M. Cornford's. In doing this, I am well aware that I am ignoring G. E. L. Owen's view of the dating of the *Timaeus* and the theory of Plato's development that goes with it. I have, however, taken as definitive Professor Cherniss's refutation of this theory (22, 23). Nor, I feel, do Professor Ryle's studies of the *Parmenides* and the *Theaetetus* necessitate so radical a change in our view of Plato's later dialectic as many British philosophers believe they do. In any event, a book on Aristotle is not the place to argue this matter; I stand here on the authority of Professor Cherniss, and if any one doubts the permissibility of this, let him read the Cherniss papers, and also the *Philebus* and the *Laws*, which nobody takes to be other than late dialogues. In short, that Plato was a Platonist to the last, and Aristotle an Aristotelian from the first, or very near it, seems to me plain from their own words.

Secondly, I should like to refer here to Erich Frank's paper on 'The Fundamental Opposition of Plato and Aristotle' (35). I have cited another paper of his (34) in which he uses, I think mistakenly, the speech of Diotima to show that Plato's view of generation is like Aristotle's; but the paper I am speaking of now brings out plainly much the same opposition that I am describing in Chapter II. In particular, Frank stresses the moral motivation of Plato's philosophy as against the more theoretical bent of Aristotle, but he speaks of Aristotle's interest in exact knowledge and in history, rather than merging both of these, as I should be inclined to do, in the concept of natural history.

I have quoted the Oxford translations for the *Metaphysics*, the *History of Animals*, *On Generation and Corruption*, and some passages from the *Parts of Animals*. For some brief passages I have given my own rendering, and in all other cases have followed the Loeb translations. All quotations therefore are from Loeb texts except where otherwise specified. I am grateful to the Clarendon Press and to the editors of the Loeb Library for permission to use their versions, and especially to the former for permission to make occasional slight revisions where a philosophical point seemed to demand it. The principal revision consists in the rendering of τὸ τί ἦν εἶναι as 'being-what-it-is' instead of 'essence'. I had intended to use Owens' 'what-IS-being', but have been persuaded by Professor Charles

Kahn to alter this to 'being-what-it-is', taking this phrase as both philosophically more intelligible and philologically closer to the probable origin of the term. There is some authority for this rendering in Hicks' edition of the *De Anima*. On reflection, I have retained 'substance' instead of adopting Owens' 'entity' for οὐσία. I admit the unfortunate connotations of 'substance', but it seems to me nevertheless to involve too much rewriting of the history of philosophy, as well as of the commentaries on Aristotle himself, if one discards it, especially in a book like this, which is meant more for the undergraduate reader or the general public than for scholars already conversant both with the text and the tradition.

BIBLIOGRAPHY

1. ALLAN, D. J., *The Philosophy of Aristotle*, Home University Library, London, 1952.
2. ALLBRITTON, Rogers, 'Forms of Particular Substances in Aristotle's Metaphysics', *Jl. Philos.* **54** (1957), pp. 699–708.
3. ANSCOMBE, G. E. M., 'Aristotle and the Sea Battle', *Mind* (NS) **65** (1956), pp. 1–15.
4. ANSCOMBE, G. E. M., 'Aristotle: The Search for Substance', in Anscombe and Geach, *Three Philosophers*, Blackwell, Oxford, 1961.
5. ANTON, J. P., *Aristotle's Theory of Contrariety*, Routledge, London, 1957.
6. APOSTLE, H., *Aristotle's Philosophy of Mathematics*, Univ. Chicago Press, Chicago, 1952.
7. ARNIM, H. von, 'Zu Werner Jaegers Grundlegung der Entwicklungsgeschichte des Aristoteles', *Wiener Stud.* **47** (1928), pp. 1–48.
8. BARR, R. R., 'The Nature of Alteration in Aristotle', *New Schol.* **30** (1956), pp. 472–484.
9. BEACH, J. D., 'Aristotle's Notion of Being', *The Thomist* **21** (1958), pp. 29–43.

10. BLACKWELL, R., 'The Methodological Function of the Categories', *New Schol.* 31 (1957), pp. 526–37.

11. BLOCK, Irving, 'Truth and Error in Aristotle's Theory of Sense Perception', *Philos. Quart.* 11 (1961), pp. 1–9.

12. BOAS, George, 'A Basic Conflict in Aristotle's Philosophy', *Amer. Jl. Philol.* 64 (1943), pp. 172ff.

13. BOAS, George, 'Aristotle's Presuppositions about Change'. *Amer. Jl. Philol.* 68 (1947), pp. 404–413.

14. BOURGEY, Louis, *Observation et Expérience chez Aristote*, Paris, 1955.

15. BRÉMOND, A., 'Le Dilemme Aristotélien', *Arch. Philos.* 10 (1933), cahier 2.

16. BRENTANO, Franz, *Aristoteles und seine Weltanschauung*, Leipzig, 1911.

17. BRÖCKER, Walter, *Aristoteles* (2nd edn.), Frankfurt a.M., 1957.

18. BRUMBAUGH, R. S., 'Aristotle's Outline of the Problems of First Philosophy', *Rev. Met.* 7 (1953–54), pp. 511–521.

19. BUCHANAN, *Aristotle's Theory of Being*, Greek, Roman and Byzantine Studies, University, Miss. and Cambridge, Mass., 1962.

20. CHARLESWORTH, M. J., *Aristotle on Art and Nature*, Auckland Univ. Coll., 1957.

21. CHERNISS, Harold, *Aristotle's Criticism of Plato and the Academy*, vol. I, Johns Hopkins, Baltimore, 1944.

22. CHERNISS, Harold, 'The Relation of the *Timaeus* to Plato's Later Dialogues', *Amer. Jl. Philol.* 78 (1957), pp. 225–266.

23. CHERNISS, Harold, 'Timaeus 38 A 8–B 5', *Jl. Hell. Stud.* 77, pt. I (1957), pp. 18–23.

24. CONRAD-MARTIUS, Hedwig, 'Le problème du temps aujourd'hui et chez Aristote', *Archives de Philosophie* 20 (1957), pp. 483–498.

25. COUSIN, D. R., 'Aristotle's Doctrine of Substance', *Mind* (NS) 42 (1933), pp. 168–185.

26. DALCQ, A. M., 'Le Dynamisme du Germe', *Sciences*, Jan.–Feb. 1961, pp. 27–29.

27. DEMOS, R., 'The Structure of Substance according to Aristotle', *Philos. and Phenom. Res.* 5 (1944–45), pp. 255–268.

28. DRONKE, E. P. M., review of Charlesworth's *Aristotle on Art and Nature*, *Austral. Jl. Philos.* 38 (1960), pp. 188–192.

29. DÜRING, Ingemar, *Aristotle's De Partibus Animalium. Critical and Literary Commentaries*, Göteborg, 1943.

30. DÜRING, Ingemar, 'Aristotle and Plato in the mid-Fourth Century', *Eranos* 54 (1956), pp. 109–120.

31. DÜRING, Ingemar, and Owen, G. E. L., (edrs.), *Aristotle and Plato in the mid-Fourth Century* (Proc. Symposium Aristotelicum, Oxford, 1957), Göteborg, 1961.

32. EAST, S. P., 'De la méthode de la biologie selon Aristote', *Laval théol.-philos.* 14 (1958), pp. 213–235.

33. EVANS, M. G., 'Causality and Explanation in the Logic of Aristotle', *Philos. and Phenom. Res.* 19 (1958–59), pp. 466–485.

34. FRANK, Erich, 'Das Problem des Lebens bei Hegel und Aristoteles', *Deutsche Vtljrsschr. f. Litwst. u. Geistesgesch.* 5 (1927), pp. 609–643.

35. FRANK, Erich, 'The Fundamental Opposition of Plato and Aristotle', *Amer. Jl. Philol.* 61 (1940), pp. 34–53, pp. 116–185.

36. GEACH, P. T., 'Aquinas', in Anscombe and Geach, *Three Philosophers*, Blackwell, Oxford, 1961.

37. GILSON, E., *L'Être et L'Essence*, Vrin, Paris, 1948.

38. GILSON, E., *Being and Some Philosophers*, Pont. Inst. Med. Stud., Toronto, 1949.

39. GOEDECKEMEYER, A., *Die Gliederung der Aristotelischen Philosophie*, Niemeyer, Halle a.S., 1912.

40. GUTHRIE, W. C. K., 'The Development of Aristotle's Theology', *Class. Quart.* 27 (1933), pp. 162–171.

41. HAMLYN, D. W., 'Aristotle's Account of Aesthesis in the De Anima', *Class. Quart.* (NS) 9 (1959), p. 6.

42. HANTZ, H. D., *The Biological Motivation in Aristotle*, Columbia, New York, 1939.

43. HARING, E. S., 'Substantial Form in Aristotle's *Metaphysics Z*', *Rev. Met.* 10 (1956–57), pp. 308–332, pp. 482–501, pp. 698–713.

44. HARING, E. S., 'A Twentieth Century Aristotle', *Rev. Met.* 14 (1960), pp. 292–299.

45. HEATH, T. L., *Mathematics in Aristotle*, Oxford, 1949.

46. HEIDEGGER, Martin, 'Vom Wesen und Begriff der φύσις. Aristoteles *Physik* B 1', *Il Pensiero* 3 (1958), pp. 131–156.

47. HICKS, R. D. (edr.), *Aristotle De Anima*, Cambridge, 1907.

48. JAEGER, Werner, *Aristotle*, 2nd Engl. edn., Oxford, 1948.

49. JAEGER, Werner, *Diokles von Karystos*, Berlin, 1937.

50. JOACHIM, H. H. (edr.), *Aristotle On Coming to Be and Passing Away*, Oxford, 1922.

51. KAPP, Ernst, *Greek Foundations of Traditional Logic*, Columbia, New York, 1942.

52. LE BLOND, J. M., *Aristote Philosophe de la Vie*, Aubier, Paris, 1945.

53. LEE, H. D. P., 'Geometrical Method and Aristotle's Account of First Principles', *Class. Quart.* 29 (1935), pp. 113–124.

54. LONES, T. E., *Aristotle's Researches in Natural Science*, London, 1912.

55. LOUIS, P., 'Remarques sur la Classification des Animaux chez Aristote', in *Autour d'Aristote*, pp. 297–304, Louvain, 1955.

56. McKEON, R. P., 'Aristotle's Concept of the Development and the Nature of Scientific Method', *Jl. Hist. Ideas* 8 (1947), pp. 3–44.

57. MANQUAT, M., *Aristote Naturaliste*, Vrin, Paris, 1932.

58. MANSION, A., *Introduction à la Physique Aristotélicienne*, Louvain, 1946.

59. MANSION, A., 'L'Objet de la Science Philosophique Suprême d'après Aristote, Met. E 1', in *Mélanges de Philos. Grecque*, pp. 151–168, Vrin, Paris, 1956.

60. MANSION, A., 'Philosophie primaire, seconde, et méta-physique chez Aristote', *Rev. philos. de Louvain* **56** (1958), pp. 165–221.

61. MANSION, S., *Le Jugement d'Existence chez Aristote*, Louvain and Paris, 1946.

62. MANSION, S., 'La Doctrine Aristotélicienne de la Substance et la Traité des Catégories', *Proc. 10th Int. Cong. Philos.*, pp. 1097–1100, Amsterdam, 1949.

63. MANSION, S., 'Les Apories de la Métaphysique Aristo-télienne', in *Autour d'Aristote*, pp. 141–179, Louvain, 1955.

64. MANSION, S., 'Les Positions Maîtresses de la Philosophie d'Aristote', in *Aristote et St. Thomas d'Aquin*, pp. 43–91, Louvain, 1957.

65. MEEHAN, F. X., *Efficient Causality in Aristotle and St. Thomas*, Cath. Univ. Amer. Press, Washington, 1940.

66. MEYER, Hans, *Der Entwicklungsgedanke bei Aristoteles*, Bonn, 1909.

67. MORAUX, P., 'L'Évolution d'Aristote', in *Aristote et St. Thomas d'Aquin*, pp. 9–41, Louvain, 1957.

68. MOREAU, J., 'L'Être et l'Essence chez Aristote', in *Autour d'Aristote*, pp. 181–204, Louvain, 1955.

69. MOREAU, J., 'L'Éloge de la Biologie chez Aristote', *Rev. des Études Anc.* **61** (1959), pp. 57–64.

70. MURE, G. R. G., *Aristotle*, Methuen, London, 1932.

71. NEEDHAM, Joseph, *A History of Embryology*, Cambridge, 1934.

72. OWENS, J., *The Doctrine of Being in the Aristotelian Metaphysics*, 2nd edn., Pont. Inst. Med. Stud., Toronto, 1957.

73. PEARSON, C. I., 'Aristotle's Dilemma', *Philos. Stud.* **9** (1959), pp. 27–35.

74. PECK, A. L. (edr.), Aristotle, *Generation of Animals*, Heinemann, London, 1953.

75. PECK, A. L. (edr.), Aristotle, *Parts of Animals*, Heinemann, London, 1955.

76. POLANYI, M., *Personal Knowledge*, Routledge, London, 1958.

77. RADL, E., *Geschichte der biologischen Theorien*, Leipzig, 1913.

78. RANDALL, J. H., Jr., *Aristotle*, Columbia, New York, 1960.

79. RIJK, L. M. de, *The Place of the Categories of Being in Aristotle's Philosophy*, Assen, 1952.

80. RITTER, Wm. E., 'Why Aristotle Invented the Word Entelecheia', *Quart. Rev. Biol.* 7 (1932), pp. 377–404.

81. ROBIN, Léon, *Greek Thought and the Origins of the Scientific Spirit*, London, 1928.

82. ROBIN, Léon, *Aristote*, Presses Univ. de la France, Paris, 1944.

83. ROSS, Sir David, *Aristotle* (5th edn.), Methuen, London, 1956.

84. ROSS, Sir David (edr.), *De Anima*, Oxford, 1961.

85. ROSS, Sir David (edr.), *Metaphysics*, 2 vols., 4th edn., Oxford, 1958.

86. ROSS, Sir David (edr.), *Parva Naturalia*, Oxford, 1955.

87. ROSS, Sir David (edr.), *Physics*, Oxford, 1936.

88. ROSS, Sir David (edr.), *Prior and Posterior Analytics*, Oxford, 1949.

89. ROSS, Sir David, 'The Development of Aristotle's Thought', *Proc. Brit. Acad.*, 1957, pp. 63–78.

90. RÜSCHE, F., *Blut, Leben und Seele*, Paderborn, 1930.

91. RUSSELL, E. S., *Form and Function*, John Murray, London, 1916.

92. SACHS, David, 'Does Aristotle Have a Doctrine of Secondary Substances?', *Mind* (NS) 57 (1948), pp. 221–225.

93. SELLARS, W., 'Substance and Form in Aristotle', *Jl. Philos.* 54 (1957), pp. 688–699.

94. SESMAT, A., 'L'Univers d'Aristote', *Rev. Philos.* 38 (1938), pp. 285–309.

95. SIEBECK, H., *Aristoteles*, 4th edn., Stuttgart, 1922.

96. SMITH, J. A., 'τόδε τι', *Class. Rev.* 35 (1921), 19.

97. SOLMSEN, F., 'The Vital Heat, the Inborn Pneuma, and the Aether', *Jl. Hell. Stud.* 77, pt. 1 (1957), pp. 119–123.

98. SOLMSEN, F., *Aristotle's System of the Physical World*, Cornell, Ithaca, 1960.

99. STALLMACH, J., *Dynamis und Energeia*, Meisenheim am Glan, 1959.

100. STEBBING, L. Susan, 'Concerning Substance', *Proc. Ar. Soc.* (NS) 30 (1930), pp. 285–308.

101. STOCKS, J. L., *Aristotelianism*, Harrap, London, 1925.

102. TAYLOR, A. E., *Aristotle*, Nelson, London, 1943. (Dover edn. revd. 1956.).

103. THEILER, Willy, *Zur Geschichte der teleologischen Naturbetrachtung bis auf Aristoteles*, Zürich and Leipzig, 1925.

104. THEILER, Willy, 'Die Entstehung der Metaphysik des Aristoteles', *Mus. Helv.* 15 (1958), pp. 85–105.

105. THOMPSON, D'Arcy W. (translr.), *Historia Animalium*, Oxford, 1910.

106. THOMPSON, D'Arcy W., 'Aristotle the Naturalist', in *Science and the Classics*, pp. 37–78, Oxford, London, 1940.

107. TORREY, H. B. and Felin, F., 'Was Aristotle an Evolutionist?', *Quart. Rev. Biol.* 12 (1937), pp. 1–18.

108. TUGENDHAT, Ernst, '*Ti Kata Tinos*', *Eine Untersuchung zur Struktur und Ursprung Aristotelischer Grundbegriffe*, Alber, Freiburg and Munich, 1958.

109. VERBEKE, G., 'La doctrine de l'être dans la Métaphysique d'Aristote', *Rev. Philos. Louv.* 50 (1952), pp. 471–478.

110. VON LEYDEN, W., ' "Existence": A Humean Point in Aristotle's Metaphysics', *Rev. Met.* 13 (1959–60), pp. 597–604.

111. VOGEL, C. de, 'The Legend of the Platonizing Aristotle', in *Plato and Aristotle in the mid-Fourth Century*, pp. 248–256, Göteborg, 1960.

112. VOGELBACHER, J., *Begriff und Erkenntnis der Substanz bei Aristoteles*, Limburg, 1932.

113. Vos, A. M. de, 'La "Vraie Substance" d'après la Métaphysique d'Aristote', *Proc. 10th Intern. Cong. Philos.* vol. I, pp. 1094–1096, Amsterdam, 1949.

114. Weiss, Helene, *Kausalität und Zufall in der Philosophie des Aristoteles*, Basle, 1942.

115. Wicksteed, P. H., and Cornford, F. M. (edrs.), *Physics*, 2 vols., Heinemann, London, 1935.

116. Wolfson, H. A., 'The Plurality of Immovable Movers in Aristotle and Averroës', *Harv. Stud. Class. Philol.* 63 (1958), pp. 233–253.

117. Wundt, Max, *Untersuchungen zur Metaphysik des Aristoteles*, Stuttgart, 1952.

118. Zürcher, J., *Aristoteles' Werk und Geist*, Paderborn, 1952.

SUPPLEMENTARY BIBLIOGRAPHY, 1967

Ackrill, J. L. (trans. and edr.), *Aristotle's 'Categories' and 'De Interpretatione'*, Oxford, 1963.

Aristote et les Problèmes de Méthode, Louvain and Paris, 1961. (Proceedings of the Symposium Aristotelicum of 1960.)

Aubenque, P., *Le Probleme de L'Etre chez Aristote*, Presses Univ. de France, Paris, 1962.

Bambrough, R. (edr.), *New Essays on Plato and Aristotle*, Routledge, London, 1965.

Bochner, S., 'Aristotle's Physics and Today's Physics', *Inter. Phil. Quart.* 4 (1964), pp. 217–244.

Brentano, Franz, *Von der mannigfachen Bedeutung des Seins bei Aristoteles*, G. Olms, Hildesheim, 1963. (Reprint of 1862 edn.)

Cherniss, H. F., *Aristotle's Criticism of Presocratic Philosophy*, Octagon, New York, 1964.

Conen, P. F., *Die Zeittheorie des Aristoteles*, Beck, Munich, 1964.

Downey, G., *Aristotle and Greek Science*, Chatto and Windus, London, 1964.

DURING, I., *Aristoteles. Darstellung und Interpretation seines Denkens*, Winter, Heidelberg, 1966.

HINTIKKA, J., 'Aristotle's Different Possibilities', *Inquiry* **6** (1963), pp. 18-29.

LACEY, A. R., οὐσία and form in Aristotle', *Phronesis* **10** (1965), pp. 97-105.

LEE, H. P. D., 'Place-names and the date of Aristotle's biological works', *Class. Quart.* **42** (1948), pp. 61-67. (This reference was inadvertently omitted from the original bibliography.)

MORAVCSIK, J. E. M., 'Aristotle on Predication', *Phil. Rev.* **76** (1967), pp. 80-96.

MORAVCSIK, J. E. M. (edr.), *Modern Studies in Philosophy: Aristotle*, Doubleday, Garden City, 1967.

MOREAU, J. *Aristote et son Ecole*, Presses Univ. de France, Paris, 1962.

OWEN, G. E. L., 'Inherence', *Phronesis* **10** (1965), pp. 97-105.

OWENS, JOSEPH, 'The Aristotelian Conception of the Sciences', *Inter. Phil. Quart.* **4** (1964), pp. 200-216.

OWENS, JOSEPH, 'The Grounds of Universality in Aristotle', *Amer. Phil. Quart.* **3** (1966), pp. 162-169.

SHUTE, G. W., *The Psychology of Aristotle: An Analysis of the Living Being*, Columbia University Studies, New York, 1964.

WIELAND, W., *Die Aristotelische Physik*, Vandenhoek and Ruprecht, Göttingen, 1962.

WOODBRIDGE, F. J. E., *Aristotle's Vision of Nature*, ed. J. H. Randall, Jr., *et al.* Columbia, New York, 1965.

INDEX

accidental, accidents, 25, 116,
117–122, 187, 207, 211;
'present in', 72–77
in science, 77–78, 81
accidental being, *see* being, accidental
action:
and actuality, 215
and passion, 120
voluntary, 51–52
actual and potential, 36, 100–103,
186, 187, 188, 229–231;
infinite, 156–157
actuality (activity), 22, 35, 131,
150–154, 217; *see also* actual
and potential
Agassiz, 154
Alcibiades, 42–43
Allan, D. J., 253
allotropy, 147
Anaximander, 15, 78
Anima, De, see *Soul, On the*
animals, see *Generation of Animals,
On the*; *Parts of Animals, On
the*; biology;
minds of, 162–163
parts of, 208–209
Anscombe, G. E. M., 80, 255
Arnim, H. von, 26, 27
art, 87, 93;
and nature, 131, 132–133, 151
atomists, 130; *see also* Democritus
attributes, 88–89, 187;
of nature, 155–160
Augustine, 15
axioms, 86, 89, 235; *see also* first
principles

being, ch. VI *passim*, 37, 64, 173;
accidental, 187, 202, 213
'predicative versus existential
is', 40, 211
being *qua* being, 20, 21, 35,
185–186, 190–192, 212
being-what-it-is, 80–85, 94, 103,
112, 149, 167, 180, 194, 195,
198, 200, 201–203, 204, 208,
211, 227, 231, 238, 240, 244
Bergson, 229
biology, 16, 32, 37, 55–58, 79–
80, 85, 108–109, 113–114,
117, 122–126, 133–155,
194–195, 212, 215, 227–229,
231, 244, 254–255;
and first philosophy, 178–179
Block, I., 108
Boyle, 107
brain, 124

Categories, 25, 37, 70–80, 81, 87,
112, 115, 117–122, 196, 197,
199, 200, 203
catfish, 79, 154
cause, causes, 94–96, 133, 140–
144, 153, 178, 179, 195,
209–211;
efficient, 16, 97, 131–132, 211
final, 16, 98, 132, 133–155,
211; *see also* teleology
formal, 211; *see also* form
material, 130, 149
chance, 145, 146, 149–153; *see
also* contingency
change, 114, 116, 118, 122, 213;
qualitative, 123–125

finite:
  and infinite, 62–64
  object of knowledge, 87
finitude, 65, 218–219, 247–251;
  in nature, 108–109, 155, 158
  of scientific discourse, 94–96
first philosophy, ch. VI *passim*,
  20, 68, 71; see also *Metaphysics*; wisdom
first principles, 89–94, 103–112,
  176–177; *see also* axioms;
  of wisdom, 192
first substance, *see* substance, first
form, 16, 20, 36, 57, 68, 69, 84,
  98, 100, 130–131, 155, 161,
  178, 180, 188, 194, 197, 198,
  199, 200, 201, 203, 204, 205,
  207, 209, 210, 216, 218, 221,
  222, 231;
  and being-what-it-is, 202
  and matter, 94–96
  pure, 212
  specific, 205
Forms, Platonic, ch. II *passim*, 14,
  24, 35, 37, 42, 53–54, 57, 61,
  65, 78, 79, 129, 162, 167,
  195, 200, 208, 237, 240
Frank, E., 58, 255

Galen, 109
Galileo, 66–67, 107, 126, 138
generation, 118–122, 201, 220;
  see also development; *Generation of Animals, On the*
Generation and Corruption, On,
  16, 58–62, 117, 126, 127
Generation of Animals, On the, 35,
  36, 60, 64, 97–103, 140–144,
  145, 255
genetics, 233
genus, 25, 76, 196, 199, 208
Gestalt, 233
Gilson, E., 215, 249

God, 17, 19, 20, 21, 65, 212, 217,
  245–247, 250
Goethe, 137
good, real and apparent, 50–53
Guthrie, W. C. K., 26

Haberling, W., 79
habit, 168–170, 173
Hamlyn, D. W., 108
Hantz, H. D., 254
Haring, E. S., 181, 200, 201, 253
heart, 23, 36, 140, 174;
  and blood, 124
Heavens, On the, 16, 117, 126, 127
Hegel, 175, 176
Heidegger, 176, 248
Heraclitus, 108, 125, 137
Hicks, R. D., 257
Hilbert, D., 91
History of Animals, The, 154
Homer, 30;
  Iliad, 92–93, 204
horns, 146–148
Hume, 44–46, 161, 162, 163, 167,
  170
Huxley, J., 147
Huxley, T. H., 231

imagination, 164
immortality, 31, 159–161, 165,
  167
individual, individuals, 24, 37, 62–
  64, 73–77, 198–199, 202,
  204, 205, 207, 208, 235
induction, 90, 103–109, 110, 114–
  115, 168, 173
infinite, 62–64, 117, 155–158,
  215, 239, 247–248;
  actual and potential, 156–157
intellect, 165; see also *nous*
intelligences, 19
Interpretation, On, 40, 73, 81
intuition, see *nous*

ontogenesis, *see* development
opinion, 24
Organon, 17, 68, 114, 219; *see also*
single titles
Ostwald, 31
Owen, G. E. L., 255
Owens, J., 30, 34, 41, 62, 82, 115,
181, 184, 194, 197, 226, 227,
249, 253

Parasilurus Aristotelis, *see* catfish
Parmenides, 15, 39, 40, 41, 78,
156–157, 189, 190, 211, 250
Parry, M., 30
Parts of Animals, On the, 22, 23,
35, 36, 56–57, 58, 68, 82, 83,
123, 131, 136, 138, 146–
148, 179, 194–195
Parva Naturalia, see *Shorter
Treatises on Nature, The*
pattern, 229–234, 240
perception, 24, 41–47, 84, 104–
109, 110, 162, 166, 169, 244
Philosophy, On, 26
physics, 179, 190–191, 192, *see
also* science, Aristotelian
Physics, ch. IV *passim*, 16, 19, 20,
26, 46, 94–95, 96, 105, 109,
173, 185, 189, 192, 194, 197,
211, 234; see also *Motion,
On; Nature, On*
physiology, Aristotelian, 123–
124, 173–174
place, 155, 158–159
Plato, ch. II *passim*, 14, 17, 19,
20, 21, 23, 24, 25, 27, 28,
31, 34, 78, 79, 82, 83, 84–
85, 86, 87, 91, 108, 120,
144, 161, 162, 167, 172,
177, 178, 179, 186, 188, 189,
190, 195, 211, 212, 230,
236–237, 240, 243, 244, 250,
255;

Gorgias, 42, 52, 78
Laws, 243
Meno, 161
Phaedo, 31, 42, 161, 263
Phaedrus, 48, 56
Philebus, 62
Republic, 42, 49, 52
Seventh Letter, 48, 84, 86
Symposium, 42–43, 58–62
Theaetetus, 39, 43, 45, 48, 91
244
Timaeus, 64, 246, 255
Platonists, 129
Plotinus, 15
Poetics, 93
Polanyi, M., 47–48
Politics, 15, 52
Posterior Analytics, 40, 68, 69,
70, 81, 82, 85–96, 103–112,
116, 128, 149, 181, 194, 198,
200
potential, 35, 207; *see* actual and
potential
predicables, 191
predication, 40, 72–78, 94, 181,
211
pre-Socratics, 130
prime matter, 200, 202
principles, *see* axioms; first principles
Prior Analytics, 67, 68, 69, 81,
200
prior, meanings of, 140–141, 142,
219
privation, *see* shortage
Progression of Animals, On the, 80
propositions, 40, 71, 73
Protagoras, 45, 163
Pythagoreans, 42, 66, 78, 188,
250

quality, *see* change; elements;
motion; physiology